HTML Crash Course for Beginners in 10 Hours or Less

(Book 1)

This book may be purchased in bulk for educational, business, fundraising, or sales promotional use.

ISBN:

Published by: Ekesy In-Outdoor Company

10B, Mufutau Opeifa Street, Oke-Odo, Ile-Epo B/Stop, Alimosho, Lagos, Nigeria

Email: care@israeljoshua.com.ng

Tel: +234 803 815 4459, +234 813 2228 534

For information, please contact us @

care@israeljoshua.com.ng

www.israeljoshua.com.ng

Call: +234 803 815 4459

Whatsapp: +234 813 2228 534

Table of Content

Dedication

By Israel Joshua Chukwubueze

I humbly and wholeheartedly **dedicate this book** to **Almighty God**, who has given me the strength, wisdom, and clarity of mind to write and teach in a way that reaches hearts and sharpens minds. Without His grace, none of this would be possible. He remains my foundation, my guide, and the ultimate source of my inspiration.

To my **precious kids**, you are the bright lights of my life. Your joy, curiosity, and boundless energy constantly motivate me to keep growing and creating. Everything I do, I do with you in mind, aiming to leave behind tools, resources, and knowledge that you can proudly use as stepping stones in your own life journey.

To my **beloved mum**, your prayers, sacrifices, and unwavering support have shaped me into the man I am today. You've always believed in me, even in moments when the path was uncertain. This book stands as a symbol of the seeds you've sown in me—seeds of diligence, discipline, and divine trust.

And to **you, my dear reader**, thank you for trusting me to guide you through your learning experience. Whether this is your first time writing code or your next attempt at finally understanding HTML, I wrote this book with you in mind. I wanted a guide that was friendly, approachable, yet thorough enough to build confidence and practical skill. You're not just reading another tech manual—you're holding a carefully crafted roadmap designed to help you build real web pages in real time.

This book was written to simplify what often seems complex. I understand how frustrating and confusing it can be to face a blank screen and not know where to begin. That's why I've filled these chapters with clear explanations, real-world examples, and quick wins that will boost your understanding and keep you moving forward. The journey to becoming a capable web developer doesn't have to feel overwhelming—and it doesn't need to take years. In just a matter of hours, you can be writing code that works, makes sense, and looks good.

I've walked this road myself, from the early days of struggling with tags and syntax, to building full-scale websites and teaching thousands. I've been where you are, and I know what you need to move ahead. This book is my way of giving back and lighting a path for others.

So as you read, type, and test your way through the pages, remember: you're not alone. This guide was made just for you—with care, clarity, and a deep belief in your potential.

May it bring you the knowledge you need, the confidence to keep going, and the joy of creating something with your own hands. May it open new doors for you, whether personally, professionally, or creatively.

To God be the glory.

To my children, my love and legacy.

To my mum, my root and strength.

To you, my reader—you are the reason this book exists.

Author: Israel Joshua Chukwubueze

(formerly known as Christopher Ekene Okade)

Preface

A Personal Welcome

Learning something new can feel overwhelming, especially when you're just starting. I wrote ***HTML Crash Course for Beginners in 10 Hours or Less*** to make your first steps into web development simple, structured, and stress-free. Whether you're an aspiring developer, a digital creative, or simply someone curious about how websites are built, this book is your guide.

My name is **Israel Joshua Chukwubueze**, and I was formerly known as **Christopher Ekene Okade**. My journey in the world of technology, education, and digital creativity spans more than two decades. Over the years, I've worked as a graphic designer, website developer, mobile app builder, digital marketing expert, educator, and mentor. I've also been privileged to teach hundreds of students one-on-one, guiding them from beginner to confident creator. This book reflects the heart of that experience.

Why I Wrote This Book

My passion for **writing and sharing knowledge** has grown over the years. I've authored over 700+ books across various subjects — from psychology to digital business — but web development remains a cornerstone of what I do and teach.

I've seen firsthand how many people feel confused or intimidated when they hear terms like "HTML," "CSS," or "coding." They assume it's too technical, too complicated, or just not for them. But the truth is: **HTML is easy to learn when it's taught the right way.** You don't need a computer science degree or years of study to understand how to build a web page. All you need is the right guide — one that speaks your language and walks you through the process one clear step at a time.

That's what this book aims to do.

What You'll Gain from This Book

By the end of this crash course, you'll be able to:

- **Create functional HTML web pages** with confidence.
- **Understand the structure** and syntax of HTML and how it interacts with CSS and JavaScript.
- **Design personal projects**, forms, navigation menus, and multimedia elements with ease.
- **Build a complete mini-portfolio website** from scratch.
- **Write clean, accessible, and SEO-friendly code** that works across different browsers and devices.

Every chapter is designed to focus on a specific skill or concept. You'll learn by doing, not just by reading. Each section builds on the last, guiding you through short, focused lessons that lead to real-world results.

Who This Book Is For

This book is perfect for:

- **Absolute beginners** who have never written a line of HTML before.
- **Students**, freelancers, bloggers, and creators who want to manage or design their own websites.
- **Professionals** who want to add web development skills to their resume.
- **Entrepreneurs** who want to understand the tech behind their business.

You don't need any previous experience — just a computer and a willingness to learn.

My Teaching Style

I wrote this book using a **friendly, practical, and no-fluff** approach. I believe learning should be straightforward and enjoyable. I don't overload you with theory. Instead, I focus on giving you what you need to know right now to take action and get results.

Expect lots of real examples, clear explanations, and practical takeaways. You'll learn how to avoid common mistakes, how to keep your code clean, and how to think like a developer from day one.

A Final Word

Writing this book has been a labor of love. It's not just a technical manual — it's a guide designed to **empower you**. HTML is the foundation of the web, and by learning it, you open the door to endless creative and career opportunities.

Whether this is your first step into the tech world or part of a larger journey, I am honored to walk alongside you.

Thank you for choosing this book.

Let's get started, and let's build something great.

With passion and purpose,
Author: Israel Joshua Chukwubueze

(formerly known as Christopher Ekene Okade)*)*

Chapter 1: Introduction to HTML

1.1 What is HTML?

Understanding HTML Fundamentals

HTML stands for HyperText Markup Language, and it serves as the foundational building block of every website on the internet. Think of HTML as the skeleton of a webpage – it provides structure, organization, and meaning to content that browsers can interpret and display to users.

Breaking Down the Acronym

HyperText refers to the ability to create links between different documents and pages. This revolutionary concept allows users to navigate seamlessly from one piece of content to another with simple clicks, creating the interconnected web of information we know today.

Markup describes the process of adding special codes or tags to regular text to give it structure and meaning. These tags tell the browser how to display different elements – whether something should appear as a heading, paragraph, image, or link.

Language indicates that HTML follows specific rules, syntax, and conventions that browsers understand and can process consistently across different platforms and devices.

How HTML Works

HTML operates through a system of elements and tags that wrap around content to define its purpose and appearance. When you visit a website, your browser downloads the HTML file, reads these tags, and renders the content according to the instructions provided.

#html

```
<!DOCTYPE html>
<html>
<head>
```

```html
    <title>My First Web Page</title>
</head>
<body>
    <h1>Welcome to My Website</h1>
    <p>This is my first paragraph of text.</p>
</body>
</html>
```

This simple example demonstrates the basic structure every HTML document follows. The browser interprets these tags and displays a webpage with a title, heading, and paragraph.

HTML as a Document Format

HTML documents are plain text files saved with a `.html` or `.htm` extension. Unlike word processing documents that require specific software to open, HTML files can be created with any basic text editor and viewed in any web browser. This universal compatibility makes HTML incredibly powerful and accessible.

The Role of HTML in Web Development

HTML serves as the content layer in modern web development. While CSS handles visual styling and JavaScript adds interactivity, HTML remains responsible for structuring information and providing semantic meaning to content. Search engines, screen readers, and other technologies rely heavily on proper HTML structure to understand and process web content effectively.

1.2 Brief History of HTML

The Birth of HTML (1990-1993)

Tim Berners-Lee created HTML in 1990 while working at CERN, the European physics research laboratory. His goal was simple yet revolutionary: create a system that would allow researchers to share documents and link between them easily. The first version of HTML contained just 18 elements, including basic tags for headings, paragraphs, lists, and links.

The original HTML specification was remarkably simple. Berners-Lee designed it to be human-readable and easy to learn, principles that continue to guide HTML development today. The first web browser, called WorldWideWeb (later renamed Nexus), could display these early HTML documents.

HTML 2.0: The First Standard (1995)

As the web gained popularity, the need for standardization became apparent. HTML 2.0, published in 1995, represented the first official standard managed by the Internet Engineering Task Force (IETF). This version included forms, which revolutionized web interaction by allowing users to input data and submit information to servers.

#html

```
<form action="/submit" method="post">
    <input type="text" name="username">
    <input type="password" name="password">
    <input type="submit" value="Login">
</form>
```

HTML 3.2: Adding Visual Elements (1997)

The World Wide Web Consortium (W3C) took over HTML development and released HTML 3.2 in 1997. This version introduced tables, which became crucial for both data presentation and page layout (though layout tables are now discouraged). Applets, text flow around images, and style sheets also made their debut.

HTML 4.0 and 4.01: Maturation (1997-1999)

HTML 4.0 brought significant improvements including better support for stylesheets, scripting languages, and accessibility features. The introduction of cascading style sheets (CSS) allowed developers to separate content from presentation more effectively. HTML 4.01, released in 1999, fixed bugs and became one of the most stable and widely-used versions.

XHTML: The XML Approach (2000-2009)

XHTML attempted to reformulate HTML as an XML application, requiring stricter syntax rules. While it introduced valuable concepts about well-formed markup, XHTML's complexity and rigid requirements made it less popular among developers than anticipated.

HTML5: The Modern Era (2008-2014)

HTML5 development began in 2008 with ambitious goals: improve semantic markup, reduce the need for proprietary plugins, and better handle rich media content. The specification introduced semantic elements like `<header>`, `<nav>`, `<article>`, and `<footer>`, along with native audio and video support.

#html

```
<article>
    <header>
        <h1>Article Title</h1>
        <time datetime="2024-01-15">January 15,
2024</time>
    </header>
    <p>Article content goes here...</p>
    <footer>
        <p>Author: John Doe</p>
    </footer>
</article>
```

Living Standard: Continuous Evolution

Rather than releasing new numbered versions, HTML now follows a "living standard" model maintained by the Web Hypertext Application Technology Working Group (WHATWG). This approach allows for continuous improvements and updates without waiting for major version releases.

1.3 Understanding Markup Language

What Makes a Markup Language

A markup language uses tags or codes to annotate text and provide instructions about how content should be structured, formatted, or processed. Unlike programming languages that execute commands, markup languages describe and organize information.

Anatomy of HTML Tags

HTML tags consist of element names enclosed in angle brackets. Most elements use both opening and closing tags, with content placed between them:

#html

```
<tagname>Content goes here</tagname>
```

Tag Structure Components

Opening Tag: `<h1>` - Marks the beginning of an element **Content**: The actual text or other elements **Closing Tag**: `</h1>` - Marks the end of an element (note the forward slash)

Self-Closing Tags

Some HTML elements don't contain content and use self-closing tags:

#html

```html
<br>        <!-- Line break -->
<img src="image.jpg" alt="Description">
<input type="text" name="username">
<hr>        <!-- Horizontal rule -->
```

Attributes: Adding Information to Tags

Attributes provide additional information about HTML elements. They appear within the opening tag and consist of a name-value pair:

#html

```html
<img src="photo.jpg" alt="A beautiful sunset" width="300"
height="200">
<a href="https://example.com" target="_blank"
title="Visit Example">Click here</a>
<div class="container" id="main-content">Content
here</div>
```

Common Attribute Types

src: Specifies the source file for images, videos, or scripts **href**: Defines the destination for links **alt**: Provides alternative text for images **class**: Assigns CSS classes for styling **id**: Provides unique identifiers for elements **title**: Offers additional information displayed on hover

Nesting and Hierarchy

HTML elements can be nested inside other elements, creating a hierarchical structure:

#html

```
<div class="article">
    <h2>Article Title</h2>
    <p>This paragraph contains <strong>bold text</strong>
and <em>italic text</em>.</p>
    <ul>
        <li>First list item</li>
        <li>Second list item with <a href="link.html">a
link</a></li>
    </ul>
</div>
```

Proper Nesting Rules

Elements must be properly nested – if element A opens before element B, then element B must close before element A closes:

#html

```
<!-- Correct nesting -->
<p>This is <strong>bold and <em>italic</em></strong>
text.</p>

<!-- Incorrect nesting -->
<p>This is <strong>bold and <em>italic</strong></em>
text.</p>
```

Block vs. Inline Elements

Block Elements: Take up the full width available and start on new lines

- `<div>`, `<p>`, `<h1>-<h6>`, `<ul>`, `<li>`, `<header>`, `<footer>`

Inline Elements: Only take up as much width as necessary and don't start new lines

- `<span>`, `<a>`, `<strong>`, `<em>`, `<img>`, `<input>`

#html

```
<div>This is a block element</div>
<div>This is another block element</div>

<span>This is inline</span> <span>This is also
inline</span>
```

1.4 HTML vs. Other Web Languages

HTML: The Content Foundation

HTML provides structure and semantic meaning to web content. It defines what content is – headings, paragraphs, lists, images – but doesn't control how it looks or behaves. HTML focuses purely on content organization and meaning.

#html

```
<article>
    <h1>Breaking News</h1>
    <p>Important information about recent events...</p>
    <ul>
        <li>Key point one</li>
        <li>Key point two</li>
    </ul>
</article>
```

CSS: The Styling Layer

Cascading Style Sheets (CSS) control the visual presentation of HTML elements. While HTML defines structure, CSS determines colors, fonts, spacing, layouts, and responsive behavior.

#css

```
article {
    background-color: #f4f4f4;
    padding: 20px;
    border-radius: 5px;
}

h1 {
    color: #333;
    font-size: 24px;
    margin-bottom: 15px;
}
```

JavaScript: The Behavior Layer

JavaScript adds interactivity and dynamic behavior to web pages. It can modify HTML content, respond to user interactions, fetch data from servers, and create complex web applications.

#javascript

```
document.getElementById('button').addEventListener('click
', function() {
    document.getElementById('message').innerHTML =
'Button clicked!';
});
```

The Three-Layer Approach

Modern web development follows a separation of concerns principle:

1. **HTML**: Structure and content
2. **CSS**: Presentation and styling
3. **JavaScript**: Behavior and interactivity

This separation makes code more maintainable, accessible, and flexible.

XML: The Strict Cousin

XML (eXtensible Markup Language) shares syntax similarities with HTML but serves different purposes. XML focuses on data storage and transport, requiring strict syntax rules and well-formed documents. HTML is more forgiving and designed specifically for web content display.

Markdown: The Simplified Alternative

Markdown provides a simpler way to create formatted text using minimal syntax. While easier to write than HTML, Markdown ultimately converts to HTML for web display:

#markdown

```
# This becomes an h1 tag
**This becomes bold text**
[This becomes a link](http://example.com)
```

Server-Side Languages

Languages like PHP, Python, Ruby, and Node.js run on web servers and can generate HTML dynamically:

#php

```php
<?php
echo "<h1>Welcome, " . $username . "!</h1>";
echo "<p>Today's date is " . date('Y-m-d') . "</p>";
?>
```

Preprocessors and Frameworks

Tools like Sass (for CSS) and frameworks like React (for JavaScript) extend basic web languages with additional features and capabilities, but ultimately compile down to standard HTML, CSS, and JavaScript that browsers understand.

1.5 Setting Up Your First HTML File

Choosing a Text Editor

The beauty of HTML lies in its simplicity – you can create HTML files using any text editor. However, specialized code editors provide features that make development much easier and more efficient.

Basic Text Editors

Notepad (Windows): The most basic option, but lacks syntax highlighting and helpful features.

TextEdit (Mac): Simple but requires configuration to save as plain text rather than rich text format.

Recommended Code Editors

Visual Studio Code: Free, powerful, and includes excellent HTML support with syntax highlighting, auto-completion, and extensive plugin ecosystem.

Sublime Text: Fast and lightweight with excellent performance and customization options.

Atom: GitHub's open-source editor with strong community support and packages.

Brackets: Adobe's editor specifically designed for web development with live preview features.

Setting Up Visual Studio Code

After installing VS Code, enhance your HTML development experience with these extensions:

- **HTML CSS Support**: Provides CSS class and ID completion
- **Auto Rename Tag**: Automatically renames paired HTML tags
- **Prettier**: Formats your HTML code consistently
- **Live Server**: Launches a local development server with live reload

Creating Your First HTML File

Open your chosen text editor and create a new file. Save it with the `.html` extension, such as `index.html` or `my-first-page.html`.

Basic HTML Document Structure

Every HTML document follows a standard structure:

#html

```
<!DOCTYPE html>
<html lang="en">
<head>
    <meta charset="UTF-8">
    <meta name="viewport" content="width=device-width,
initial-scale=1.0">
```

```
    <title>My First HTML Page</title>
</head>
<body>
    <h1>Hello, World!</h1>
    <p>This is my first HTML page.</p>
</body>
</html>
```

Understanding the Document Structure

DOCTYPE Declaration: `<!DOCTYPE html>` tells the browser this is an HTML5 document and ensures it renders in standards mode.

HTML Element: `<html lang="en">` is the root element that contains all other elements. The `lang` attribute specifies the document language.

Head Section: Contains metadata about the document that doesn't display on the page:

- `<meta charset="UTF-8">`: Specifies character encoding for proper text display
- `<meta name="viewport" content="width=device-width, initial-scale=1.0">`: Ensures proper mobile responsiveness
- `<title>`: Sets the text displayed in browser tabs and search results

Body Section: Contains all visible content that appears on the webpage.

Creating a More Complete Example

#html

```
<!DOCTYPE html>
<html lang="en">
<head>
```

```
    <meta charset="UTF-8">
    <meta name="viewport" content="width=device-width,
initial-scale=1.0">
    <meta name="description" content="A beginner's first
HTML page">
    <title>Learning HTML - My First Page</title>
</head>
<body>
    <header>
        <h1>Welcome to My Website</h1>
        <nav>
            <ul>
                <li><a href="#about">About</a></li>
                <li><a href="#contact">Contact</a></li>
            </ul>
        </nav>
    </header>

    <main>
        <section id="about">
            <h2>About Me</h2>
            <p>I'm learning HTML and this is my first
webpage. It's exciting to see how markup language creates
structure and meaning for web content.</p>

            <h3>My Interests</h3>
            <ul>
                <li>Web Development</li>
                <li>Technology</li>
                <li>Learning New Skills</li>
            </ul>
        </section>
```

```html
        <section id="contact">
            <h2>Contact Information</h2>
            <p>You can reach me at: <a
href="mailto:example@email.com">example@email.com</a></p>
        </section>
    </main>

    <footer>
        <p>&copy; 2024 My First Website. All rights
reserved.</p>
    </footer>
</body>
</html>
```

File Organization Best Practices

Create a dedicated folder for your HTML project:

```
my-website/
├── index.html
├── about.html
├── contact.html
├── images/
│   ├── logo.png
│   └── photo.jpg
├── css/
│   └── styles.css
└── js/
    └── scripts.js
```

Viewing Your HTML File

To see your HTML file in action:

1. **Double-click the file**: This opens it in your default browser
2. **Right-click and choose "Open with"**: Select your preferred browser
3. **Drag and drop**: Drag the HTML file onto a browser window
4. **Use a local server**: Tools like VS Code's Live Server extension provide better development experience

Browser Developer Tools

All modern browsers include developer tools that help you inspect and debug HTML:

- **Chrome**: Press F12 or right-click and select "Inspect"
- **Firefox**: Press F12 or right-click and select "Inspect Element"
- **Safari**: Enable Developer menu in preferences, then press Cmd+Option+I
- **Edge**: Press F12 or right-click and select "Inspect"

Common Beginner Mistakes to Avoid

Forgetting closing tags: Always close elements that require closing tags **Incorrect nesting**: Ensure elements are properly nested **Missing DOCTYPE**: Always include the DOCTYPE declaration **Incorrect file extension**: Save files with `.html` or `.htm` extension **Case sensitivity**: While HTML is not case sensitive, use consistent lowercase for better practices

Testing Across Different Browsers

Different browsers may render HTML slightly differently. Test your pages in:

- Chrome
- Firefox
- Safari
- Edge

This ensures your content displays correctly for all users.

Version Control Considerations

As you create more HTML files, consider using version control systems like Git to track changes and maintain project history. This becomes invaluable as your projects grow in complexity.

Essential Tips for HTML Beginners

- Always include the DOCTYPE declaration at the beginning of every HTML document to ensure browsers render your page in standards mode and avoid compatibility issues.
- Use semantic HTML elements like `<header>`, `<nav>`, `<main>`, `<article>`, and `<footer>` instead of generic `<div>` elements to improve accessibility and search engine optimization.
- Validate your HTML code regularly using online validators or browser developer tools to catch errors early and ensure your markup follows proper standards.
- Keep your HTML clean and well-indented for better readability and easier maintenance, especially when working on larger projects or collaborating with others.
- Always provide alternative text for images using the `alt` attribute to make your content accessible to screen readers and improve user experience when images fail to load.

Actionable Strategies for HTML Success

- Set up a dedicated workspace with a proper code editor like Visual Studio Code, install helpful extensions, and organize your project files in a logical folder structure from day one.
- Practice writing HTML by hand rather than relying on visual editors or generators to build muscle memory and truly understand how elements work together.
- Study the source code of websites you admire by right-clicking and selecting "View Page Source" to see how professional developers structure their HTML.

- Create a personal HTML reference sheet with commonly used elements, attributes, and code snippets that you can quickly reference while learning.
- Build small projects regularly, starting with simple single-page websites and gradually adding more complex features and multiple pages as your skills improve.
- Join HTML and web development communities online, participate in forums, and ask questions when you encounter challenges rather than struggling alone.
- Focus on writing accessible HTML from the beginning by using proper heading hierarchies, meaningful link text, and semantic elements rather than trying to retrofit accessibility later.

Chapter 2: Basic Structure of an HTML Document

2.1 The `<!DOCTYPE>` Declaration

Understanding the DOCTYPE Declaration

The DOCTYPE declaration stands as the very first line of every HTML document, serving as a crucial instruction that tells the web browser which version of HTML the document uses. This declaration prevents browsers from entering "quirks mode," a compatibility state that attempts to render pages like older, non-standard browsers did in the past.

#html

```
<!DOCTYPE html>
```

The modern HTML5 DOCTYPE declaration is remarkably simple compared to its predecessors. This simplicity represents years of evolution in web standards, moving away from complex declarations that referenced Document Type Definitions (DTDs) to a clean, memorable format.

Historical Context of DOCTYPE Declarations

Before HTML5, DOCTYPE declarations were verbose and difficult to remember. HTML 4.01 required different declarations depending on whether you used Strict, Transitional, or Frameset versions:

#html

```
<!-- HTML 4.01 Strict -->
<!DOCTYPE HTML PUBLIC "-//W3C//DTD HTML 4.01//EN"
"http://www.w3.org/TR/html4/strict.dtd">

<!-- HTML 4.01 Transitional -->
<!DOCTYPE HTML PUBLIC "-//W3C//DTD HTML 4.01
Transitional//EN" "http://www.w3.org/TR/html4/loose.dtd">
```

```
<!-- XHTML 1.0 Strict -->
<!DOCTYPE html PUBLIC "-//W3C//DTD XHTML 1.0 Strict//EN"
"http://www.w3.org/TR/xhtml1/DTD/xhtml1-strict.dtd">
```

These complex declarations often caused developers to copy and paste rather than understand their purpose. HTML5 designers recognized this problem and created the current simplified version.

How Browsers Interpret DOCTYPE

When a browser encounters a webpage, it first reads the DOCTYPE declaration to determine how to render the content. This process happens before any HTML parsing begins:

Standards Mode: Modern DOCTYPE triggers standards-compliant rendering **Quirks Mode**: Missing or outdated DOCTYPE triggers legacy compatibility mode **Almost Standards Mode**: Some browsers use an intermediate mode for certain older DOCTYPEs

The Impact of Missing DOCTYPE

Without a proper DOCTYPE declaration, browsers enter quirks mode, which can cause:

- Inconsistent box model behavior
- Different default styling across browsers
- Unpredictable layout rendering
- CSS compatibility issues
- JavaScript behavior differences

#html

```
<!-- This triggers quirks mode -->
<html>
```

```
<head>
    <title>No DOCTYPE Example</title>
</head>
<body>
    <p>This page may render inconsistently</p>
</body>
</html>
```

DOCTYPE Case Sensitivity and Variations

The DOCTYPE declaration is case-insensitive, meaning these variations all work identically:

#html

```
<!DOCTYPE html>
<!doctype html>
<!DocType html>
<!DOCTYPE HTML>
```

However, the standard convention uses uppercase "DOCTYPE" and lowercase "html" for consistency across the web development community.

Placement Rules for DOCTYPE

The DOCTYPE declaration must appear:

- As the very first line of the HTML document
- Before any HTML tags
- Before any whitespace or comments
- Without any content preceding it

#html

```
<!-- Correct placement -->
<!DOCTYPE html>
<html>
<!-- Document continues -->

<!-- Incorrect - has content before DOCTYPE -->
<!-- This is a comment -->
<!DOCTYPE html>
<html>
```

Modern DOCTYPE Benefits

The HTML5 DOCTYPE provides several advantages:

- **Simplicity**: Easy to remember and type
- **Future-proof**: Works with current and future HTML specifications
- **Universal compatibility**: Recognized by all modern browsers
- **Standards compliance**: Ensures consistent rendering behavior

2.2 The `<html>` Tag

The Root Element Foundation

The `<html>` tag serves as the root element of every HTML document, acting as the container that holds all other HTML elements. Every piece of content, metadata, and structure within an HTML document must exist inside this fundamental element.

#html

```
<!DOCTYPE html>
<html lang="en">
```

```html
    <!-- All content goes here -->
</html>
```

Essential Attributes of the HTML Tag

The lang Attribute

The `lang` attribute specifies the primary language of the document content, providing crucial information for browsers, search engines, and assistive technologies:

#html

```html
<html lang="en">          <!-- English -->
<html lang="es">          <!-- Spanish -->
<html lang="fr">          <!-- French -->
<html lang="de">          <!-- German -->
<html lang="zh-CN">       <!-- Chinese (Simplified) -->
<html lang="ar">          <!-- Arabic -->
```

Language codes follow the ISO 639-1 standard for two-letter language codes, with optional country codes using ISO 3166-1 alpha-2 format:

#html

```html
<html lang="en-US">       <!-- English (United States) -->
<html lang="en-GB">       <!-- English (Great Britain) -->
<html lang="pt-BR">       <!-- Portuguese (Brazil) -->
<html lang="fr-CA">       <!-- French (Canada) -->
```

The dir Attribute

The `dir` attribute controls text direction, particularly important for languages that read right-to-left:

#html

```
<html lang="ar" dir="rtl">    <!-- Arabic, right-to-left
-->
<html lang="he" dir="rtl">    <!-- Hebrew, right-to-left
-->
<html lang="en" dir="ltr">    <!-- English, left-to-right
-->
```

Accessibility Impact of HTML Attributes

Screen readers and other assistive technologies rely heavily on the `lang` attribute to:

- Select appropriate pronunciation rules
- Choose correct voice synthesis settings
- Provide language-specific navigation features
- Announce language changes to users

#html

```
<html lang="en">
<head>
    <title>Multilingual Content Example</title>
</head>
<body>
    <h1>Welcome to Our Site</h1>
    <p>This content is in English.</p>
    <p lang="es">Este contenido está en español.</p>
```

```
    <p lang="fr">Ce contenu est en français.</p>
</body>
</html>
```

SEO Benefits of Proper HTML Tag Usage

Search engines use the `lang` attribute to:

- Understand content language for regional search results
- Provide appropriate search results based on user language preferences
- Index content correctly for international SEO
- Deliver localized search experiences

XML Namespace Considerations

While not commonly used in HTML5, the `xmlns` attribute defines XML namespaces, particularly relevant when embedding other XML-based languages:

#html

```
<html xmlns="http://www.w3.org/1999/xhtml" lang="en">
    <!-- XHTML-style declaration -->
</html>
```

Multiple Language Support

For documents containing multiple languages, the primary language goes in the `<html>` tag, with specific language changes marked using `lang` attributes on individual elements:

#html

```
<html lang="en">
<body>
    <h1>International Recipe Collection</h1>
    <section>
        <h2>French Recipe</h2>
        <p lang="fr">Bouillabaisse est une soupe de
poisson traditionnelle.</p>
    </section>
    <section>
        <h2>Italian Recipe</h2>
        <p lang="it">La carbonara è un piatto tipico
della cucina romana.</p>
    </section>
</body>
</html>
```

2.3 The <head> Element

Understanding the Head Section Purpose

The <head> element contains metadata about the HTML document that doesn't display directly on the webpage but provides essential information to browsers, search engines, and other web services. Think of the head section as the document's information center where you configure how the page behaves and appears in various contexts.

#html

```
<head>
    <meta charset="UTF-8">
    <meta name="viewport" content="width=device-width,
initial-scale=1.0">
    <title>Complete Head Section Example</title>
```

```html
    <meta name="description" content="A comprehensive example of HTML head elements">
    <link rel="stylesheet" href="styles.css">
    <script src="script.js"></script>
</head>
```

The Title Element

The <title> element defines the document title that appears in browser tabs, bookmarks, and search engine results. This element significantly impacts user experience and SEO performance:

#html

```html
<title>HTML Crash Course for Beginners | Learn Web Development</title>
```

Title Best Practices

Length Guidelines: Keep titles between 50-60 characters to prevent truncation in search results and browser tabs.

Descriptive Content: Make titles specific and descriptive rather than generic.

Brand Positioning: Include brand names strategically, typically at the end.

#html

```html
<!-- Good title examples -->
<title>Chocolate Chip Cookie Recipe - Easy Homemade Cookies</title>
<title>2024 Web Development Trends | TechBlog</title>
<title>Contact Us - Smith & Associates Law Firm</title>
```

```
<!-- Poor title examples -->
<title>Home</title>
<title>Page 1</title>
<title>Welcome</title>
```

Meta Elements and Attributes

Meta elements provide metadata about the HTML document using name-value pairs. Different types of meta elements serve various purposes:

Character Encoding

The charset meta element specifies how the browser should interpret text characters:

#html

```
<meta charset="UTF-8">
```

UTF-8 encoding supports virtually all languages and special characters, making it the standard choice for modern websites.

Viewport Configuration

The viewport meta element controls how pages display on mobile devices:

#html

```
<meta name="viewport" content="width=device-width,
initial-scale=1.0">
```

This declaration ensures responsive design functionality across different screen sizes.

SEO Meta Elements

Search engines use specific meta elements to understand and index page content:

#html

```html
<meta name="description" content="Learn HTML basics with our comprehensive crash course. Perfect for beginners who want to master web development fundamentals in 10 hours or less.">
<meta name="keywords" content="HTML, web development, beginner tutorial, crash course">
<meta name="author" content="Web Development Academy">
<meta name="robots" content="index, follow">
```

Social Media Meta Elements

Open Graph and Twitter Card meta elements control how content appears when shared on social platforms:

#html

```html
<!-- Open Graph for Facebook -->
<meta property="og:title" content="HTML Crash Course for Beginners">
<meta property="og:description" content="Master HTML fundamentals in 10 hours or less">
<meta property="og:image" content="https://example.com/course-image.jpg">
<meta property="og:url" content="https://example.com/html-course">
<meta property="og:type" content="website">
```

```
<!-- Twitter Cards -->
<meta name="twitter:card" content="summary_large_image">
<meta name="twitter:title" content="HTML Crash Course for Beginners">
<meta name="twitter:description" content="Master HTML fundamentals in 10 hours or less">
<meta name="twitter:image" content="https://example.com/course-image.jpg">
```

Link Elements

Link elements establish relationships between the current document and external resources:

Stylesheet Links

#html

```
<link rel="stylesheet" href="styles.css">
<link rel="stylesheet" href="https://fonts.googleapis.com/css2?family=Roboto:wght@300;400;700&display=swap">
```

Favicon Links

#html

```
<link rel="icon" type="image/x-icon" href="/favicon.ico">
<link rel="icon" type="image/png" sizes="32x32" href="/favicon-32x32.png">
<link rel="icon" type="image/png" sizes="16x16" href="/favicon-16x16.png">
```

```
<link rel="apple-touch-icon" sizes="180x180"
href="/apple-touch-icon.png">
```

Canonical URLs

#html

```
<link rel="canonical"
href="https://example.com/preferred-url">
```

Script Elements in Head

JavaScript files can be included in the head section, though placement affects loading behavior:

#html

```
<script src="analytics.js"></script>
<script defer src="main.js"></script>
<script async src="tracking.js"></script>
```

defer: Script executes after HTML parsing completes **async**: Script executes as soon as it's downloaded

Complete Head Section Example

#html

```
<head>
    <!-- Essential meta elements -->
    <meta charset="UTF-8">
```

```
    <meta name="viewport" content="width=device-width,
initial-scale=1.0">

    <!-- Title and SEO meta -->
    <title>Professional Web Development Services |
YourCompany</title>
    <meta name="description" content="Expert web
development services including HTML, CSS, and JavaScript
solutions for businesses worldwide.">
    <meta name="keywords" content="web development, HTML,
CSS, JavaScript, responsive design">
    <meta name="author" content="YourCompany Development
Team">

    <!-- Social media meta -->
    <meta property="og:title" content="Professional Web
Development Services">
    <meta property="og:description" content="Expert web
development services for businesses worldwide">
    <meta property="og:image"
content="https://yourcompany.com/social-image.jpg">
    <meta property="og:url"
content="https://yourcompany.com">

    <!-- External resources -->
    <link rel="stylesheet" href="css/main.css">
    <link rel="preconnect"
href="https://fonts.googleapis.com">
    <link rel="stylesheet"
href="https://fonts.googleapis.com/css2?family=Inter:wght
@300;400;600;700&display=swap">

    <!-- Favicon -->
```

```
    <link rel="icon" type="image/png" sizes="32x32"
href="/favicon-32x32.png">

    <!-- Scripts -->
    <script defer src="js/main.js"></script>
</head>
```

2.4 The <body> Element

The Visible Content Container

The <body> element contains all visible content that appears on the webpage. Everything users see and interact with - text, images, videos, forms, navigation menus, and interactive elements - must be placed within the body section.

#html

```
<body>
    <header>
        <h1>Welcome to My Website</h1>
    </header>

    <main>
        <p>This is the main content area.</p>
    </main>

    <footer>
        <p>&copy; 2024 My Website</p>
    </footer>
</body>
```

Body Element Attributes

Global Attributes

The body element supports all global HTML attributes, but several deserve special attention:

#html

```
<body class="dark-theme" id="main-page" data-page="home">
```

Event Handler Attributes

Body elements can include event handlers for page-level interactions:

#html

```
<body onload="initializePage()" onresize="handleResize()"
onbeforeunload="confirmLeave()">
```

Modern development practices prefer adding event listeners through JavaScript rather than inline event handlers:

#html

```
<body>
    <script>
        document.body.addEventListener('load', function()
{
            console.log('Page loaded');
        });
    </script>
</body>
```

Semantic Structure Within Body

Modern HTML emphasizes semantic structure using elements that describe content meaning rather than just appearance:

#html

```html
<body>
    <header>
        <nav>
            <ul>
                <li><a href="#home">Home</a></li>
                <li><a href="#about">About</a></li>
                <li><a href="#services">Services</a></li>
                <li><a href="#contact">Contact</a></li>
            </ul>
        </nav>
    </header>

    <main>
        <section id="home">
            <h1>Welcome to Our Company</h1>
            <p>We provide excellent services...</p>
        </section>

        <section id="about">
            <h2>About Us</h2>
            <article>
                <h3>Our Story</h3>
                <p>Founded in 2020...</p>
            </article>
        </section>
```

```
        <aside>
            <h3>Latest News</h3>
            <ul>
                <li>Company milestone achieved</li>
                <li>New service launched</li>
            </ul>
        </aside>
    </main>

    <footer>
        <p>&copy; 2024 Our Company. All rights
reserved.</p>
        <address>
            <p>123 Business Street<br>
            City, State 12345<br>
            <a
href="mailto:info@company.com">info@company.com</a></p>
        </address>
    </footer>
</body>
```

Content Organization Principles

Logical Document Flow

Content should follow a logical reading order that makes sense when CSS styling is removed:

#html

```
<body>
    <!-- Header content first -->
```

```
    <header>
        <h1>Site Title</h1>
        <nav>Navigation menu</nav>
    </header>

    <!-- Main content second -->
    <main>
        <h2>Page Heading</h2>
        <p>Primary content...</p>
    </main>

    <!-- Footer content last -->
    <footer>
        <p>Footer information</p>
    </footer>
</body>
```

Heading Hierarchy

Maintain proper heading structure for accessibility and SEO:

html

```
<body>
    <h1>Main Page Title</h1>

    <section>
        <h2>Major Section</h2>
        <p>Section content...</p>

        <section>
```

```
            <h3>Subsection</h3>
            <p>Subsection content...</p>

            <section>
                <h4>Sub-subsection</h4>
                <p>More specific content...</p>
            </section>
        </section>
    </section>
</body>
```

Interactive Elements in Body

The body section contains all interactive elements users can engage with:

#html

```
<body>
    <form action="/submit" method="post">
        <label for="username">Username:</label>
        <input type="text" id="username" name="username"
required>

        <label for="email">Email:</label>
        <input type="email" id="email" name="email"
required>

        <label for="message">Message:</label>
        <textarea id="message" name="message" rows="4"
cols="50"></textarea>

        <button type="submit">Send Message</button>
```

```
    </form>


    <details>
        <summary>Click to expand</summary>
        <p>Hidden content that appears when expanded.</p>
    </details>


    <dialog id="myDialog">
        <p>This is a modal dialog</p>
        <button
onclick="document.getElementById('myDialog').close()">Clo
se</button>
    </dialog>
</body>
```

Multimedia Content Integration

The body element houses all multimedia content:

#html

```
<body>
    <section>
        <h2>Our Gallery</h2>


        <figure>
            <img src="images/product1.jpg" alt="Premium
product showcase">
            <figcaption>Our flagship product in
action</figcaption>
        </figure>
```

```
        <figure>
            <video controls width="640" height="360">
                <source src="videos/demo.mp4"
type="video/mp4">
                <source src="videos/demo.webm"
type="video/webm">
                <p>Your browser doesn't support video
playback.</p>
            </video>
            <figcaption>Product demonstration
video</figcaption>
        </figure>

        <figure>
            <audio controls>
                <source src="audio/podcast.mp3"
type="audio/mpeg">
                <source src="audio/podcast.ogg"
type="audio/ogg">
                <p>Your browser doesn't support audio
playback.</p>
            </audio>
            <figcaption>Latest podcast
episode</figcaption>
        </figure>
    </section>
</body>
```

2.5 Saving and Opening HTML Files

File Naming Conventions

Proper file naming ensures compatibility across different operating systems and web servers. HTML files should follow these conventions:

Extension Requirements

HTML files must use either `.html` or `.htm` extensions:

```
index.html          ✓ Preferred
about.html          ✓ Standard
contact.htm         ✓ Acceptable but less common
homepage.HTML       ✓ Works but inconsistent
page.txt            ✗ Wrong extension
```

Naming Best Practices

Use lowercase: Many web servers are case-sensitive, so consistent lowercase prevents issues.

```
about.html          ✓ Recommended
About.html          ⚠ Potential issues
ABOUT.HTML          ⚠ Potential issues
```

Avoid spaces: Use hyphens or underscores instead of spaces.

```
contact-us.html     ✓ SEO-friendly
contact_us.html     ✓ Acceptable
contact us.html     ✗ Causes problems
```

Use descriptive names: File names should clearly indicate content purpose.

```
services.html       ✓ Clear and descriptive
pricing.html        ✓ Indicates content type
page2.html          ✗ Generic and unclear
temp.html           ✗ Not descriptive
```

File Structure Organization

Organize HTML files in a logical directory structure:

```
website-project/
├── index.html
├── about.html
├── contact.html
├── services/
│   ├── web-design.html
│   ├── seo-services.html
│   └── maintenance.html
├── blog/
│   ├── index.html
│   ├── 2024/
│   │   ├── january/
│   │   │   └── new-year-post.html
│   │   └── february/
│   │       └── valentine-tips.html
├── assets/
│   ├── css/
│   │   ├── main.css
│   │   └── responsive.css
│   ├── js/
│   │   ├── main.js
│   │   └── analytics.js
│   ├── images/
│   │   ├── logo.png
│   │   ├── hero-banner.jpg
│   │   └── gallery/
│   │       ├── photo1.jpg
```

```
│   │       └── photo2.jpg
│   └── fonts/
│       ├── custom-font.woff2
│       └── icons.woff
```

Character Encoding Considerations

Save HTML files with proper character encoding to ensure text displays correctly:

UTF-8 Encoding

Always save HTML files using UTF-8 encoding, which supports international characters:

#html

```
<!DOCTYPE html>
<html lang="en">
<head>
    <meta charset="UTF-8">
    <title>International Content Example</title>
</head>
<body>
    <h1>Welcome - Bienvenido - 欢迎 - مرحبا</h1>
    <p>This page displays text in multiple languages
correctly.</p>
</body>
</html>
```

Text Editor Encoding Settings

Visual Studio Code: File → Preferences → Settings → Search "encoding" → Set to UTF-8 **Sublime Text**: File → Save with Encoding → UTF-8 **Notepad++**: Encoding → Convert to UTF-8

Opening HTML Files in Browsers

Multiple methods exist for viewing HTML files in web browsers:

Direct File Opening

Double-click method: Double-clicking an HTML file opens it in the default browser.

Right-click method: Right-click the file and select "Open with" to choose a specific browser.

Drag and drop: Drag the HTML file directly onto a browser window.

Browser Address Bar Method

Type the file path directly in the browser's address bar:

```
file:///C:/Users/YourName/Documents/website/index.html
file:///Users/YourName/Documents/website/index.html (Mac)
file:///home/username/Documents/website/index.html (Linux)
```

Local Development Server

Using a local server provides better development experience:

VS Code Live Server Extension:

1. Install Live Server extension
2. Right-click HTML file
3. Select "Open with Live Server"

Python Simple Server:

```bash
# Python 3
```

```
python -m http.server 8000
```

```
# Python 2
```

```
python -m SimpleHTTPServer 8000
```

Node.js http-server:

#bash

```
npm install -g http-server
http-server
```

Browser Developer Tools Usage

Access developer tools to inspect and debug HTML:

Chrome/Edge: F12 or Ctrl+Shift+I (Cmd+Option+I on Mac) **Firefox**: F12 or Ctrl+Shift+I (Cmd+Option+I on Mac) **Safari**: Cmd+Option+I (enable Developer menu first)

Elements Panel

The Elements panel shows the HTML structure with live editing capabilities:

#html

```html
<!-- Original HTML -->
```

```html
<div class="container">
    <h1>Original Title</h1>
    <p>Original paragraph text.</p>
</div>

<!-- You can edit directly in DevTools -->
<div class="container modified">
    <h1>Modified Title</h1>
    <p>Updated paragraph text with new content.</p>
</div>
```

Console Panel

Use the console to test JavaScript interactions with HTML elements:

javascript

// Access elements by ID

```javascript
document.getElementById('myElement')
```

// Access elements by class

```javascript
document.getElementsByClassName('myClass')
```

// Access elements by tag name

```javascript
document.getElementsByTagName('p')
```

// Modern query selectors

```
document.querySelector('.myClass')
document.querySelectorAll('p')
```

File Management Best Practices

Version Control Integration

Use version control systems like Git to track changes:

#bash

```
git init
git add index.html
git commit -m "Initial HTML structure"
git add about.html contact.html
git commit -m "Added about and contact pages"
```

Backup Strategies

Implement regular backup procedures:

- Cloud storage synchronization (Google Drive, Dropbox, OneDrive)
- External hard drive backups
- Repository hosting (GitHub, GitLab, Bitbucket)

File Linking Considerations

Use relative paths for internal links to maintain portability:

#html

```
<!-- Relative paths (recommended) -->
<a href="about.html">About Us</a>
<a href="services/web-design.html">Web Design</a>
<a href="../index.html">Back to Home</a>
<img src="assets/images/logo.png" alt="Company Logo">
<link rel="stylesheet" href="assets/css/main.css">

<!-- Absolute paths (avoid for internal links) -->
<a href="https://yoursite.com/about.html">About Us</a>
<img src="C:/website/images/logo.png" alt="Logo">
```

Testing Across Different Environments

Test HTML files in various scenarios:

- Different browsers (Chrome, Firefox, Safari, Edge)
- Different operating systems (Windows, Mac, Linux)
- Different devices (desktop, tablet, mobile)
- With and without internet connection
- On actual web servers vs. local file system

Essential Tips

- Place the DOCTYPE declaration as the absolute first line of every HTML document without any preceding whitespace, comments, or other content to ensure browsers render in standards mode.
- Always include the lang attribute in your html tag with the appropriate language code to improve accessibility for screen readers and help search engines understand your content's primary language.
- Keep your head section organized by grouping similar meta elements together - charset and viewport first, then SEO meta tags, followed by external resources like stylesheets and scripts.
- Use semantic HTML5 elements like header, nav, main, article, section, aside, and footer within your body element instead of generic divs to

create meaningful document structure that benefits both accessibility and SEO.

- Save all HTML files with UTF-8 encoding and use consistent lowercase naming conventions with hyphens instead of spaces to ensure cross-platform compatibility and avoid server issues.

Actionable Strategies

- Create a standardized HTML template with complete DOCTYPE, html, head, and body structure that you can copy and modify for new pages, ensuring consistency across your entire website project.
- Establish a clear file and folder organization system from the start of any project, separating HTML files, CSS stylesheets, JavaScript files, and images into logical directories that scale as your site grows.
- Set up your text editor with proper encoding settings, syntax highlighting, and useful extensions like auto-completion and bracket matching to streamline your HTML writing process and catch errors early.
- Use browser developer tools regularly to inspect your HTML structure, test changes in real-time, and understand how browsers interpret your markup before making permanent modifications to your files.
- Implement a consistent workflow for testing HTML files across multiple browsers and devices, creating a checklist that includes viewing pages with and without CSS to verify proper semantic structure.
- Maintain proper heading hierarchy throughout your documents by using h1 for main page titles, h2 for major sections, and h3-h6 for subsections, never skipping heading levels for styling purposes.
- Develop the habit of validating your HTML markup using online validators or browser extensions to catch syntax errors, missing closing tags, and other structural issues that could affect page rendering and accessibility.

Chapter 3: Headings and Paragraphs

Text forms the backbone of every website. Whether you're building a personal blog, a corporate site, or an e-commerce platform, the way you structure and present textual content determines how users interact with your pages. HTML provides several fundamental elements specifically designed for organizing and displaying text content effectively.

Understanding how to properly implement headings, paragraphs, line breaks, and horizontal rules creates the foundation for readable, accessible, and well-structured web pages. These elements work together to establish visual hierarchy, improve readability, and enhance the overall user experience.

3.1 Using `<h1>` to `<h6>`

Understanding HTML Heading Hierarchy

HTML offers six levels of headings, numbered from 1 to 6, with `<h1>` being the most important and `<h6>` being the least significant. These heading elements create a structured hierarchy that helps both users and search engines understand the organization of your content.

The heading hierarchy follows a top-down approach where each level represents a different degree of importance or section depth. Think of headings as the outline of a research paper or book - they provide structure and make content scannable.

Syntax and Basic Implementation

Each heading element follows the same basic syntax pattern:

#html

```
<h1>Main Title</h1>
<h2>Section Title</h2>
```

```
<h3>Subsection Title</h3>
<h4>Sub-subsection Title</h4>
<h5>Minor Heading</h5>
<h6>Smallest Heading</h6>
```

Practical Examples of Heading Usage

Here's a comprehensive example showing how headings work together to structure a webpage about web development:

#html

```
<!DOCTYPE html>
<html lang="en">
<head>
    <meta charset="UTF-8">
    <meta name="viewport" content="width=device-width,
initial-scale=1.0">
    <title>Web Development Guide</title>
</head>
<body>
    <h1>Complete Guide to Web Development</h1>

    <h2>Frontend Technologies</h2>
    <h3>HTML</h3>
    <h4>Semantic Elements</h4>
    <h5>Form Elements</h5>
    <h6>Input Types</h6>

    <h3>CSS</h3>
    <h4>Selectors</h4>
```

```
    <h4>Flexbox Layout</h4>
    <h4>Grid Layout</h4>

    <h3>JavaScript</h3>
    <h4>Variables and Data Types</h4>
    <h4>Functions</h4>
    <h4>DOM Manipulation</h4>

    <h2>Backend Technologies</h2>
    <h3>Server-Side Languages</h3>
    <h4>Node.js</h4>
    <h4>Python</h4>
    <h4>PHP</h4>
</body>
</html>
```

Visual Hierarchy and Default Styling

Each heading level has default styling that creates visual distinction:

- `<h1>`: Largest font size, typically 32px, bold weight
- `<h2>`: Second largest, typically 24px, bold weight
- `<h3>`: Medium-large size, typically 19px, bold weight
- `<h4>`: Medium size, typically 16px, bold weight
- `<h5>`: Small size, typically 13px, bold weight
- `<h6>`: Smallest size, typically 11px, bold weight

SEO and Accessibility Considerations

Search engines use heading structure to understand page content and hierarchy. Proper heading usage improves SEO rankings and makes content accessible to screen readers and assistive technologies.

Screen readers use headings to create a navigable outline, allowing users to jump between sections quickly. This makes proper heading hierarchy crucial for accessibility compliance.

Common Heading Mistakes to Avoid

Never skip heading levels for visual purposes. Instead of jumping from `<h2>` to `<h5>` because you prefer the visual appearance, use CSS to modify the styling while maintaining proper semantic structure.

Avoid using multiple `<h1>` elements on a single page unless you're implementing HTML5 sectioning elements. Each page should typically have one main `<h1>` that describes the primary content.

3.2 Creating Paragraphs with <p>

Understanding the Paragraph Element

The `<p>` element represents a paragraph of text and is one of the most frequently used HTML elements. It automatically adds spacing before and after the content, creating visual separation between blocks of text.

Paragraphs are block-level elements, meaning they take up the full width available and create a new line before and after their content. This behavior makes them ideal for structuring readable text content.

Basic Paragraph Syntax

```
#html
```

```
<p>This is a paragraph of text. It can contain multiple
sentences and will be displayed as a cohesive block of
content with automatic spacing.</p>
<p>This is another paragraph. Notice how there's
automatic spacing between this paragraph and the previous
one.</p>
```

Advanced Paragraph Usage

Paragraphs can contain various inline elements to enhance text formatting and meaning:

#html

```
<p>This paragraph contains <strong>bold text</strong>,
<em>emphasized text</em>, and even <a
href="https://example.com">links to other pages</a>.</p>


<p>You can also include <code>inline code</code>,
<mark>highlighted text</mark>, and <span style="color:
blue;">styled text</span> within paragraphs.</p>


<p>Paragraphs can contain <abbr title="HyperText Markup
Language">HTML</abbr> abbreviations and <q>short
quotations</q> as well.</p>
```

Paragraph Content Guidelines

Each paragraph should focus on a single idea or concept. When the topic changes or when you're introducing a new point, start a new paragraph. This approach improves readability and helps users scan content more effectively.

Avoid creating overly long paragraphs that might overwhelm readers. Generally, paragraphs containing 3-5 sentences work well for web content, though this can vary based on your audience and content type.

Nesting and Block-Level Restrictions

Paragraphs cannot contain other block-level elements like headings, other paragraphs, or structural elements. They're designed specifically for text content and inline elements.

#html

```
<!-- Correct paragraph usage -->
<p>This paragraph contains only text and <em>inline elements</em>.</p>


<!-- Incorrect - don't nest block elements in paragraphs -->
<p>This is wrong: <div>Block elements don't belong here</div></p>
```

Styling Paragraphs with CSS

While paragraphs have default styling, you can customize their appearance using CSS:

#html

```
<!DOCTYPE html>
<html lang="en">
<head>
    <meta charset="UTF-8">
    <meta name="viewport" content="width=device-width, initial-scale=1.0">
    <title>Styled Paragraphs</title>
```

```
    <style>
        .intro {
            font-size: 18px;
            line-height: 1.6;
            color: #333;
            margin-bottom: 20px;
        }

        .highlight {
            background-color: #f0f8ff;
            padding: 15px;
            border-left: 4px solid #007acc;
        }
    </style>
</head>
<body>
    <p class="intro">This is an introductory paragraph
with custom styling.</p>
    <p class="highlight">This paragraph has a highlighted
background and border.</p>
    <p>This is a regular paragraph with default
styling.</p>
</body>
</html>
```

3.3 Line Breaks with `<br>`

Understanding Line Breaks

The `<br>` element creates a line break within text content. Unlike paragraphs, which create block-level separation with margins, line breaks simply move content to the next line without adding extra spacing.

Line breaks are self-closing elements, meaning they don't require a closing tag. In XHTML and XML-style HTML, you might see them written as `<br />`, but in HTML5, `<br>` is sufficient.

When to Use Line Breaks

Line breaks are appropriate for content where line separation is meaningful, such as:

- Postal addresses
- Poetry or song lyrics
- Short lists where paragraph separation would be excessive
- Contact information

Basic Line Break Syntax

#html

```
<p>
    John Smith<br>
    123 Main Street<br>
    Anytown, ST 12345<br>
    United States
</p>

<p>
    Email: john@example.com<br>
    Phone: (555) 123-4567<br>
    Fax: (555) 123-4568
</p>
```

Line Breaks in Poetry and Formatted Text

When displaying poetry or other formatted text where line breaks are semantically important:

#html

```html
<p>
    Two roads diverged in a yellow wood,<br>
    And sorry I could not travel both<br>
    And be one traveler, long I stood<br>
    And looked down one as far as I could<br>
    To where it bent in the undergrowth;
</p>
```

Avoiding Line Break Misuse

Don't use multiple line breaks to create spacing between paragraphs. This practice makes content harder to maintain and style consistently:

#html

```html
<!-- Wrong way to create spacing -->
<p>First paragraph</p>
<br><br><br>
<p>Second paragraph</p>

<!-- Correct way using proper paragraph separation -->
<p>First paragraph</p>
<p>Second paragraph</p>
```

Responsive Considerations

Line breaks create fixed line endings that might not work well on different screen sizes. Consider whether your line breaks will make sense on mobile devices where text might reflow differently.

For responsive design, sometimes it's better to use CSS to control text flow rather than hard-coded line breaks:

#html

```
<style>
    .address {
        line-height: 1.4;
    }

    .address span {
        display: block;
    }

    @media (min-width: 768px) {
        .address span {
            display: inline;
        }

        .address span:after {
            content: " | ";
        }

        .address span:last-child:after {
            content: "";
        }
    }
</style>
```

```html
<div class="address">
    <span>123 Main Street</span>
    <span>Anytown, ST 12345</span>
    <span>United States</span>
</div>
```

3.4 Horizontal Rules with <hr>

Understanding Horizontal Rules

The `<hr>` element creates a horizontal rule or line that represents a thematic break between content sections. It's a self-closing element that provides visual separation while also carrying semantic meaning about content structure.

Horizontal rules help break up long content sections and indicate topic changes or transitions between different types of content within the same page.

Basic Horizontal Rule Syntax

#html

```html
<p>This is the first section of content.</p>
<hr>
<p>This is a new section of content, separated by a horizontal rule.</p>
```

Semantic Usage of Horizontal Rules

Use horizontal rules to separate content sections that are related but distinct:

#html

```html
<article>
    <h1>Product Review: Smartphone XYZ</h1>

    <h2>Design and Build Quality</h2>
    <p>The smartphone features premium materials and excellent craftsmanship...</p>

    <hr>

    <h2>Performance and Speed</h2>
    <p>Testing revealed impressive benchmark scores and smooth operation...</p>

    <hr>

    <h2>Camera Quality</h2>
    <p>The camera system delivers outstanding results in various lighting conditions...</p>

    <hr>

    <h2>Final Verdict</h2>
    <p>Overall, this smartphone offers excellent value and performance...</p>
</article>
```

Styling Horizontal Rules

Default horizontal rules appear as simple gray lines, but CSS allows extensive customization:

#html

```
<!DOCTYPE html>
<html lang="en">
<head>
    <meta charset="UTF-8">
    <meta name="viewport" content="width=device-width,
initial-scale=1.0">
    <title>Styled Horizontal Rules</title>
    <style>
        .fancy-hr {
            border: none;
            height: 3px;
            background: linear-gradient(to right,
#ff6b6b, #4ecdc4, #ffe66d);
            margin: 30px 0;
        }

        .dotted-hr {
            border: none;
            border-top: 3px dotted #333;
            margin: 20px 0;
        }

        .centered-hr {
            border: none;
            height: 2px;
            background-color: #ccc;
            width: 50%;
            margin: 25px auto;
        }
```

```
        .text-hr {
            border: none;
            position: relative;
            text-align: center;
            margin: 30px 0;
        }

        .text-hr:before {
            content: "• • •";
            color: #666;
            font-size: 18px;
        }
    </style>
</head>
<body>
    <p>Content before the first rule</p>
    <hr class="fancy-hr">

    <p>Content between rules</p>
    <hr class="dotted-hr">

    <p>More content</p>
    <hr class="centered-hr">

    <p>Final content section</p>
    <hr class="text-hr">

    <p>Content after the last rule</p>
</body>
</html>
```

Horizontal Rules in Document Structure

Horizontal rules work well in blog posts, articles, and documentation to separate major sections:

#html

```
<article>
    <header>
        <h1>Understanding Climate Change</h1>
        <p>Published on March 15, 2024</p>
    </header>

    <section>
        <h2>Introduction</h2>
        <p>Climate change represents one of the most 
pressing challenges...</p>
    </section>

    <hr>

    <section>
        <h2>Scientific Evidence</h2>
        <p>Multiple lines of evidence support the reality 
of climate change...</p>
    </section>

    <hr>

    <section>
        <h2>Potential Solutions</h2>
```

```
        <p>Addressing climate change requires coordinated global action...</p>
    </section>

    <hr>

    <footer>
        <p>Author: Dr. Jane Smith, Environmental Science Department</p>
    </footer>
</article>
```

Accessibility Considerations

Screen readers handle horizontal rules appropriately, announcing them as separators or breaks. However, ensure that the content structure makes sense even without the visual separation provided by the horizontal rule.

3.5 Best Practices for Text Content

Creating Scannable Content Structure

Modern web users scan content rather than reading every word. Structure your text content to support this behavior by using clear headings, short paragraphs, and logical information hierarchy.

Break up large blocks of text with subheadings, bullet points, and white space. This approach makes content more digestible and improves user engagement.

Maintaining Consistent Heading Hierarchy

Always follow proper heading hierarchy without skipping levels. This practice benefits both SEO and accessibility:

#html

```html
<!-- Correct hierarchy -->
<h1>Main Topic</h1>
<h2>Section Topic</h2>
<h3>Subsection Topic</h3>
<h4>Sub-subsection Topic</h4>

<!-- Incorrect - don't skip levels -->
<h1>Main Topic</h1>
<h4>This skips h2 and h3</h4>
```

Writing Effective Headings

Create headings that accurately describe the content they introduce. Good headings help users understand what they'll learn in each section:

#html

```html
<!-- Vague headings -->
<h2>Things to Know</h2>
<h2>More Information</h2>

<!-- Descriptive headings -->
<h2>Required Equipment for Installation</h2>
<h2>Step-by-Step Installation Process</h2>
```

Optimizing Paragraph Length and Structure

Keep paragraphs focused on single ideas. Web content generally works best with shorter paragraphs than print content:

#html

```
<!-- Too long for web content -->
<p>This paragraph contains multiple ideas about web design, user experience, responsive layouts, color theory, typography choices, navigation patterns, content strategy, and performance optimization, making it difficult for users to scan and understand the key points being presented.</p>


<!-- Better approach -->
<p>Effective web design considers multiple interconnected factors that impact user experience.</p>


<p>Responsive layouts ensure content works across different devices and screen sizes.</p>


<p>Typography and color choices affect readability and visual appeal.</p>


<p>Well-planned navigation patterns help users find information efficiently.</p>
```

Implementing Semantic HTML

Use HTML elements for their semantic meaning rather than their default appearance. This approach improves accessibility and SEO while making your code more maintainable:

#html

```
<!-- Using elements for meaning, not appearance -->
```

```html
<h2>Important Section</h2>
<p>This paragraph introduces the <strong>most critical information</strong> and includes <em>emphasized details</em>.</p>

<!-- Avoid using elements just for styling -->
<h3>Don't use headings just to make text bigger</h3>
```

Content Accessibility Guidelines

Ensure text content meets accessibility standards by providing sufficient color contrast, using clear language, and structuring content logically.

Include alternative text for images that complement your text content, and ensure that your heading structure creates a logical outline that screen reader users can navigate effectively.

Cross-Browser Compatibility

Test your text content across different browsers and devices to ensure consistent appearance and functionality. While modern browsers handle basic text elements consistently, custom styling might require testing and adjustment.

Performance Considerations

Optimize text content for fast loading by minimizing unnecessary HTML, using efficient CSS, and considering the impact of web fonts on load times.

Large amounts of text content can affect page load speed, especially on mobile connections. Consider implementing progressive loading or pagination for very long content.

Mobile-First Text Design

Design text content with mobile users as the primary consideration. This means using larger font sizes, adequate line spacing, and touch-friendly interactive elements.

Test how your headings, paragraphs, and line breaks work on different screen sizes to ensure readability across all devices.

Essential Tips

- Always start with `<h1>` and follow sequential heading hierarchy without skipping levels to maintain proper document structure and accessibility compliance.
- Keep paragraphs focused on single ideas with 3-5 sentences each to improve readability and scanning behavior for web users.
- Use line breaks sparingly and only when line position carries semantic meaning, such as in addresses, poetry, or contact information blocks.
- Implement horizontal rules to create meaningful content separation while avoiding overuse that might fragment the reading experience unnecessarily.
- Write descriptive headings that accurately preview the content users will find in each section, helping them navigate and understand your information architecture.

Actionable Strategies

- Structure your content outline using only headings before writing paragraphs to ensure logical information flow and proper hierarchy establishment.
- Test heading hierarchy by using a screen reader or accessibility tool to verify that your content structure makes sense when navigated by assistive technology.
- Implement a consistent paragraph length standard across your website, aiming for 50-75 words per paragraph for optimal web readability.

- Create a style guide that defines when to use line breaks versus paragraph breaks to maintain consistency across all content creators and editors.
- Use horizontal rules strategically to separate major content sections while avoiding their use within closely related information that should flow together.
- Audit existing content regularly to identify overly long paragraphs, missing heading hierarchy, or unclear section breaks that could benefit from restructuring.
- Optimize text content for mobile-first design by testing how headings, paragraphs, and breaks appear on small screens before finalizing desktop layouts.

Chapter 4: Text Formatting

Text formatting transforms plain content into visually engaging and semantically meaningful communication. HTML provides numerous elements that allow you to emphasize important information, mark special content types, and create visual hierarchy through typography. Understanding these formatting options helps you create professional-looking web pages that effectively communicate your message.

Proper text formatting goes beyond making content look attractive. It conveys meaning, improves readability, and enhances accessibility for users with different needs. Modern web development requires balancing visual presentation with semantic accuracy to create content that works across all devices and assistive technologies.

4.1 Bold and Italics

Understanding Strong Emphasis with `<strong>`

The `<strong>` element indicates content with strong importance or urgency. Unlike visual-only formatting, `<strong>` carries semantic meaning that screen readers and other assistive technologies can interpret and announce appropriately to users.

Screen readers typically announce strongly emphasized text with increased emphasis or different vocal inflection, helping visually impaired users understand the content hierarchy and importance.

Basic Strong Element Syntax

#html

```html
<p>This is normal text with <strong>strongly emphasized content</strong> within the paragraph.</p>
```

```
<p><strong>Warning:</strong> Always backup your data
before making system changes.</p>

<p>The <strong>most important point</strong> to remember
is proper file organization.</p>
```

Visual Bold Formatting with <b>

The <b> element provides visual bold formatting without semantic meaning. Use this element when you need bold appearance for stylistic purposes rather than to convey importance or emphasis.

Common use cases for <b> include product names, keywords in technical documentation, or lead-in words that need visual distinction without semantic emphasis.

#html

```
<p>The <b>iPhone 15 Pro</b> features advanced camera
capabilities.</p>

<p><b>Installation:</b> Follow these steps to complete
the setup process.</p>

<p>Key terms: <b>HTML</b>, <b>CSS</b>, and
<b>JavaScript</b> form the foundation of web
development.</p>
```

Emphasizing Text with <em>

The <em> element provides emphasis that changes the meaning of the sentence. It indicates stress emphasis that would be pronounced differently when speaking aloud.

Screen readers recognize <em> elements and typically announce them with vocal stress or inflection, making the emphasis clear to users who cannot see the visual formatting.

#html

```
<p>I <em>really</em> need to finish this project
today.</p>


<p>The meeting is scheduled for <em>next</em> Tuesday,
not this Tuesday.</p>


<p>You should <em>always</em> validate your HTML code
before publishing.</p>
```

Visual Italic Formatting with <i>

The <i> element provides italic visual formatting for content that needs stylistic distinction without semantic emphasis. This includes foreign phrases, technical terms, thoughts, or ship names.

#html

```
<p>The restaurant serves authentic <i>cuisine
française</i> in an elegant setting.</p>


<p>The <i>Titanic</i> remains one of the most famous
ships in history.</p>


<p>The term <i>responsive design</i> refers to layouts
that adapt to different screen sizes.</p>


<p><i>She wondered if the meeting would ever end,</i>
thinking to herself as the presentation continued.</p>
```

Combining Bold and Italic Formatting

You can combine different formatting elements to achieve specific visual and semantic effects:

#html

```
<p>This is <strong><em>very important and
emphasized</em></strong> information.</p>


<p>The <strong><i>Enterprise</i></strong> was the most
famous starship in the fleet.</p>


<p><em>Remember:</em> <strong>Never share your
password</strong> with anyone.</p>
```

Nested Formatting Examples

Complex formatting scenarios often require nesting multiple elements:

#html

```
<article>
    <h2>Product Review: <strong>Premium
Headphones</strong></h2>


    <p>The <b>Sony WH-1000XM4</b> headphones offer
<strong>exceptional</strong> noise cancellation. The
<i>Active Noise Canceling</i> technology works
<em>remarkably</em> well in busy environments.</p>
```

```
    <p><strong>Pros:</strong> <em>Outstanding</em> sound
quality, <em>comfortable</em> fit, and <em>long</em>
battery life.</p>

    <p><strong>Cons:</strong> The <i>touch controls</i>
can be <em>overly</em> sensitive in cold weather.</p>
</article>
```

Accessibility Considerations for Bold and Italic

Screen readers handle semantic elements (`<strong>` and `<em>`) differently from visual elements (`<b>` and `<i>`). Choose elements based on meaning rather than appearance to ensure accessibility compliance.

When styling text for visual users, consider that some users might have difficulty distinguishing italic text, especially at smaller font sizes or on low-resolution displays.

4.2 Underline and Strikethrough

Creating Underlined Text with <u>

The `<u>` element creates underlined text, though its use has evolved significantly in modern web development. Originally used for emphasis, underlined text now primarily indicates proper nouns in some languages or marks text that should be stylistically distinct.

Avoid using `<u>` for emphasis since users expect underlined text to be clickable links. This confusion can create poor user experience and accessibility issues.

`#html`

```
<p>The Chinese name <u>李小明</u> translates to Li
Xiaoming in English.</p>


<p>Proper nouns like <u>Beijing</u> and <u>Shanghai</u>
are major Chinese cities.</p>


<p>The misspelled word <u>recieve</u> should be corrected
to "receive".</p>
```

Indicating Deleted Content with `<del>`

The `<del>` element marks content that has been deleted or removed from a document. It typically displays with strikethrough formatting and carries semantic meaning about content changes.

This element is particularly useful for showing edits, corrections, or version changes in documents:

#html

```
<p>The meeting is scheduled for <del>Monday</del> Tuesday
at 3 PM.</p>


<p>Original price: <del>$99.99</del> Sale price:
$79.99</p>


<p>The project deadline is <del>March 15th</del> March
22nd due to additional requirements.</p>
```

Marking Inserted Content with `<ins>`

The <ins> element indicates content that has been added to a document. It often appears with underlined formatting and works well in combination with <del> to show document revisions:

#html

```
<p>The <del>old</del> <ins>new</ins> policy takes effect
immediately.</p>


<p>Team members: John, Sarah, <ins>Michael</ins>, and
Lisa.</p>


<p>The budget has been <del>reduced</del>
<ins>increased</ins> by 15%.</p>
```

Visual Strikethrough with <s>

The <s> element provides visual strikethrough formatting for content that is no longer accurate or relevant but should remain visible for context. Unlike <del>, it doesn't carry semantic meaning about document changes.

#html

```
<p>Today's special: <s>Grilled salmon</s> Sold out!</p>


<p>Available colors: Red, Blue, <s>Green</s>, Yellow</p>


<p>Event status: <s>Registration open</s> Registration
closed</p>
```

Combining Deletion and Insertion Elements

Show complex edits and revisions by combining different elements:

#html

```
<article>
    <h2>Contract Amendment</h2>

    <p>The contract duration is <del>12 months</del>
<ins>18 months</ins> starting from the effective
date.</p>

    <p>Monthly payment: <del>$2,500</del>
<ins>$3,200</ins></p>

    <p>Deliverables include:
        <ul>
            <li>Initial design mockups</li>
            <li><del>Basic functionality</del>
<ins>Complete application with advanced
features</ins></li>
            <li>Testing and documentation</li>
            <li><ins>Six months of maintenance
support</ins></li>
        </ul>
    </p>
</article>
```

Styling Underline and Strikethrough Elements

Custom CSS can enhance the appearance of these elements while maintaining their semantic meaning:

#html

```
<!DOCTYPE html>
```

```
<html lang="en">
<head>
    <meta charset="UTF-8">
    <meta name="viewport" content="width=device-width,
initial-scale=1.0">
    <title>Styled Text Formatting</title>
    <style>
        .highlight-insert {
            background-color: #d4edda;
            color: #155724;
            text-decoration: underline;
            padding: 2px 4px;
        }

        .highlight-delete {
            background-color: #f8d7da;
            color: #721c24;
            text-decoration: line-through;
            padding: 2px 4px;
        }

        .special-underline {
            text-decoration: underline wavy #ff6b6b;
        }

        .double-strike {
            text-decoration: line-through;
            position: relative;
        }

        .double-strike::after {
```

```
            content: '';
            position: absolute;
            top: 60%;
            left: 0;
            right: 0;
            height: 1px;
            background: currentColor;
        }
    </style>
</head>
<body>
    <p>The price was <del class="highlight-
delete">$150</del> <ins class="highlight-
insert">$120</ins> after the discount.</p>

    <p>Important terms: <u class="special-underline">API
documentation</u> and <u class="special-underline">user
authentication</u>.</p>

    <p>This item is <s class="double-strike">no longer
available</s> for purchase.</p>
</body>
</html>
```

4.3 Superscript and Subscript

Creating Superscript Text with `<sup>`

The `<sup>` element raises text above the baseline, creating superscript formatting. This is essential for mathematical expressions, footnote references, ordinal numbers, and scientific notation.

Superscript text appears smaller and higher than normal text, making it ideal for references and mathematical notation:

#html

```
<p>Einstein's famous equation: E = mc<sup>2</sup></p>


<p>The area of a square is calculated as
length<sup>2</sup>.</p>


<p>See footnote reference<sup>1</sup> for additional
information.</p>


<p>Today is March 21<sup>st</sup>, 2024.</p>
```

Mathematical and Scientific Applications

Superscript is crucial for properly displaying mathematical and scientific content:

#html

```
<div>
    <h3>Mathematical Expressions</h3>
    <p>Quadratic formula: x = (-b ± √(b<sup>2</sup> -
4ac)) / 2a</p>
    <p>Power of ten: 10<sup>6</sup> = 1,000,000</p>
    <p>Square root: √x = x<sup>1/2</sup></p>

    <h3>Chemical Formulas</h3>
    <p>Water molecule: H<sub>2</sub>O</p>
    <p>Carbon dioxide: CO<sub>2</sub></p>
    <p>Sulfuric acid: H<sub>2</sub>SO<sub>4</sub></p>
</div>
```

Creating Subscript Text with <sub>

The <sub> element lowers text below the baseline, creating subscript formatting. This is essential for chemical formulas, mathematical notation, and specialized terminology.

#html

```
<p>Chemical formula for glucose:
C<sub>6</sub>H<sub>12</sub>O<sub>6</sub></p>


<p>Mathematical sequence: a<sub>1</sub>, a<sub>2</sub>,
a<sub>3</sub>, ..., a<sub>n</sub></p>


<p>Base conversion: 1010<sub>2</sub> =
10<sub>10</sub></p>


<p>Log notation: log<sub>10</sub>(100) = 2</p>
```

Complex Scientific Notation

Combine superscript and subscript for complex scientific expressions:

#html

```
<article>
    <h2>Advanced Chemistry Examples</h2>


    <p>Balanced chemical equation:</p>
    <p>2H<sub>2</sub> + O<sub>2</sub> →
2H<sub>2</sub>O</p>
```

```
    <p>Ionic compound: Ca<sup>2+</sup> + 2Cl<sup>-</sup>
→ CaCl<sub>2</sub></p>

    <p>Radioactive decay: <sup>238</sup>U →
<sup>234</sup>Th + <sup>4</sup>He</p>

    <h2>Mathematical Sequences</h2>

    <p>Geometric series: S<sub>n</sub> = a(1 -
r<sup>n</sup>) / (1 - r)</p>

    <p>Exponential function: f(x) = ae<sup>bx</sup> +
c</p>

    <p>Matrix notation: A<sub>ij</sub> represents element
at row i, column j</p>
</article>
```

Footnote and Reference Systems

Create professional footnote systems using superscript:

#html

```
<article>
    <h1>The Impact of Climate Change</h1>

    <p>Global temperatures have risen significantly over
the past century<sup>1</sup>. This warming trend affects
weather patterns<sup>2</sup> and sea levels<sup>3</sup>
worldwide.</p>
```

```html
    <p>Scientists agree that human activities contribute
to these changes<sup>4</sup>, particularly through
greenhouse gas emissions<sup>5</sup>.</p>


    <hr>


    <section>
        <h2>References</h2>
        <p><sup>1</sup> IPCC Climate Change Report,
2023</p>
        <p><sup>2</sup> National Weather Service
Analysis, 2024</p>
        <p><sup>3</sup> Ocean Research Institute
Findings, 2024</p>
        <p><sup>4</sup> Global Scientific Consensus
Study, 2023</p>
        <p><sup>5</sup> Environmental Protection Agency
Data, 2024</p>
    </section>
</article>
```

Accessibility and Superscript/Subscript

Screen readers handle superscript and subscript elements appropriately, often announcing them as "superscript" or "subscript" followed by the content. This helps users understand the formatting context.

Consider providing alternative text or explanations for complex mathematical or scientific notation to ensure accessibility for all users.

4.4 Quotations and Blockquotes

Inline Quotations with <q>

The <q> element marks short quotations that appear within a paragraph or line of text. Browsers automatically add appropriate quotation marks based on the document's language settings.

#html

```
<p>Shakespeare wrote, <q>To be or not to be, that is the question.</q></p>


<p>The customer said, <q>This is exactly what I was looking for!</q></p>


<p>According to the manual, <q>Regular maintenance extends equipment life significantly.</q></p>
```

Language-Specific Quotation Marks

The <q> element automatically uses appropriate quotation marks for different languages:

#html

```
<p lang="en">English quote: <q>Hello, world!</q></p>
<p lang="fr">French quote: <q>Bonjour le monde!</q></p>
<p lang="de">German quote: <q>Hallo Welt!</q></p>
```

Block Quotations with <blockquote>

The <blockquote> element is used for longer quotations that should be displayed as separate blocks of content. These typically include substantial excerpts from other sources.

#html

```
<blockquote>
    <p>The best way to predict the future is to create it. Innovation comes from those who dare to think differently and act boldly in the face of uncertainty.</p>
</blockquote>


<blockquote cite="https://example.com/source">
    <p>Web accessibility is not just about making websites usable for people with disabilities. It's about creating a better user experience for everyone, regardless of their abilities or the devices they use.</p>
</blockquote>
```

Adding Citation Information

Use the `cite` attribute to provide source information, and the `<cite>` element to mark the title of works:

#html

```
<blockquote cite="https://www.w3.org/WAI/">
    <p>The power of the Web is in its universality. Access by everyone regardless of disability is an essential aspect.</p>
    <footer>
        — <cite>Tim Berners-Lee, W3C Director and inventor of the World Wide Web</cite>
    </footer>
</blockquote>
```

```
<p>In his book <cite>Don't Make Me Think</cite>, Steve Krug emphasizes the importance of intuitive web design.</p>
```

Complex Blockquote Structures

Create sophisticated quotation layouts with proper attribution:

#html

```
<article>
    <h2>Industry Expert Opinions</h2>

    <blockquote>
        <p>Artificial intelligence will transform how we work, but it won't replace human creativity and emotional intelligence. The future belongs to those who can effectively collaborate with AI tools.</p>
        <footer>
            <cite>Dr. Sarah Johnson</cite>,
            <span>AI Research Director</span>,
            <time datetime="2024-03-15">March 15, 2024</time>
        </footer>
    </blockquote>

    <blockquote>
        <p>Sustainable web development isn't just about reducing server loads and optimizing code. It's about creating digital experiences that serve users efficiently while minimizing environmental impact.</p>
        <footer>
            <cite>Marcus Chen</cite>,
```

```
            <span>Green Tech Advocate</span>
            <time datetime="2024-03-20">March 20,
2024</time>
        </footer>
    </blockquote>
</article>
```

Styling Quotations with CSS

Enhance quotation appearance while maintaining semantic meaning:

#html

```
<!DOCTYPE html>
<html lang="en">
<head>
    <meta charset="UTF-8">
    <meta name="viewport" content="width=device-width,
initial-scale=1.0">
    <title>Styled Quotations</title>
    <style>
        blockquote {
            margin: 20px 0;
            padding: 20px;
            border-left: 4px solid #007acc;
            background-color: #f8f9fa;
            font-style: italic;
            position: relative;
        }

        blockquote::before {
```

```
        content: '"';
        font-size: 4em;
        color: #007acc;
        position: absolute;
        top: -10px;
        left: 10px;
        font-family: serif;
    }

    blockquote footer {
        margin-top: 15px;
        font-style: normal;
        font-size: 0.9em;
        color: #666;
    }

    q {
        font-style: italic;
        color: #555;
    }

    cite {
        font-weight: bold;
        color: #007acc;
    }

    .pullquote {
        float: right;
        width: 300px;
        margin: 0 0 20px 20px;
        padding: 15px;
```

```
            border: 2px solid #ddd;
            background-color: #fff;
            font-size: 1.2em;
            text-align: center;
        }
    </style>
</head>
<body>
    <article>
        <h1>The Future of Web Development</h1>

        <p>The industry continues to evolve rapidly. As
one expert noted, <q>Staying current with web
technologies requires continuous learning and
adaptation.</q></p>

        <blockquote class="pullquote">
            <p>The best websites don't just look good—
they solve real problems for real people.</p>
            <footer>— <cite>UX Design
Principles</cite></footer>
        </blockquote>

        <p>Modern web development requires understanding
both technical implementation and user experience
design.</p>

        <blockquote>
            <p>Code is read much more often than it is
written. Write code that tells a story, not just code
that works.</p>
            <footer>— <cite>Clean Code
Philosophy</cite></footer>
```

```
        </blockquote>
    </article>
</body>
</html>
```

Nested Quotations

Handle complex quotation scenarios with proper nesting:

#html

```
<blockquote>
    <p>The conference speaker explained, <q>When users say the interface is intuitive, they mean it matches their mental model of how things should work.</q></p>
    <p>This insight changed how our team approaches user interface design.</p>
    <footer>— Conference Notes, UX Summit 2024</footer>
</blockquote>
```

4.5 Semantic Meaning vs. Visual Styling

Understanding Semantic HTML

Semantic HTML means using elements for their intended meaning rather than their default visual appearance. This approach improves accessibility, SEO, and code maintainability while ensuring content works across different devices and contexts.

Search engines and assistive technologies rely on semantic markup to understand content structure and meaning. Proper semantic usage helps your content reach wider audiences and rank better in search results.

Choosing Between Semantic and Visual Elements

Always prioritize semantic meaning when selecting HTML elements:

#html

```html
<!-- Semantic approach - recommended -->
<p>This is <strong>very important</strong> information that requires <em>careful attention</em>.</p>

<p>The book <cite>HTML5 Specification</cite> provides detailed technical information.</p>

<p>The chemical formula is H<sub>2</sub>SO<sub>4</sub>.</p>

<!-- Visual-only approach - avoid -->
<p>This is <b>very important</b> information that requires <i>careful attention</i>.</p>
```

CSS for Visual Styling

Use CSS to control visual appearance while maintaining semantic HTML structure:

#html

```html
<!DOCTYPE html>
<html lang="en">
<head>
    <meta charset="UTF-8">
    <meta name="viewport" content="width=device-width, initial-scale=1.0">
    <title>Semantic Styling</title>
```

```
    <style>
        /* Style semantic elements to match design needs
*/
        strong {
            color: #d32f2f;
            font-weight: 600;
            text-transform: uppercase;
            letter-spacing: 0.5px;
        }

        em {
            color: #1976d2;
            font-style: normal;
            background-color: #e3f2fd;
            padding: 2px 4px;
            border-radius: 3px;
        }

        cite {
            font-style: normal;
            font-weight: bold;
            color: #388e3c;
        }

        .brand-name {
            font-weight: bold;
            color: #ff5722;
            /* Visual styling without semantic emphasis
*/
        }
```

```
        .technical-term {
            font-style: italic;
            color: #795548;
            border-bottom: 1px dotted #795548;
        }
    </style>
</head>
<body>
    <article>
        <h1>Product Documentation</h1>

        <p><strong>Warning:</strong> Always backup your
data before proceeding with <em>system updates</em>.</p>

        <p>For detailed instructions, refer to the
<cite>Administrator's Guide</cite>.</p>

        <p>The <span class="brand-name">SuperTech
Pro</span> system uses <span class="technical-
term">distributed architecture</span> for improved
performance.</p>

        <p>Key benefits include <strong>enhanced
security</strong> and <em>simplified
maintenance</em>.</p>
    </article>
</body>
</html>
```

Screen Reader and Accessibility Impact

Semantic elements provide crucial information to assistive technologies:

#html

```
<!-- Screen readers announce this appropriately -->
<p>The <strong>most critical step</strong> is to <em>verify all connections</em> before powering on the device.</p>


<!-- Screen readers may not convey the intended emphasis -->
<p>The <span style="font-weight: bold;">most critical step</span> is to <span style="font-style: italic;">verify all connections</span> before powering on the device.</p>
```

SEO Benefits of Semantic Markup

Search engines better understand content when proper semantic elements are used:

#html

```
<article>
    <h1>Complete Guide to Web Performance</h1>


    <p>Website speed affects user experience and search rankings. <strong>Page load time</strong> is a critical factor in user satisfaction.</p>


    <blockquote>
        <p>A one-second delay in page response can result in a 7% reduction in conversions.</p>
        <footer>– <cite>Web Performance Research Study</cite></footer>
    </blockquote>
```

```
    <p>Key optimization techniques include <em>image compression</em>, <em>code minification</em>, and <em>browser caching</em>.</p>
</article>
```

Creating Consistent Semantic Patterns

Establish consistent patterns for using semantic elements throughout your project:

#html

```
<section class="product-features">
    <h2>Product Features</h2>

    <div class="feature">
        <h3><strong>Advanced Security</strong></h3>
        <p>Our system provides <em>enterprise-grade protection</em> against cyber threats.</p>
        <p><strong>Key benefit:</strong> <q>Peace of mind through comprehensive security.</q></p>
    </div>

    <div class="feature">
        <h3><strong>Scalable Architecture</strong></h3>
        <p>Built to handle growth from startup to <em>enterprise scale</em>.</p>
        <p><strong>Key benefit:</strong> <q>Grow without system limitations.</q></p>
    </div>

    <div class="feature">
        <h3><strong>24/7 Support</strong></h3>
```

```
        <p>Expert assistance whenever you need it,
<em>around the clock</em>.</p>
        <p><strong>Key benefit:</strong> <q>Never face
technical challenges alone.</q></p>
    </div>
</section>
```

Future-Proofing with Semantic HTML

Semantic markup ensures your content remains accessible and meaningful as technologies evolve:

#html

```
<main>
    <article>
        <header>
            <h1>Understanding Machine Learning</h1>
            <p>Published on <time datetime="2024-03-
21">March 21, 2024</time></p>
        </header>

        <section>
            <h2>Key Concepts</h2>
            <p><strong>Machine learning</strong> enables
computers to learn without explicit programming. The
field includes <em>supervised learning</em>,
<em>unsupervised learning</em>, and <em>reinforcement
learning</em>.</p>

            <blockquote>
                <p>Machine learning is the future of data
analysis and decision-making systems.</p>
```

```
                <footer>— <cite>AI Research
Quarterly</cite></footer>
            </blockquote>
        </section>

        <section>
            <h2>Practical Applications</h2>
            <p>Real-world applications include
<strong>image recognition</strong>, <strong>natural
language processing</strong>, and <strong>predictive
analytics</strong>.</p>
        </section>
    </article>
</main>
```

Essential Tips

- Choose `<strong>` over `<b>` and `<em>` over `<i>` when the formatting conveys importance or emphasis, ensuring screen readers properly announce the semantic meaning to users.
- Use `<del>` and `<ins>` elements to show document changes and revisions, providing clear visual and semantic indication of content modifications for both users and version control systems.
- Implement `<sup>` and `<sub>` elements for mathematical expressions, chemical formulas, and footnote references to maintain proper scientific notation and academic formatting standards.
- Apply `<blockquote>` for substantial quotations and `<q>` for inline quotes, always including proper citation information using the `cite` attribute and `<cite>` element for source attribution.
- Prioritize semantic HTML elements over visual styling, using CSS to achieve desired appearances while maintaining the underlying meaning and accessibility of your content structure.

Actionable Strategies

- Create a comprehensive style guide that specifies when to use each formatting element, establishing consistent patterns across your entire website or application for all content creators and developers.
- Test all formatted content with screen readers and accessibility tools to verify that semantic elements properly convey meaning and emphasis to users with visual impairments or other accessibility needs.
- Implement CSS classes for common formatting patterns while maintaining semantic HTML, allowing designers to achieve visual goals without compromising the underlying content structure and meaning.
- Establish clear guidelines for quotation formatting including citation requirements, source attribution standards, and consistent styling patterns that work across different content types and page layouts.
- Audit existing content regularly to identify instances where visual formatting elements were used instead of semantic alternatives, converting them to improve accessibility and SEO performance.
- Document semantic formatting decisions in your project's technical documentation, helping team members understand when and why to choose specific elements for different content scenarios and formatting needs.
- Validate formatted content across multiple browsers and devices to ensure consistent appearance and functionality, paying special attention to how superscript, subscript, and quotation elements render on different screen sizes.

Chapter 5: Links and Anchors

Links form the backbone of the World Wide Web, creating the interconnected network that allows users to navigate seamlessly between different pages, sections, and resources. The HTML anchor element (`<a>`) serves as the fundamental building block for creating these connections, enabling developers to craft interactive experiences that guide users through digital content with precision and purpose.

5.1 Introduction to <a> Tags

Understanding the Anchor Element

The anchor element (`<a>`) represents one of the most essential HTML tags, serving as the primary mechanism for creating hyperlinks within web documents. This element derives its name from the nautical concept of an anchor, symbolizing a fixed point of reference that connects different locations across the vast ocean of digital information.

The basic structure of an anchor tag consists of opening and closing tags that wrap around the content you want to make clickable. The most critical attribute of the anchor element is the `href` attribute, which specifies the destination of the link.

#html

```
<a href="destination">Link text</a>
```

Essential Attributes of Anchor Tags

The `href` attribute stands as the cornerstone of anchor functionality, accepting various types of values depending on the intended destination. This attribute can contain absolute URLs, relative paths, fragment identifiers, or special protocol schemes.

#html

```html
<!-- Basic link structure -->
<a href="https://www.example.com">Visit Example
Website</a>

<!-- Link with title attribute for accessibility -->
<a href="contact.html" title="Get in touch with our
team">Contact Us</a>

<!-- Link with multiple attributes -->
<a href="products.html" title="Browse our product
catalog" id="product-link">Our Products</a>
```

The `title` attribute provides additional context about the link destination, appearing as a tooltip when users hover over the link. This attribute significantly enhances user experience and accessibility, particularly for screen reader users who rely on descriptive information to understand link purposes.

Semantic Importance of Link Text

The content placed between opening and closing anchor tags, known as link text or anchor text, carries substantial semantic weight. Search engines and assistive technologies rely heavily on this text to understand the context and purpose of the link. Effective link text should be descriptive, concise, and provide clear indication of what users can expect when they follow the link.

#html

```html
<!-- Poor link text -->
<a href="report.pdf">Click here</a>

<!-- Improved link text -->
<a href="annual-report-2024.pdf">Download 2024 Annual
Report (PDF, 2.3MB)</a>
```

Styling Anchor Elements

Anchor elements can be styled using CSS to match your website's design aesthetic while maintaining usability and accessibility standards. The CSS pseudo-classes `:link`, `:visited`, `:hover`, and `:active` allow developers to create distinct visual states for different link interactions.

#html

```
<style>
a {
    color: #0066cc;
    text-decoration: none;
    transition: color 0.3s ease;
}

a:hover {
    color: #004499;
    text-decoration: underline;
}

a:visited {
    color: #551a8b;
}

a:active {
    color: #ff0000;
}
</style>

<a href="example.html">Styled Link Example</a>
```

5.2 Internal and External Links

Understanding Link Types

Web navigation relies on two primary categories of links: internal links that connect pages within the same website, and external links that direct users to different domains or websites. Each type serves distinct purposes and requires different implementation approaches to ensure optimal functionality and user experience.

Internal Links: Connecting Your Website

Internal links create pathways between different pages within your website, establishing a logical navigation structure that helps users discover related content and enables search engines to understand your site's architecture. These links use relative URLs, which reference file locations relative to the current page's position within the directory structure.

#html

```html
<!-- Relative path to a file in the same directory -->
<a href="about.html">About Us</a>

<!-- Relative path to a file in a subdirectory -->
<a href="products/laptops.html">Laptop Collection</a>

<!-- Relative path to a file in a parent directory -->
<a href="../index.html">Return to Home</a>

<!-- Relative path with multiple directory levels -->
<a href="../../images/gallery/photo1.jpg">View Photo</a>
```

Directory Structure Navigation

Understanding directory structures becomes crucial when implementing internal links effectively. The forward slash (/) represents directory separators, while two periods (..) indicate moving up one directory level in the file hierarchy.

#html

```
<!-- Current directory structure:
     /website
       /pages
         current-page.html
         about.html
       /products
         /laptops
           gaming.html
       index.html
-->

<!-- From current-page.html, linking to different locations -->
<a href="about.html">About Page (same directory)</a>
<a href="../index.html">Home Page (parent directory)</a>
<a href="../products/laptops/gaming.html">Gaming Laptops (nested directories)</a>
```

External Links: Connecting to the World

External links direct users to resources located on different domains, requiring absolute URLs that include the complete web address including the protocol (http:// or https://). These links expand your website's reach by connecting to relevant external resources, references, and partner sites.

#html

```
<!-- Basic external link -->
```

```html
<a href="https://www.wikipedia.org">Wikipedia</a>

<!-- External link with secure protocol -->
<a href="https://www.github.com">GitHub Repository</a>

<!-- External link to a specific page -->
<a href="https://developer.mozilla.org/en-US/docs/Web/HTML">HTML Documentation</a>
```

Best Practices for External Links

External links require careful consideration to maintain user trust and website performance. Adding the `rel="noopener"` attribute prevents potential security vulnerabilities when opening links in new tabs, while `rel="nofollow"` instructs search engines not to follow the link for ranking purposes.

#html

```html
<!-- Secure external link opening in new tab -->
<a href="https://www.example.com" target="_blank" rel="noopener noreferrer">
    External Resource
</a>

<!-- External link with no-follow attribute -->
<a href="https://www.sponsored-content.com" rel="nofollow">
    Sponsored Link
</a>
```

Mixed Navigation Strategies

Effective websites typically employ a combination of internal and external links to create comprehensive navigation experiences. Internal links keep users engaged within your site ecosystem, while carefully selected external links provide additional value and context.

#html

```html
<article>
    <h2>Web Development Resources</h2>
    <p>
        Start with our <a href="html-basics.html">HTML Basics Guide</a>
        to understand fundamental concepts. For advanced techniques,
        consult the official
        <a href="https://www.w3.org/TR/html52/" target="_blank" rel="noopener">
            W3C HTML5.2 Specification
        </a>.
    </p>
    <p>
        Check out our <a href="../tutorials/css-tutorial.html">CSS Tutorial</a>
        next, or explore external resources like
        <a href="https://css-tricks.com" target="_blank" rel="noopener">
            CSS-Tricks
        </a> for inspiration.
    </p>
</article>
```

5.3 Opening Links in New Tabs

The Target Attribute

The `target` attribute controls how and where linked documents open when users click on anchor elements. This attribute accepts several values, with `_blank` being the most commonly used to open links in new browser tabs or windows.

#html

```html
<!-- Open link in new tab -->
<a href="https://www.example.com" target="_blank">Open in New Tab</a>

<!-- Open link in same tab (default behavior) -->
<a href="example.html" target="_self">Open in Same Tab</a>

<!-- Open link in parent frame -->
<a href="parent-page.html" target="_parent">Open in Parent</a>

<!-- Open link in top-level window -->
<a href="top-level.html" target="_top">Open in Top Window</a>
```

Security Considerations

Opening links in new tabs introduces potential security vulnerabilities through the `window.opener` property, which grants the newly opened page access to the original page's window object. The `rel="noopener"` attribute prevents this access, while `rel="noreferrer"` additionally prevents the destination page from receiving referrer information.

#html

```
<!-- Secure new tab opening -->
<a href="https://www.external-site.com"
   target="_blank"
   rel="noopener noreferrer">
    Secure External Link
</a>

<!-- Multiple security attributes -->
<a href="https://www.partner-site.com"
   target="_blank"
   rel="noopener noreferrer nofollow">
    Partner Site (Secure & No-Follow)
</a>
```

User Experience Considerations

The decision to open links in new tabs should align with user expectations and website functionality. Internal navigation typically benefits from same-tab opening to maintain the user's browsing flow, while external links often warrant new tab opening to prevent users from leaving your site entirely.

#html

```
<nav>
    <!-- Internal navigation - same tab -->
    <a href="home.html">Home</a>
    <a href="about.html">About</a>
    <a href="contact.html">Contact</a>
</nav>

<article>
```

```
    <p>
        Read our <a href="privacy-policy.html">Privacy
Policy</a>
        for detailed information, or visit
        <a href="https://www.gdpr.eu" target="_blank"
rel="noopener">
            GDPR.eu
        </a> for general data protection regulations.
    </p>
</article>
```

Accessibility and New Tab Links

When opening links in new tabs, providing clear indication to users, especially those using assistive technologies, becomes essential. Screen readers may not automatically announce that a link opens in a new tab, potentially causing confusion.

#html

```
<!-- Accessible new tab link with visual and screen
reader indication -->
<a href="https://www.external-resource.com"
   target="_blank"
   rel="noopener noreferrer"
   aria-label="External resource (opens in new tab)">
    External Resource <span aria-hidden="true">↗</span>
</a>

<!-- Alternative approach with title attribute -->
<a href="https://www.reference.com"
   target="_blank"
   rel="noopener"
```

```
    title="Reference site (opens in new tab)">
     Reference Site
</a>
```

5.4 Anchor Links within a Page

Understanding Fragment Identifiers

Anchor links within a page, also known as fragment identifiers or jump links, allow users to navigate directly to specific sections of long documents. These links use the hash symbol (#) followed by an identifier that corresponds to an element's `id` attribute within the same page.

#html

```html
<!-- Table of contents with anchor links -->
<nav>
    <h3>Table of Contents</h3>
    <ul>
        <li><a href="#introduction">Introduction</a></li>
        <li><a href="#methodology">Methodology</a></li>
        <li><a href="#results">Results</a></li>
        <li><a href="#conclusion">Conclusion</a></li>
    </ul>
</nav>

<!-- Document sections with corresponding IDs -->
<section id="introduction">
    <h2>Introduction</h2>
    <p>This section introduces the topic...</p>
</section>
```

```
<section id="methodology">
    <h2>Methodology</h2>
    <p>Our research methodology involved...</p>
</section>

<section id="results">
    <h2>Results</h2>
    <p>The results of our study show...</p>
</section>

<section id="conclusion">
    <h2>Conclusion</h2>
    <p>In conclusion, we found that...</p>
</section>
```

Creating Effective ID Attributes

ID attributes must be unique within each HTML document and should follow naming conventions that make them meaningful and maintainable. Use descriptive names that clearly indicate the section's content or purpose.

#html

```
<!-- Well-structured page with descriptive IDs -->
<article>
    <header id="article-header">
        <h1>Complete Guide to Web Accessibility</h1>
        <nav id="quick-navigation">
            <a href="#wcag-guidelines">WCAG
Guidelines</a>
            <a href="#implementation-
strategies">Implementation</a>
```

```
            <a href="#testing-methods">Testing
Methods</a>
            <a href="#common-mistakes">Common
Mistakes</a>
        </nav>
    </header>

    <section id="wcag-guidelines">
        <h2>WCAG Guidelines Overview</h2>
        <p>The Web Content Accessibility
Guidelines...</p>
    </section>

    <section id="implementation-strategies">
        <h2>Implementation Strategies</h2>
        <p>Successful accessibility implementation
requires...</p>
    </section>

    <section id="testing-methods">
        <h2>Testing Methods</h2>
        <p>Various testing approaches help ensure...</p>
    </section>

    <section id="common-mistakes">
        <h2>Common Mistakes to Avoid</h2>
        <p>Many developers inadvertently create
barriers...</p>
    </section>
</article>
```

Smooth Scrolling Enhancement

Modern browsers support smooth scrolling behavior that creates elegant transitions when users click anchor links. This can be implemented using CSS to enhance the user experience.

#html

```
<style>
html {
    scroll-behavior: smooth;
}

/* Alternative: targeting specific elements */
.smooth-scroll {
    scroll-behavior: smooth;
}
</style>

<!-- Anchor links with smooth scrolling -->
<nav class="table-of-contents">
    <a href="#section-one">Section One</a>
    <a href="#section-two">Section Two</a>
    <a href="#section-three">Section Three</a>
</nav>

<div id="section-one">
    <h2>Section One</h2>
    <p>Content for section one...</p>
    <a href="#top">Back to Top</a>
</div>

<div id="section-two">
```

```
    <h2>Section Two</h2>
    <p>Content for section two...</p>
    <a href="#top">Back to Top</a>
</div>

<div id="section-three">
    <h2>Section Three</h2>
    <p>Content for section three...</p>
    <a href="#top">Back to Top</a>
</div>
```

Skip Links for Accessibility

Skip links provide crucial accessibility features, allowing keyboard and screen reader users to bypass repetitive navigation elements and jump directly to main content areas.

#html

```
<!-- Skip Link at the beginning of the page -->
<a href="#main-content" class="skip-link">Skip to main
content</a>

<nav id="main-navigation">
    <!-- Navigation items -->
    <a href="home.html">Home</a>
    <a href="about.html">About</a>
    <a href="services.html">Services</a>
</nav>

<main id="main-content">
    <h1>Welcome to Our Website</h1>
```

```
    <p>This is the main content area...</p>
</main>

<style>
.skip-link {
    position: absolute;
    top: -40px;
    left: 6px;
    background: #000;
    color: #fff;
    padding: 8px;
    text-decoration: none;
    transition: top 0.3s;
}

.skip-link:focus {
    top: 6px;
}
</style>
```

5.5 Linking to Email and Phone

Email Links with Mailto Protocol

The `mailto:` protocol enables direct email composition by launching the user's default email client with pre-populated recipient information. This functionality streamlines communication by removing the need for users to manually copy email addresses.

#html

```
<!-- Basic email link -->
```

```html
<a href="mailto:contact@example.com">Send Email</a>


<!-- Email link with subject line -->
<a href="mailto:support@example.com?subject=Website
Support Request">
    Contact Support
</a>


<!-- Email link with subject and body -->
<a href="mailto:info@example.com?subject=Product
Inquiry&body=Hello, I would like to know more about your
products.">
    Product Inquiry
</a>
```

Advanced Email Link Parameters

Email links support multiple parameters that can pre-populate various fields in the email client, including carbon copy (CC), blind carbon copy (BCC), subject lines, and message body content.

#html

```html
<!-- Comprehensive email link with multiple parameters --
>
<a
href="mailto:sales@example.com?cc=manager@example.com&bcc
=records@example.com&subject=Sales Inquiry -
Website&body=Dear Sales Team,%0A%0AI am interested in
learning more about your services.%0A%0ABest regards">
    Contact Sales Team
</a>


<!-- Multiple recipients -->
```

```
<a
href="mailto:support@example.com,billing@example.com?subj
ect=Account Issue">
    Contact Support and Billing
</a>
```

URL Encoding for Email Content

Special characters in email subjects and body content require URL encoding to ensure proper transmission. Common characters like spaces (%20), line breaks (%0A), and symbols need appropriate encoding.

#html

```
<!-- Email with properly encoded content -->
<a
href="mailto:feedback@example.com?subject=Website%20Feedb
ack%20-
%20Page%20Not%20Found&body=Hello,%0A%0AI%20encountered%20
an%20error%20on%20your%20website.%0A%0APage%20URL:%20http
s://example.com/missing-
page%0AError%20Code:%20404%0A%0APlease%20investigate.%0A%
0AThank%20you!">
    Report Website Issue
</a>
```

Phone Links with Tel Protocol

The `tel:` protocol creates clickable phone number links that initiate phone calls on mobile devices or launch calling applications on desktop systems. This functionality particularly benefits mobile users who can call directly by tapping the link.

#html

```html
<!-- Basic phone link -->
<a href="tel:+1234567890">Call Us: (123) 456-7890</a>

<!-- International phone number -->
<a href="tel:+44203123456">UK Office: +44 20 3123 456</a>

<!-- Phone link with extension -->
<a href="tel:+12345678901234">Call Sales: (123) 456-7890
ext. 1234</a>
```

SMS Links with SMS Protocol

The `sms:` protocol enables users to send text messages directly from web links, pre-populating the recipient's phone number and optionally including message content.

#html

```html
<!-- Basic SMS link -->
<a href="sms:+1234567890">Send Text Message</a>

<!-- SMS link with pre-filled message -->
<a href="sms:+1234567890?body=Hello, I would like more
information about your services.">
    Text for Info
</a>

<!-- SMS link for multiple recipients -->
<a href="sms:+1234567890,+0987654321?body=Group message
content">
    Send Group Message
</a>
```

Combining Communication Methods

Effective contact sections often combine multiple communication methods, providing users with various options to reach out based on their preferences and device capabilities.

#html

```
<section id="contact-information">
    <h2>Get in Touch</h2>

    <div class="contact-methods">
        <div class="contact-item">
            <h3>Email</h3>
            <a
href="mailto:hello@example.com?subject=General Inquiry">
                hello@example.com
            </a>
        </div>

        <div class="contact-item">
            <h3>Phone</h3>
            <a href="tel:+1234567890">(123) 456-7890</a>
        </div>

        <div class="contact-item">
            <h3>Text Message</h3>
            <a href="sms:+1234567890?body=Hi, I have a
question about your services.">
                Send SMS
            </a>
```

```
        </div>

        <div class="contact-item">
            <h3>Emergency Support</h3>
            <a href="tel:+1234567899">Emergency Line:
(123) 456-7899</a>
        </div>
    </div>
</section>
```

Accessibility for Communication Links

Communication links should include clear labeling and context to help all users understand the action that will occur when they activate the link.

#html

```
<!-- Accessible communication links with clear context --
>
<section class="contact-info">
    <h2>Contact Methods</h2>

    <p>
        <strong>Email:</strong>
        <a
href="mailto:support@example.com?subject=Website Support"
           aria-label="Send email to support team">
            support@example.com
        </a>
    </p>

    <p>
```

```
        <strong>Phone:</strong>
        <a href="tel:+1234567890"
           aria-label="Call our main office">
            (123) 456-7890
        </a>
    </p>

    <p>
        <strong>Text Support:</strong>
        <a href="sms:+1234567891?body=I need help
with..."
           aria-label="Send text message to support">
            Text us for quick help
        </a>
    </p>
</section>
```

Essential Tips

- Always write descriptive link text that clearly indicates the destination or action, avoiding generic phrases like "click here" or "read more" that provide no context about what users will find when they follow the link.
- Test all links regularly to ensure they remain functional, as broken links create poor user experiences and can negatively impact search engine rankings and site credibility.
- Use the `title` attribute sparingly and meaningfully, providing additional context only when it adds value beyond what the link text already conveys, as overuse can create unnecessary noise for screen reader users.
- Implement consistent link styling throughout your website to help users recognize clickable elements, maintaining visual distinction between visited and unvisited links while ensuring sufficient color contrast for accessibility.

- Consider the user's journey when placing links within content, positioning them logically within the text flow and grouping related links together to create intuitive navigation paths.

Actionable Strategies

- Conduct regular link audits using automated tools and manual testing to identify and fix broken internal and external links, maintaining a schedule for checking high-traffic pages and critical navigation elements.
- Implement a clear hierarchy for different link types by using distinct visual styling for internal links, external links, and special actions like downloads or email contacts, helping users understand what to expect before clicking.
- Create comprehensive anchor link navigation for long-form content by adding a table of contents at the beginning of articles or documents, enabling users to jump directly to sections that interest them most.
- Optimize for mobile users by ensuring link targets are appropriately sized for touch interaction, maintaining at least 44x44 pixel touch targets and providing adequate spacing between adjacent links.
- Use analytics to track link performance and user behavior, identifying which links receive the most clicks and which pages have high exit rates to inform improvements to your linking strategy.
- Implement progressive enhancement for communication links by providing fallback options for users whose devices may not support tel: or mailto: protocols, ensuring everyone can access contact information.
- Create logical link relationships using HTML attributes like `rel="prev"` and `rel="next"` for paginated content, helping search engines understand content relationships and potentially improving search result presentation with site links.

Chapter 6: Images in HTML

Images form the visual backbone of modern web experiences, transforming static text into engaging, dynamic content that captures attention and communicates messages effectively. Understanding how to implement images correctly in HTML requires mastering not just the basic syntax, but also the nuances of accessibility, performance optimization, and responsive design principles that ensure your images work seamlessly across all devices and user contexts.

6.1 The `<img>` Tag

Understanding the Image Element Structure

The `<img>` tag represents one of HTML's most fundamental self-closing elements, designed specifically for embedding images directly into web pages. Unlike container elements that require opening and closing tags, the image element stands alone as a void element, meaning it cannot contain any content between opening and closing tags.

#html

```
<img src="path/to/image.jpg" alt="Description of the
image">
```

Core Attributes of the Image Tag

The image element relies heavily on attributes to define its behavior and appearance. The most critical attributes include `src` for specifying the image source and `alt` for providing alternative text, but several other attributes enhance functionality and accessibility.

#html

```
<img
  src="images/landscape.jpg"
```

```
  alt="Beautiful mountain landscape with snow-capped
peaks"
  width="800"
  height="600"
  title="Mountain Landscape Photography"
  loading="lazy"
>
```

Image Element Positioning and Flow

Images in HTML follow the normal document flow by default, appearing inline with surrounding text content. However, their behavior can be modified through CSS styling to achieve different layout effects.

#html

```
<p>This paragraph contains an inline image
<img src="icon.png" alt="Small icon" style="vertical-
align: middle;">
that flows with the text content.</p>

<div>
  <img src="hero-image.jpg" alt="Hero banner image"
style="display: block; width: 100%;">
</div>
```

Multiple Image Sources and Fallbacks

Modern HTML supports advanced image loading techniques through the `<picture>` element, which works in conjunction with `<img>` tags to provide multiple source options based on different conditions.

#html

```
<picture>
  <source media="(min-width: 800px)" srcset="large-
image.jpg">
  <source media="(min-width: 400px)" srcset="medium-
image.jpg">
  <img src="small-image.jpg" alt="Responsive image
example">
</picture>
```

6.2 Adding src and alt Attributes

The src Attribute: Image Source Specification

The `src` attribute defines the path or URL to the image file that should be displayed. This attribute accepts both relative and absolute paths, allowing flexibility in how images are referenced and organized within your project structure.

Relative Path Examples

#html

```
<!-- Image in the same directory -->
<img src="photo.jpg" alt="Local photo">

<!-- Image in a subdirectory -->
<img src="images/gallery/vacation.png" alt="Vacation
photo">

<!-- Image in parent directory -->
<img src="../assets/logo.svg" alt="Company logo">
```

Absolute Path and URL Examples

#html

```html
<!-- Absolute local path -->
<img src="/images/header-banner.jpg" alt="Header banner">


<!-- External URL -->
<img src="https://example.com/images/product.jpg"
alt="Product image">


<!-- Data URL (base64 encoded) -->
<img
src="data:image/svg+xml;base64,PHN2ZyB3aWR0aD0iMTAwIiBoZW
lnaHQ9IjEwMCI+..." alt="Inline SVG">
```

The alt Attribute: Alternative Text Implementation

The `alt` attribute provides crucial alternative text that describes the image content for users who cannot see images, including those using screen readers, experiencing slow internet connections, or when images fail to load.

Writing Effective Alt Text

#html

```html
<!-- Descriptive alt text -->
<img src="dog-playing.jpg" alt="Golden retriever catching
a frisbee in a sunny park">


<!-- Decorative images -->
<img src="decorative-border.png" alt=""
role="presentation">
```

```html
<!-- Functional images -->
<img src="search-icon.png" alt="Search">

<!-- Complex images -->
<img src="sales-chart.png" alt="Monthly sales increased 25% from January to March 2024">
```

Alt Text Best Practices and Guidelines

Different types of images require different approaches to alternative text. Informative images need descriptive text that conveys the essential information, while decorative images should have empty alt attributes to avoid cluttering screen reader output.

#html

```html
<!-- Logo with text -->
<img src="company-logo.png" alt="TechCorp Solutions">

<!-- Image button -->
<button>
  <img src="download-icon.svg" alt="Download PDF report">
</button>

<!-- Image with caption -->
<figure>
  <img src="experiment-results.jpg" alt="Bar chart showing experiment results">
  <figcaption>Figure 1: Comparison of treatment groups A, B, and C</figcaption>
</figure>
```

Error Handling and Fallback Strategies

When images fail to load, browsers display the alt text in place of the image. Planning for these scenarios ensures your content remains accessible and meaningful even when technical issues occur.

#html

```
<img
  src="important-diagram.jpg"
  alt="Process flow diagram: Customer inquiry →
Assessment → Proposal → Implementation → Review"
  onerror="this.src='fallback-image.jpg';
this.onerror=null;"
>
```

6.3 Image Sizes and Responsiveness

Setting Image Dimensions

Controlling image dimensions prevents layout shifts and ensures consistent visual presentation across different viewing contexts. HTML provides both attribute-based and CSS-based approaches for dimension control.

HTML Width and Height Attributes

#html

```
<!-- Fixed dimensions -->
<img src="portrait.jpg" alt="Team member portrait"
width="300" height="400">


<!-- Maintaining aspect ratio -->
<img src="landscape.jpg" alt="Scenic landscape"
width="800" height="600">
```

CSS-Based Sizing Approaches

#html

```
<style>
.responsive-image {
  max-width: 100%;
  height: auto;
}

.fixed-size {
  width: 250px;
  height: 250px;
  object-fit: cover;
}

.container-fill {
  width: 100%;
  height: 100%;
  object-fit: contain;
}
</style>

<img src="flexible-image.jpg" alt="Flexible sizing
example" class="responsive-image">
<img src="profile-pic.jpg" alt="Profile picture"
class="fixed-size">
<img src="banner.jpg" alt="Banner image"
class="container-fill">
```

Responsive Image Techniques

Creating images that adapt seamlessly to different screen sizes and resolutions requires understanding several HTML and CSS techniques that work together to deliver optimal user experiences.

CSS Media Queries for Image Control

#html

```html
<style>
.hero-image {
  width: 100%;
  height: 300px;
  object-fit: cover;
}

@media (min-width: 768px) {
  .hero-image {
    height: 500px;
  }
}

@media (min-width: 1200px) {
  .hero-image {
    height: 700px;
  }
}
</style>

<img src="hero-banner.jpg" alt="Hero banner" class="hero-image">
```

Flexible Image Containers

#html

```
<style>
.image-container {
  position: relative;
  width: 100%;
  max-width: 800px;
  margin: 0 auto;
}

.image-container img {
  width: 100%;
  height: auto;
  display: block;
}
</style>

<div class="image-container">
  <img src="content-image.jpg" alt="Main content image">
</div>
```

Advanced Responsive Techniques

Modern responsive image implementation goes beyond simple CSS scaling to include art direction, resolution switching, and performance optimization strategies.

The srcset Attribute

#html

```
<!-- Resolution switching -->
<img
```

```
  src="image-400w.jpg"
  srcset="image-400w.jpg 400w,
          image-800w.jpg 800w,
          image-1200w.jpg 1200w"
  sizes="(max-width: 600px) 400px,
         (max-width: 900px) 800px,
         1200px"
  alt="Responsive image with multiple resolutions"
>
```

Art Direction with Picture Element

#html

```
<picture>
  <source
    media="(min-width: 1200px)"
    srcset="wide-landscape.jpg"
  >
  <source
    media="(min-width: 600px)"
    srcset="medium-crop.jpg"
  >
  <img
    src="mobile-portrait.jpg"
    alt="Adaptive image showing different crops for
different screen sizes"
  >
</picture>
```

6.4 Image File Formats

Understanding Common Web Image Formats

Different image formats serve specific purposes and offer unique advantages in terms of file size, quality, and browser support. Choosing the appropriate format significantly impacts loading performance and visual quality.

JPEG Format Characteristics

JPEG excels at compressing photographic images with many colors and gradual transitions. This format uses lossy compression, reducing file sizes at the cost of some image quality.

#html

```
<!-- Best for photographs -->
<img src="portrait-photo.jpg" alt="Professional headshot photograph">
<img src="nature-scene.jpg" alt="Natural landscape with varied colors">
```

PNG Format Applications

PNG provides lossless compression and supports transparency, making it ideal for images requiring sharp edges, text, or transparent backgrounds.

#html

```
<!-- Best for graphics with transparency -->
<img src="company-logo.png" alt="Company logo with transparent background">
<img src="ui-icon.png" alt="User interface icon">
```

WebP Format Advantages

WebP offers superior compression compared to JPEG and PNG while maintaining high quality, though browser support varies.

#html

```html
<picture>
  <source srcset="optimized-image.webp"
type="image/webp">
  <img src="fallback-image.jpg" alt="Modern image with
WebP optimization">
</picture>
```

SVG for Scalable Graphics

Scalable Vector Graphics provide resolution-independent images perfect for icons, logos, and simple illustrations.

#html

```html
<img src="vector-icon.svg" alt="Scalable vector icon">

<!-- Inline SVG -->
<svg width="100" height="100" viewBox="0 0 100 100">
  <circle cx="50" cy="50" r="40" fill="blue" />
  <text x="50" y="55" text-anchor="middle"
fill="white">Logo</text>
</svg>
```

Format Selection Guidelines

Choosing the optimal image format depends on image content, quality requirements, file size constraints, and target browser compatibility.

Decision Matrix for Format Selection

#html

```
<!-- Photographs: Use JPEG -->
<img src="wedding-photo.jpg" alt="Wedding ceremony photograph">

<!-- Graphics with transparency: Use PNG -->
<img src="product-cutout.png" alt="Product image with transparent background">

<!-- Simple graphics and logos: Use SVG -->
<img src="brand-logo.svg" alt="Scalable brand logo">

<!-- Modern browsers with fallback: Use WebP -->
<picture>
  <source srcset="hero-image.webp" type="image/webp">
  <source srcset="hero-image.jpg" type="image/jpeg">
  <img src="hero-image.jpg" alt="Hero image with modern format optimization">
</picture>
```

Optimization Strategies for Different Formats

Each image format benefits from specific optimization techniques that balance quality and file size for optimal web performance.

JPEG Optimization Techniques

#html

```html
<!-- Progressive JPEG loading -->
<img src="progressive-photo.jpg" alt="Photo optimized for progressive loading">

<!-- Quality-optimized images -->
<img
  src="photo-80-quality.jpg"
  alt="Photograph compressed at 80% quality for web optimization"
>
```

PNG Optimization Methods
#html

```html
<!-- 8-bit PNG for limited colors -->
<img src="simple-graphic.png" alt="Simple graphic with limited color palette">

<!-- 24-bit PNG for complex graphics -->
<img src="detailed-illustration.png" alt="Detailed illustration requiring full color range">
```

6.5 Best Practices for SEO and Accessibility

Search Engine Optimization for Images

Images significantly impact search engine optimization when properly implemented with descriptive filenames, appropriate alt attributes, and structured markup that helps search engines understand image content and context.

SEO-Friendly Image Implementation

#html

```html
<!-- Descriptive filename and alt text -->
<img
  src="red-leather-handbag-designer-collection.jpg"
  alt="Red leather designer handbag from premium
collection"
  title="Premium Red Leather Handbag"
>

<!-- Structured data markup -->
<div itemscope itemtype="https://schema.org/Product">
  <img
    src="product-image.jpg"
    alt="Blue wireless headphones with noise
cancellation"
    itemprop="image"
  >
  <h2 itemprop="name">Professional Wireless
Headphones</h2>
</div>
```

Image Sitemaps and Metadata

#html

```html
<!-- Image with comprehensive metadata -->
<figure>
  <img
    src="infographic-social-media-trends-2024.jpg"
```

```
    alt="Infographic showing social media platform usage trends in 2024"
    width="800"
    height="1200"
  >
  <figcaption>
    Social Media Trends 2024: Platform Usage Statistics and Growth Patterns
  </figcaption>
</figure>
```

Accessibility Implementation Standards

Creating accessible images requires understanding how assistive technologies interact with image content and implementing markup that provides equivalent information for all users.

Screen Reader Optimization

#html

```
<!-- Informative image with descriptive alt text -->
<img
  src="quarterly-sales-chart.png"
  alt="Bar chart showing quarterly sales growth: Q1 $50k, Q2 $65k, Q3 $80k, Q4 $95k"
>

<!-- Decorative image with empty alt -->
<img src="decorative-flourish.png" alt="" role="presentation">

<!-- Complex image with detailed description -->
```

```
<img
  src="complex-diagram.jpg"
  alt="Organizational chart showing company hierarchy"
  aria-describedby="chart-description"
>
<div id="chart-description" class="sr-only">
  Detailed description: CEO at top level, three VPs below
(Sales, Marketing, Operations),
  with department managers and staff members shown in
subsequent levels.
</div>
```

Focus Management and Keyboard Navigation
#html

```
<!-- Clickable images with proper focus -->
<a href="product-details.html">
  <img
    src="product-thumbnail.jpg"
    alt="Blue ceramic vase - Click to view details"
    tabindex="0"
  >
</a>

<!-- Image buttons with accessible labels -->
<button type="submit" aria-label="Search products">
  <img src="search-icon.svg" alt="" role="presentation">
</button>
```

Performance Optimization Strategies

Image performance directly affects user experience and search engine rankings, making optimization techniques essential for successful web development.

Lazy Loading Implementation

#html

```html
<!-- Native lazy loading -->
<img
  src="below-fold-image.jpg"
  alt="Image that loads when scrolled into view"
  loading="lazy"
  width="800"
  height="600"
>

<!-- Progressive enhancement with fallback -->
<img
  src="placeholder.jpg"
  data-src="full-resolution-image.jpg"
  alt="Image with progressive loading enhancement"
  class="lazy-load"
>
```

Preloading Critical Images

#html

```html
<head>
  <!-- Preload hero image -->
  <link rel="preload" as="image" href="hero-banner.jpg">
```

```
  <!-- Preload responsive image variants -->
  <link rel="preload" as="image" href="hero-mobile.jpg"
media="(max-width: 600px)">
  <link rel="preload" as="image" href="hero-desktop.jpg"
media="(min-width: 601px)">
</head>


<body>
  <img src="hero-banner.jpg" alt="Hero banner image"
class="hero-image">
</body>
```

Content Delivery and Caching Strategies

Optimizing image delivery involves implementing caching headers, content delivery networks, and compression techniques that reduce loading times while maintaining visual quality.

CDN Integration Examples

#html

```
<!-- CDN-hosted images with optimization parameters -->
<img

src="https://cdn.example.com/images/product.jpg?w=400&h=3
00&q=85&f=webp"
  alt="Product image served from CDN with automatic
optimization"
>


<!-- Responsive images through CDN -->
```

```
<img
  src="https://cdn.example.com/images/hero.jpg?w=400"
  srcset="https://cdn.example.com/images/hero.jpg?w=400
400w,
          https://cdn.example.com/images/hero.jpg?w=800
800w,
          https://cdn.example.com/images/hero.jpg?w=1200
1200w"
  sizes="(max-width: 600px) 400px, (max-width: 900px)
800px, 1200px"
  alt="CDN-optimized responsive hero image"
>
```

Essential Tips

- Choose image formats based on content type: JPEG for photographs, PNG for graphics with transparency, SVG for scalable icons and logos, and WebP for modern browsers with JPEG/PNG fallbacks.
- Always include meaningful alt text that describes the image content or function, using empty alt attributes only for purely decorative images that add no informational value.
- Implement responsive images using srcset and sizes attributes or the picture element to serve appropriate image sizes for different devices and screen resolutions.
- Optimize image file sizes through compression while maintaining acceptable quality levels, typically 80-85% quality for JPEG images and appropriate bit depths for PNG images.
- Use descriptive, SEO-friendly filenames that include relevant keywords and accurately describe the image content, avoiding generic names like "image1.jpg" or "photo.png".

Actionable Strategies

- Establish a consistent image naming convention across your project that includes descriptive keywords, version numbers if applicable, and clear organizational structure for easy maintenance and SEO benefits.
- Create multiple image variants for different use cases during the design phase, including mobile-optimized versions, thumbnail sizes, and high-resolution variants for different display contexts.
- Implement lazy loading for images below the fold while preloading critical above-the-fold images to optimize initial page load performance and user experience.
- Set up automated image optimization workflows using build tools or content delivery networks that automatically compress and convert images to optimal formats based on browser support.
- Develop comprehensive alt text guidelines for your team that specify how to write effective alternative text for different image types, including photographs, charts, diagrams, and decorative elements.
- Test image accessibility using screen readers and keyboard navigation to ensure all users can access and understand your visual content effectively.
- Monitor image performance metrics including loading times, compression ratios, and user engagement data to continuously optimize your image implementation strategy and improve overall site performance.

Chapter 7: Lists and Navigation

Lists form the backbone of structured content presentation in HTML, providing developers with powerful tools to organize information hierarchically and create intuitive navigation systems. This chapter covers the essential list elements and demonstrates how to transform simple lists into sophisticated navigation components that enhance user experience across web applications.

7.1 Ordered Lists `<ol>`

Understanding Ordered Lists

Ordered lists present information in a sequential, numbered format where the arrangement of items carries specific meaning. The `<ol>` element automatically generates numerical indicators for each list item, making it ideal for step-by-step instructions, rankings, procedures, or any content where order matters significantly.

Basic Ordered List Structure

#html

```
<ol>
    <li>First item in the sequence</li>
    <li>Second item follows logically</li>
    <li>Third item continues the pattern</li>
    <li>Fourth item completes the list</li>
</ol>
```

This basic structure produces a numbered list starting from 1 and incrementing automatically for each subsequent item.

Customizing Ordered List Attributes

The **type** Attribute

The `type` attribute modifies the numbering system used in ordered lists:

#html

```html
<!-- Numeric numbering (default) -->
<ol type="1">
    <li>Analyze the problem</li>
    <li>Design the solution</li>
    <li>Implement the code</li>
    <li>Test thoroughly</li>
</ol>

<!-- Uppercase letters -->
<ol type="A">
    <li>Primary objective</li>
    <li>Secondary goal</li>
    <li>Tertiary consideration</li>
</ol>

<!-- Lowercase letters -->
<ol type="a">
    <li>Initial phase</li>
    <li>Development phase</li>
    <li>Testing phase</li>
</ol>

<!-- Uppercase Roman numerals -->
<ol type="I">
    <li>Introduction</li>
    <li>Main content</li>
```

```
    <li>Conclusion</li>
</ol>

<!-- Lowercase Roman numerals -->
<ol type="i">
    <li>Background research</li>
    <li>Data collection</li>
    <li>Analysis results</li>
</ol>
```

The `start` Attribute

The `start` attribute specifies the beginning number for the list sequence:

#html

```
<ol start="5">
    <li>Continue from step five</li>
    <li>This becomes step six</li>
    <li>This becomes step seven</li>
</ol>

<ol type="A" start="3">
    <li>This displays as "C"</li>
    <li>This displays as "D"</li>
    <li>This displays as "E"</li>
</ol>
```

The `reversed` Attribute

The `reversed` attribute creates countdown lists:

#html

```
<ol reversed>
    <li>Third place finisher</li>
    <li>Second place finisher</li>
    <li>First place winner</li>
</ol>
```

Advanced Ordered List Techniques

Custom Starting Values with Individual Items

Individual list items can override the automatic numbering using the `value` attribute:

#html

```
<ol>
    <li value="10">Start at ten</li>
    <li>This becomes eleven</li>
    <li value="50">Jump to fifty</li>
    <li>This becomes fifty-one</li>
</ol>
```

Styling Ordered Lists with CSS

#html

```
<style>
    .custom-ordered {
        counter-reset: section;
        list-style: none;
        padding-left: 0;
```

```
    }

    .custom-ordered li {
        counter-increment: section;
        margin-bottom: 10px;
        padding-left: 40px;
        position: relative;
    }

    .custom-ordered li::before {
        content: counter(section, decimal-leading-zero)
".";
        position: absolute;
        left: 0;
        top: 0;
        color: #007acc;
        font-weight: bold;
    }
</style>

<ol class="custom-ordered">
    <li>Custom numbered item with zero padding</li>
    <li>Another beautifully formatted item</li>
    <li>Third item maintains consistent styling</li>
</ol>
```

7.2 Unordered Lists <ul>

Understanding Unordered Lists

Unordered lists present information without inherent sequence or hierarchy, using bullet points or other markers to distinguish individual items. The `<ul>` element serves perfectly for collections of related items where order doesn't convey meaning, such as feature lists, ingredient collections, or navigation menus.

Basic Unordered List Structure

#html

```
<ul>
    <li>Fresh vegetables</li>
    <li>Organic fruits</li>
    <li>Whole grain products</li>
    <li>Lean proteins</li>
</ul>
```

Customizing Unordered List Markers

CSS List Style Types

#html

```
<style>
    .disc-bullets { list-style-type: disc; }
    .circle-bullets { list-style-type: circle; }
    .square-bullets { list-style-type: square; }
    .no-bullets { list-style-type: none; }
</style>

<ul class="disc-bullets">
    <li>Default solid bullet point</li>
    <li>Another solid bullet item</li>
```

```
</ul>

<ul class="circle-bullets">
    <li>Hollow circle marker</li>
    <li>Another hollow circle item</li>
</ul>

<ul class="square-bullets">
    <li>Square bullet marker</li>
    <li>Another square bullet item</li>
</ul>

<ul class="no-bullets">
    <li>No visible bullet marker</li>
    <li>Clean list without markers</li>
</ul>
```

Advanced Unordered List Styling

Custom Image Bullets
#html

```
<style>
    .image-bullets {
        list-style-image: url('custom-bullet.png');
        padding-left: 20px;
    }

    .icon-bullets {
```

```
        list-style: none;
        padding-left: 0;
    }

    .icon-bullets li {
        padding-left: 25px;
        position: relative;
    }

    .icon-bullets li::before {
        content: "→";
        position: absolute;
        left: 0;
        color: #28a745;
        font-weight: bold;
    }
</style>

<ul class="image-bullets">
    <li>Custom image bullet point</li>
    <li>Another custom image item</li>
</ul>

<ul class="icon-bullets">
    <li>Arrow bullet using CSS content</li>
    <li>Another arrow bullet item</li>
    <li>Consistent custom styling</li>
</ul>
```

Horizontal Unordered Lists
#html

```
<style>
    .horizontal-list {
        list-style: none;
        padding: 0;
        display: flex;
        gap: 20px;
    }

    .horizontal-list li {
        padding: 10px 15px;
        background-color: #f8f9fa;
        border-radius: 5px;
        border: 1px solid #dee2e6;
    }
</style>

<ul class="horizontal-list">
    <li>First item</li>
    <li>Second item</li>
    <li>Third item</li>
    <li>Fourth item</li>
</ul>
```

7.3 List Items `<li>`

Understanding List Items

The `<li>` element represents individual items within both ordered and unordered lists. Each list item can contain various HTML elements, including text, images, links, and even nested lists, making them versatile containers for complex content structures.

Basic List Item Usage

#html

```
<ul>
    <li>Simple text content</li>
    <li><strong>Bold text</strong> with emphasis</li>
    <li><em>Italicized content</em> for emphasis</li>
    <li><a href="https://example.com">Linked
content</a></li>
</ul>
```

Complex List Item Content

List Items with Multiple Elements
#html

```
<ul>
    <li>
        <h3>Product Title</h3>
        <p>Detailed description of the product with
multiple sentences explaining features and benefits.</p>
        <p><strong>Price:</strong> $29.99</p>
        <a href="product-details.html">View Details</a>
    </li>
    <li>
        <h3>Another Product</h3>
```

```
        <p>Different product description with unique selling points and feature highlights.</p>
        <p><strong>Price:</strong> $39.99</p>
        <a href="another-product.html">View Details</a>
    </li>
</ul>
```

List Items with Images
#html

```
<ul>
    <li>
        <img src="team-member1.jpg" alt="John Smith" width="100" height="100">
        <h4>John Smith</h4>
        <p>Senior Developer with 8 years experience in web technologies.</p>
        <p>Email: john.smith@company.com</p>
    </li>
    <li>
        <img src="team-member2.jpg" alt="Sarah Johnson" width="100" height="100">
        <h4>Sarah Johnson</h4>
        <p>UX Designer specializing in user-centered design principles.</p>
        <p>Email: sarah.johnson@company.com</p>
    </li>
</ul>
```

List Item Styling Techniques

Individual List Item Styling

#html

```
<style>
    .special-item {
        background-color: #fff3cd;
        border: 1px solid #ffeaa7;
        padding: 15px;
        margin: 5px 0;
        border-radius: 8px;
    }

    .highlight-item {
        background: linear-gradient(90deg, #667eea 0%,
#764ba2 100%);
        color: white;
        padding: 12px;
        margin: 8px 0;
        border-radius: 6px;
    }
</style>

<ul>
    <li>Regular list item</li>
    <li class="special-item">Special highlighted item
with custom styling</li>
    <li>Another regular item</li>
    <li class="highlight-item">Gradient background item
with white text</li>
</ul>
```

Interactive List Items
#html

```
<style>
    .interactive-item {
        padding: 12px;
        margin: 5px 0;
        border: 2px solid transparent;
        border-radius: 5px;
        transition: all 0.3s ease;
        cursor: pointer;
    }

    .interactive-item:hover {
        background-color: #e9ecef;
        border-color: #007bff;
        transform: translateX(5px);
    }
</style>

<ul>
    <li class="interactive-item">Hover over this item to
see the effect</li>
    <li class="interactive-item">Another interactive list
item</li>
    <li class="interactive-item">Third item with hover
animations</li>
</ul>
```

7.4 Nested Lists

Understanding List Nesting

Nested lists create hierarchical structures by placing complete list elements inside list items. This technique proves invaluable for organizing complex information, creating detailed outlines, representing organizational charts, or building multi-level navigation systems.

Basic Nested List Structure

#html

```
<ul>
    <li>Main Category One
        <ul>
            <li>Subcategory A</li>
            <li>Subcategory B</li>
            <li>Subcategory C</li>
        </ul>
    </li>
    <li>Main Category Two
        <ul>
            <li>Subcategory X</li>
            <li>Subcategory Y</li>
        </ul>
    </li>
    <li>Main Category Three</li>
</ul>
```

Mixed List Type Nesting

#html

```
<ol>
    <li>First Major Step
        <ul>
            <li>Preparatory task alpha</li>
            <li>Preparatory task beta</li>
            <li>Preparatory task gamma</li>
        </ul>
    </li>
    <li>Second Major Step
        <ol type="a">
            <li>Detailed sub-step one</li>
            <li>Detailed sub-step two
                <ul>
                    <li>Additional consideration</li>
                    <li>Alternative approach</li>
                </ul>
            </li>
            <li>Detailed sub-step three</li>
        </ol>
    </li>
    <li>Final Major Step</li>
</ol>
```

Deep Nesting Examples

Multi-Level Content Organization
#html

```
<ul>
    <li>Web Development
```

```
        <ul>
            <li>Frontend Technologies
                <ul>
                    <li>HTML
                        <ul>
                            <li>Semantic Elements</li>
                            <li>Forms and Input</li>
                            <li>Multimedia
Integration</li>
                        </ul>
                    </li>
                    <li>CSS
                        <ul>
                            <li>Selectors and
Properties</li>
                            <li>Layout Techniques</li>
                            <li>Responsive Design</li>
                        </ul>
                    </li>
                    <li>JavaScript
                        <ul>
                            <li>DOM Manipulation</li>
                            <li>Event Handling</li>
                            <li>Asynchronous
Programming</li>
                        </ul>
                    </li>
                </ul>
            </li>
            <li>Backend Technologies
                <ul>
```

```
                    <li>Server-Side Languages</li>
                    <li>Database Management</li>
                    <li>API Development</li>
                </ul>
            </li>
        </ul>
    </li>
</ul>
```

Styling Nested Lists

Visual Hierarchy with CSS
#html

```
<style>
    .nested-list {
        line-height: 1.6;
    }

    .nested-list ul {
        margin: 8px 0;
        padding-left: 25px;
    }

    .nested-list > li {
        font-weight: bold;
        color: #2c3e50;
        margin-bottom: 10px;
    }
```

```
    .nested-list > li > ul > li {
        font-weight: normal;
        color: #34495e;
        margin-bottom: 5px;
    }

    .nested-list > li > ul > li > ul > li {
        color: #7f8c8d;
        font-size: 0.9em;
    }
</style>

<ul class="nested-list">
    <li>Primary Level Item
        <ul>
            <li>Secondary Level Item
                <ul>
                    <li>Tertiary level detail</li>
                    <li>Another tertiary detail</li>
                </ul>
            </li>
            <li>Another Secondary Item</li>
        </ul>
    </li>
</ul>
```

Collapsible Nested Lists

#html

```
<style>
```

```
    .collapsible-list details {
        margin: 5px 0;
    }

    .collapsible-list summary {
        cursor: pointer;
        font-weight: bold;
        padding: 8px;
        background-color: #f8f9fa;
        border-radius: 4px;
        border: 1px solid #dee2e6;
    }

    .collapsible-list summary:hover {
        background-color: #e9ecef;
    }

    .collapsible-list ul {
        margin: 10px 0;
        padding-left: 20px;
    }
</style>

<ul class="collapsible-list">
    <li>
        <details>
            <summary>Expandable Category One</summary>
            <ul>
                <li>Hidden item alpha</li>
                <li>Hidden item beta</li>
                <li>Hidden item gamma</li>
```

```
            </ul>
        </details>
    </li>
    <li>
        <details>
            <summary>Expandable Category Two</summary>
            <ul>
                <li>Another hidden item</li>
                <li>Yet another hidden item</li>
            </ul>
        </details>
    </li>
</ul>
```

7.5 Creating Navigation Menus

Understanding Navigation Menu Fundamentals

Navigation menus transform simple unordered lists into interactive user interface elements that guide visitors through website content. Effective navigation menus balance visual appeal with functional accessibility, providing clear pathways while maintaining responsive design principles across various devices and screen sizes.

Basic Horizontal Navigation Menu

#html

```
<style>
    .nav-menu {
        list-style: none;
        margin: 0;
```

```
        padding: 0;
        display: flex;
        background-color: #333;
        border-radius: 8px;
        overflow: hidden;
    }

    .nav-menu li {
        flex: 1;
    }

    .nav-menu a {
        display: block;
        padding: 15px 20px;
        color: white;
        text-decoration: none;
        text-align: center;
        transition: background-color 0.3s ease;
    }

    .nav-menu a:hover {
        background-color: #555;
    }

    .nav-menu .active {
        background-color: #007bff;
    }
</style>

<ul class="nav-menu">
    <li><a href="home.html" class="active">Home</a></li>
```

```
    <li><a href="about.html">About Us</a></li>
    <li><a href="services.html">Services</a></li>
    <li><a href="portfolio.html">Portfolio</a></li>
    <li><a href="contact.html">Contact</a></li>
</ul>
```

Vertical Navigation Menu

#html

```
<style>
    .vertical-nav {
        list-style: none;
        margin: 0;
        padding: 0;
        width: 250px;
        background-color: #f8f9fa;
        border: 1px solid #dee2e6;
        border-radius: 8px;
    }

    .vertical-nav li {
        border-bottom: 1px solid #dee2e6;
    }

    .vertical-nav li:last-child {
        border-bottom: none;
    }

    .vertical-nav a {
```

```
        display: block;
        padding: 12px 20px;
        color: #333;
        text-decoration: none;
        transition: all 0.3s ease;
    }

    .vertical-nav a:hover {
        background-color: #007bff;
        color: white;
        padding-left: 30px;
    }
</style>

<ul class="vertical-nav">
    <li><a href="dashboard.html">Dashboard</a></li>
    <li><a href="profile.html">User Profile</a></li>
    <li><a href="settings.html">Account Settings</a></li>
    <li><a
href="notifications.html">Notifications</a></li>
    <li><a href="logout.html">Sign Out</a></li>
</ul>
```

Dropdown Navigation Menu

#html

```
<style>
    .dropdown-nav {
        list-style: none;
```

```
    margin: 0;
    padding: 0;
    display: flex;
    background-color: #2c3e50;
    position: relative;
}

.dropdown-nav > li {
    position: relative;
}

.dropdown-nav a {
    display: block;
    padding: 15px 20px;
    color: white;
    text-decoration: none;
    transition: background-color 0.3s ease;
}

.dropdown-nav > li:hover > a {
    background-color: #34495e;
}

.dropdown-nav .dropdown {
    position: absolute;
    top: 100%;
    left: 0;
    background-color: #34495e;
    min-width: 200px;
    opacity: 0;
    visibility: hidden;
```

```
        transform: translateY(-10px);
        transition: all 0.3s ease;
        border-radius: 0 0 8px 8px;
        box-shadow: 0 4px 6px rgba(0,0,0,0.1);
    }

    .dropdown-nav li:hover .dropdown {
        opacity: 1;
        visibility: visible;
        transform: translateY(0);
    }

    .dropdown li {
        border-bottom: 1px solid #2c3e50;
    }

    .dropdown li:last-child {
        border-bottom: none;
    }

    .dropdown a:hover {
        background-color: #2c3e50;
    }
</style>

<ul class="dropdown-nav">
    <li>
        <a href="home.html">Home</a>
    </li>
    <li>
        <a href="services.html">Services</a>
```

```
        <ul class="dropdown">
            <li><a href="web-design.html">Web
Design</a></li>
            <li><a href="web-development.html">Web
Development</a></li>
            <li><a href="seo-services.html">SEO
Services</a></li>
            <li><a href="digital-marketing.html">Digital
Marketing</a></li>
        </ul>
    </li>
    <li>
        <a href="portfolio.html">Portfolio</a>
        <ul class="dropdown">
            <li><a href="recent-projects.html">Recent
Projects</a></li>
            <li><a href="case-studies.html">Case
Studies</a></li>
            <li><a href="client-
testimonials.html">Testimonials</a></li>
        </ul>
    </li>
    <li>
        <a href="contact.html">Contact</a>
    </li>
</ul>
```

Mobile-Responsive Navigation Menu

#html

```
<style>
```

```
.mobile-nav {
    list-style: none;
    margin: 0;
    padding: 0;
    background-color: #333;
}

.mobile-nav-toggle {
    display: none;
    background-color: #333;
    color: white;
    border: none;
    padding: 15px 20px;
    font-size: 18px;
    cursor: pointer;
    width: 100%;
    text-align: left;
}

.mobile-nav-toggle:hover {
    background-color: #555;
}

.mobile-nav-items {
    display: flex;
}

.mobile-nav li {
    flex: 1;
}
```

```
.mobile-nav a {
    display: block;
    padding: 15px 20px;
    color: white;
    text-decoration: none;
    text-align: center;
    transition: background-color 0.3s ease;
}

.mobile-nav a:hover {
    background-color: #555;
}

@media (max-width: 768px) {
    .mobile-nav-toggle {
        display: block;
    }

    .mobile-nav-items {
        display: none;
        flex-direction: column;
    }

    .mobile-nav-items.active {
        display: flex;
    }

    .mobile-nav li {
        flex: none;
    }
```

```
        .mobile-nav a {
            text-align: left;
            border-bottom: 1px solid #555;
        }
    }
</style>

<nav class="mobile-nav">
    <button class="mobile-nav-toggle"
onclick="toggleMenu()">☰ Menu</button>
    <ul class="mobile-nav-items" id="mobileNavItems">
        <li><a href="home.html">Home</a></li>
        <li><a href="about.html">About</a></li>
        <li><a href="services.html">Services</a></li>
        <li><a href="portfolio.html">Portfolio</a></li>
        <li><a href="contact.html">Contact</a></li>
    </ul>
</nav>

<script>
    function toggleMenu() {
        const navItems =
document.getElementById('mobileNavItems');
        navItems.classList.toggle('active');
    }
</script>
```

Breadcrumb Navigation

#html

```
<style>
    .breadcrumb {
        list-style: none;
        margin: 0;
        padding: 10px 0;
        display: flex;
        align-items: center;
        background-color: #f8f9fa;
        border-radius: 6px;
        padding: 12px 20px;
    }

    .breadcrumb li {
        display: flex;
        align-items: center;
    }

    .breadcrumb li:not(:last-child)::after {
        content: ">";
        margin: 0 12px;
        color: #6c757d;
        font-weight: bold;
    }

    .breadcrumb a {
        color: #007bff;
        text-decoration: none;
        transition: color 0.3s ease;
    }
```

```
    .breadcrumb a:hover {
        color: #0056b3;
        text-decoration: underline;
    }

    .breadcrumb .current {
        color: #6c757d;
        font-weight: 500;
    }
</style>

<ul class="breadcrumb">
    <li><a href="home.html">Home</a></li>
    <li><a href="products.html">Products</a></li>
    <li><a href="electronics.html">Electronics</a></li>
    <li><span class="current">Smartphones</span></li>
</ul>
```

Tab Navigation

#html

```
<style>
    .tab-nav {
        list-style: none;
        margin: 0;
        padding: 0;
        display: flex;
        border-bottom: 2px solid #dee2e6;
        background-color: #f8f9fa;
```

```
    }

    .tab-nav li {
        margin-right: 5px;
    }

    .tab-nav a {
        display: block;
        padding: 12px 24px;
        color: #495057;
        text-decoration: none;
        border: 2px solid transparent;
        border-bottom: none;
        border-radius: 8px 8px 0 0;
        transition: all 0.3s ease;
        position: relative;
        top: 2px;
    }

    .tab-nav a:hover {
        background-color: #e9ecef;
        color: #007bff;
    }

    .tab-nav .active {
        background-color: white;
        border-color: #dee2e6;
        border-bottom: 2px solid white;
        color: #007bff;
        font-weight: 600;
    }
```

```
</style>

<ul class="tab-nav">
    <li><a href="#overview"
class="active">Overview</a></li>
    <li><a href="#specifications">Specifications</a></li>
    <li><a href="#reviews">Customer Reviews</a></li>
    <li><a href="#support">Support</a></li>
    <li><a href="#warranty">Warranty</a></li>
</ul>
```

Essential Tips

- Use semantic list types appropriately - ordered lists for sequential content and unordered lists for collections without inherent order.
- Maintain consistent styling across similar list elements throughout your website to create cohesive user experiences.
- Implement proper keyboard navigation support in interactive menus by ensuring all links are focusable and visible when tabbed through.
- Test navigation menus across different devices and screen sizes to ensure responsive functionality and accessibility.
- Keep nested list structures logical and not overly deep, as excessive nesting can confuse users and impact accessibility.

Actionable Strategies

- Structure complex information hierarchically using nested lists to create clear content organization that users can easily scan and understand.
- Create responsive navigation systems that adapt seamlessly between desktop horizontal layouts and mobile vertical or hamburger menu patterns.
- Implement hover effects and visual feedback on interactive list elements to provide immediate user response and improve engagement.
- Use CSS custom properties for consistent theming across all list-based components, enabling easy maintenance and brand consistency.

- Combine lists with modern CSS features like Flexbox and Grid for sophisticated layouts that maintain semantic HTML structure.
- Optimize list accessibility by including proper ARIA labels, keyboard navigation support, and screen reader compatibility.
- Test list functionality across different browsers and devices to ensure consistent behavior and appearance for all users.

Chapter 8: HTML Tables

HTML tables provide a powerful way to display structured data in rows and columns, making information easy to read and compare. Tables are essential for presenting data like financial reports, comparison charts, schedules, and any information that benefits from a grid-like structure. Understanding how to create and style tables effectively is crucial for web developers who need to present data clearly and professionally.

8.1 Basic Table Structure

Understanding Table Elements

HTML tables are built using a specific hierarchy of elements that work together to create the complete table structure. The foundation of every table begins with the `<table>` element, which serves as the container for all table content.

The basic structure follows this pattern:

- `<table>` - The main container element
- `<tr>` - Table row elements that create horizontal rows
- `<td>` - Table data cells that contain the actual content
- `<th>` - Table header cells for column or row headings

Creating Your First Table

Let's start with a simple table that displays basic information:

#html

```html
<table>
    <tr>
        <td>Apple</td>
        <td>$2.50</td>
        <td>Fresh</td>
    </tr>
    <tr>
```

```
        <td>Banana</td>
        <td>$1.20</td>
        <td>Ripe</td>
    </tr>
    <tr>
        <td>Orange</td>
        <td>$3.00</td>
        <td>Juicy</td>
    </tr>
</table>
```

This creates a basic three-row, three-column table displaying fruit information. Each `<tr>` element creates a new row, and each `<td>` element within that row creates a new cell.

Table Semantic Structure

HTML5 introduced semantic table elements that provide better structure and accessibility:

#html

```
<table>
    <caption>Monthly Sales Report</caption>
    <thead>
        <tr>
            <th>Product</th>
            <th>Units Sold</th>
            <th>Revenue</th>
        </tr>
    </thead>
    <tbody>
```

```
        <tr>
            <td>Laptops</td>
            <td>45</td>
            <td>$22,500</td>
        </tr>
        <tr>
            <td>Tablets</td>
            <td>67</td>
            <td>$20,100</td>
        </tr>
    </tbody>
    <tfoot>
        <tr>
            <td>Total</td>
            <td>112</td>
            <td>$42,600</td>
        </tr>
    </tfoot>
</table>
```

Semantic Elements Explained

The `<caption>` element provides a title or description for the table, which is particularly important for accessibility. Screen readers use captions to help users understand what the table contains before reading through the data.

The `<thead>` element groups header content and typically contains column headings. This section often remains visible when scrolling through long tables.

The `<tbody>` element contains the main data rows of the table. This is where your primary content lives.

The <tfoot> element groups footer content, often containing summary information like totals or averages.

Table Accessibility Considerations

Proper table structure improves accessibility for users with screen readers and other assistive technologies. Always use semantic elements appropriately and consider adding scope attributes to headers:

#html

```
<table>
    <thead>
        <tr>
            <th scope="col">Name</th>
            <th scope="col">Age</th>
            <th scope="col">Department</th>
        </tr>
    </thead>
    <tbody>
        <tr>
            <th scope="row">John Smith</th>
            <td>28</td>
            <td>Marketing</td>
        </tr>
        <tr>
            <th scope="row">Sarah Johnson</th>
            <td>34</td>
            <td>Engineering</td>
        </tr>
    </tbody>
</table>
```

8.2 Table Rows and Data

Working with Table Rows

Table rows (<tr>) define the horizontal structure of your table. Each row can contain multiple cells, and the number of cells in each row should typically be consistent to maintain proper table alignment.

#html

```html
<table>
    <tr>
        <td>Monday</td>
        <td>9:00 AM</td>
        <td>Team Meeting</td>
        <td>Conference Room A</td>
    </tr>
    <tr>
        <td>Tuesday</td>
        <td>2:00 PM</td>
        <td>Client Presentation</td>
        <td>Main Office</td>
    </tr>
    <tr>
        <td>Wednesday</td>
        <td>10:30 AM</td>
        <td>Project Review</td>
        <td>Conference Room B</td>
    </tr>
</table>
```

Table Data Cells

Table data cells (<td>) contain the actual content of your table. These cells can hold various types of content including text, numbers, images, links, and even other HTML elements.

#html

```
<table>
    <tr>
        <td>
            <img src="product1.jpg" alt="Wireless
Headphones" width="50">
        </td>
        <td>
            <strong>Wireless Headphones</strong><br>
            <small>Model: WH-1000XM4</small>
        </td>
        <td>$299.99</td>
        <td>
            <a href="buy-now.html">Buy Now</a>
        </td>
    </tr>
    <tr>
        <td>
            <img src="product2.jpg" alt="Bluetooth
Speaker" width="50">
        </td>
        <td>
            <strong>Bluetooth Speaker</strong><br>
            <small>Model: SRS-XB43</small>
        </td>
        <td>$149.99</td>
        <td>
```

```
            <a href="buy-now.html">Buy Now</a>
        </td>
    </tr>
</table>
```

Cell Alignment and Content

By default, table cells inherit text alignment from their parent elements, but you can control alignment using CSS or the deprecated `align` attribute (CSS is preferred):

#html

```
<style>
    .number-cell {
        text-align: right;
    }
    .center-cell {
        text-align: center;
    }
    .left-cell {
        text-align: left;
    }
</style>

<table>
    <tr>
        <td class="left-cell">Product Name</td>
        <td class="center-cell">Category</td>
        <td class="number-cell">Price</td>
    </tr>
```

```
    <tr>
        <td class="left-cell">Gaming Mouse</td>
        <td class="center-cell">Electronics</td>
        <td class="number-cell">$79.99</td>
    </tr>
</table>
```

Empty Cells and Data Handling

Sometimes you'll have empty cells in your table. It's important to handle these properly for both visual presentation and accessibility:

#html

```
<table>
    <tr>
        <td>John Doe</td>
        <td>Manager</td>
        <td>$75,000</td>
    </tr>
    <tr>
        <td>Jane Smith</td>
        <td>Developer</td>
        <td> </td> <!-- Empty cell with non-breaking space -->
    </tr>
    <tr>
        <td>Bob Wilson</td>
        <td></td> <!-- Truly empty cell -->
        <td>$45,000</td>
    </tr>
```

```
</table>
```

Dynamic Row Creation

While not purely HTML, understanding how table rows work with dynamic content is valuable. Here's how you might structure a table that will be populated with JavaScript:

#html

```
<table id="data-table">
    <thead>
        <tr>
            <th>ID</th>
            <th>Name</th>
            <th>Status</th>
            <th>Actions</th>
        </tr>
    </thead>
    <tbody id="table-body">
        <!-- Rows will be inserted here dynamically -->
    </tbody>
</table>
```

8.3 Table Headers

Understanding Header Cells

Table headers (`<th>`) serve as labels for columns or rows, providing context for the data in your table. Headers are crucial for accessibility and help users understand what each column or row represents.

#html

```
<table>
    <tr>
        <th>First Name</th>
        <th>Last Name</th>
        <th>Email</th>
        <th>Phone</th>
    </tr>
    <tr>
        <td>Michael</td>
        <td>Johnson</td>
        <td>m.johnson@email.com</td>
        <td>(555) 123-4567</td>
    </tr>
    <tr>
        <td>Emily</td>
        <td>Davis</td>
        <td>e.davis@email.com</td>
        <td>(555) 987-6543</td>
    </tr>
</table>
```

Column Headers vs Row Headers

Headers can serve as column labels (most common) or row labels. When using row headers, place the `<th>` element as the first cell in each row:

#html

```
<table>
    <tr>
        <th></th>
```

```
        <th>Q1</th>
        <th>Q2</th>
        <th>Q3</th>
        <th>Q4</th>
    </tr>
    <tr>
        <th>Sales</th>
        <td>$125K</td>
        <td>$143K</td>
        <td>$167K</td>
        <td>$189K</td>
    </tr>
    <tr>
        <th>Marketing</th>
        <td>$45K</td>
        <td>$52K</td>
        <td>$48K</td>
        <td>$61K</td>
    </tr>
    <tr>
        <th>Operations</th>
        <td>$78K</td>
        <td>$82K</td>
        <td>$91K</td>
        <td>$95K</td>
    </tr>
</table>
```

Header Scope Attributes

The `scope` attribute helps screen readers understand which cells a header applies to. This is essential for complex tables:

#html

```html
<table>
    <thead>
        <tr>
            <th scope="col">Product</th>
            <th scope="col">January</th>
            <th scope="col">February</th>
            <th scope="col">March</th>
        </tr>
    </thead>
    <tbody>
        <tr>
            <th scope="row">Widgets</th>
            <td>150</td>
            <td>175</td>
            <td>200</td>
        </tr>
        <tr>
            <th scope="row">Gadgets</th>
            <td>89</td>
            <td>95</td>
            <td>102</td>
        </tr>
    </tbody>
</table>
```

Complex Header Structures

For more complex tables, you might need headers that span multiple columns or rows, or tables with multiple levels of headers:

#html

```
<table>
    <thead>
        <tr>
            <th rowspan="2">Employee</th>
            <th colspan="2">Q1</th>
            <th colspan="2">Q2</th>
        </tr>
        <tr>
            <th>Sales</th>
            <th>Target</th>
            <th>Sales</th>
            <th>Target</th>
        </tr>
    </thead>
    <tbody>
        <tr>
            <th>Alice</th>
            <td>$15K</td>
            <td>$12K</td>
            <td>$18K</td>
            <td>$15K</td>
        </tr>
        <tr>
            <th>Bob</th>
            <td>$22K</td>
            <td>$20K</td>
            <td>$25K</td>
```

```
            <td>$23K</td>
        </tr>
    </tbody>
</table>
```

Header Styling Considerations

Headers typically receive different styling than regular data cells. They're often bold, centered, or have different background colors:

#html

```
<style>
    th {
        background-color: #f2f2f2;
        font-weight: bold;
        padding: 10px;
        text-align: center;
        border: 1px solid #ddd;
    }

    td {
        padding: 8px;
        border: 1px solid #ddd;
    }

    .row-header {
        background-color: #e8f4f8;
        font-weight: bold;
        text-align: left;
    }
```

```
</style>

<table>
    <tr>
        <th>Category</th>
        <th>Item</th>
        <th>Price</th>
    </tr>
    <tr>
        <td class="row-header">Fruits</td>
        <td>Apples</td>
        <td>$3.99/lb</td>
    </tr>
    <tr>
        <td class="row-header">Vegetables</td>
        <td>Carrots</td>
        <td>$2.49/lb</td>
    </tr>
</table>
```

8.4 Table Borders and Cell Spacing

Basic Border Implementation

Table borders help define the structure and improve readability of your data. You can apply borders to the entire table, individual rows, or specific cells:

#html

```
<style>
    .bordered-table {
        border: 2px solid #333;
```

```
        border-collapse: collapse;
        width: 100%;
    }

    .bordered-table th,
    .bordered-table td {
        border: 1px solid #666;
        padding: 8px;
    }
</style>

<table class="bordered-table">
    <tr>
        <th>Name</th>
        <th>Position</th>
        <th>Salary</th>
    </tr>
    <tr>
        <td>John Smith</td>
        <td>Developer</td>
        <td>$65,000</td>
    </tr>
    <tr>
        <td>Mary Jones</td>
        <td>Designer</td>
        <td>$58,000</td>
    </tr>
</table>
```

Border Collapse Property

The `border-collapse` property determines how adjacent borders are handled. The two main values are `separate` (default) and `collapse`:

#html

```
<style>
    .separate-borders {
        border-collapse: separate;
        border-spacing: 5px;
        border: 2px solid #000;
    }

    .separate-borders th,
    .separate-borders td {
        border: 1px solid #666;
        padding: 10px;
    }

    .collapsed-borders {
        border-collapse: collapse;
        border: 2px solid #000;
    }

    .collapsed-borders th,
    .collapsed-borders td {
        border: 1px solid #666;
        padding: 10px;
    }
</style>

<h3>Separate Borders</h3>
```

```
<table class="separate-borders">
    <tr>
        <th>Column 1</th>
        <th>Column 2</th>
    </tr>
    <tr>
        <td>Data 1</td>
        <td>Data 2</td>
    </tr>
</table>

<h3>Collapsed Borders</h3>
<table class="collapsed-borders">
    <tr>
        <th>Column 1</th>
        <th>Column 2</th>
    </tr>
    <tr>
        <td>Data 1</td>
        <td>Data 2</td>
    </tr>
</table>
```

Cell Spacing and Padding

Cell spacing controls the space between cells, while padding controls the space inside each cell:

#html

```
<style>
```

```
    .spaced-table {
        border-collapse: separate;
        border-spacing: 10px 5px; /* horizontal, vertical
*/
        background-color: #f0f0f0;
    }

    .spaced-table th,
    .spaced-table td {
        background-color: white;
        padding: 15px 20px;
        border: 1px solid #ccc;
    }

    .padded-table {
        border-collapse: collapse;
    }

    .padded-table th {
        padding: 15px;
        background-color: #4CAF50;
        color: white;
    }

    .padded-table td {
        padding: 12px;
        border-bottom: 1px solid #ddd;
    }
</style>

<table class="spaced-table">
```

```
    <tr>
        <th>Product</th>
        <th>Price</th>
        <th>Stock</th>
    </tr>
    <tr>
        <td>Laptop</td>
        <td>$899</td>
        <td>15</td>
    </tr>
    <tr>
        <td>Mouse</td>
        <td>$25</td>
        <td>43</td>
    </tr>
</table>
```

Advanced Border Styling

You can create sophisticated border effects using different border styles, colors, and widths:

#html

```
<style>
    .fancy-table {
        border-collapse: collapse;
        width: 100%;
        font-family: Arial, sans-serif;
    }
```

```
    .fancy-table th {
        background: linear-gradient(135deg, #667eea 0%,
#764ba2 100%);
        color: white;
        padding: 12px;
        text-align: left;
        border-bottom: 3px solid #4a5568;
    }

    .fancy-table td {
        padding: 12px;
        border-bottom: 1px solid #e2e8f0;
    }

    .fancy-table tr:nth-child(even) {
        background-color: #f7fafc;
    }

    .fancy-table tr:hover {
        background-color: #edf2f7;
    }

    .fancy-table .number-cell {
        text-align: right;
        font-weight: bold;
        color: #2d3748;
    }
</style>

<table class="fancy-table">
    <tr>
```

```
        <th>Customer</th>
        <th>Order Date</th>
        <th>Amount</th>
        <th>Status</th>
    </tr>
    <tr>
        <td>Acme Corporation</td>
        <td>2024-01-15</td>
        <td class="number-cell">$2,450.00</td>
        <td>Completed</td>
    </tr>
    <tr>
        <td>Tech Solutions Inc</td>
        <td>2024-01-16</td>
        <td class="number-cell">$1,875.50</td>
        <td>Pending</td>
    </tr>
    <tr>
        <td>Global Industries</td>
        <td>2024-01-17</td>
        <td class="number-cell">$3,200.75</td>
        <td>Shipped</td>
    </tr>
</table>
```

Responsive Border Considerations

When designing tables for responsive layouts, consider how borders will appear on different screen sizes:

#html

```
<style>
    .responsive-table {
        border-collapse: collapse;
        width: 100%;
        margin: 20px 0;
    }

    .responsive-table th,
    .responsive-table td {
        border: 1px solid #ddd;
        padding: 8px;
        text-align: left;
    }

    @media screen and (max-width: 600px) {
        .responsive-table {
            border: 0;
        }

        .responsive-table th,
        .responsive-table td {
            border: none;
            border-bottom: 1px solid #eee;
            display: block;
            padding: 10px;
        }

        .responsive-table th {
            background-color: #f2f2f2;
            font-weight: bold;
```

```
        }
    }
</style>
```

8.5 Spanning Rows and Columns

Column Spanning with Colspan

The `colspan` attribute allows a cell to span across multiple columns, which is useful for creating headers that cover multiple data columns or for grouping related information:

#html

```
<table>
    <tr>
        <th colspan="3">Sales Report Q1 2024</th>
    </tr>
    <tr>
        <th>Month</th>
        <th>Revenue</th>
        <th>Growth %</th>
    </tr>
    <tr>
        <td>January</td>
        <td>$125,000</td>
        <td>12%</td>
    </tr>
    <tr>
        <td>February</td>
        <td>$140,000</td>
        <td>15%</td>
```

```
    </tr>
    <tr>
        <td>March</td>
        <td>$158,000</td>
        <td>18%</td>
    </tr>
    <tr>
        <td colspan="2"><strong>Total
Revenue</strong></td>
        <td><strong>$423,000</strong></td>
    </tr>
</table>
```

Row Spanning with Rowspan

The `rowspan` attribute enables a cell to span across multiple rows, perfect for creating categories or grouping related data vertically:

#html

```
<table>
    <tr>
        <th>Department</th>
        <th>Employee</th>
        <th>Role</th>
        <th>Salary</th>
    </tr>
    <tr>
        <td rowspan="3">Engineering</td>
        <td>John Smith</td>
        <td>Senior Developer</td>
```

```
        <td>$85,000</td>
    </tr>
    <tr>
        <td>Sarah Johnson</td>
        <td>Frontend Developer</td>
        <td>$72,000</td>
    </tr>
    <tr>
        <td>Mike Wilson</td>
        <td>DevOps Engineer</td>
        <td>$78,000</td>
    </tr>
    <tr>
        <td rowspan="2">Marketing</td>
        <td>Lisa Brown</td>
        <td>Marketing Manager</td>
        <td>$65,000</td>
    </tr>
    <tr>
        <td>Tom Davis</td>
        <td>Content Specialist</td>
        <td>$48,000</td>
    </tr>
</table>
```

Combining Colspan and Rowspan

You can combine both colspan and rowspan attributes to create complex table layouts:

#html

```
<style>
    .complex-table {
        border-collapse: collapse;
        width: 100%;
        margin: 20px 0;
    }

    .complex-table th,
    .complex-table td {
        border: 1px solid #333;
        padding: 10px;
        text-align: center;
    }

    .complex-table th {
        background-color: #f0f0f0;
        font-weight: bold;
    }

    .category-cell {
        background-color: #e8f4f8;
        font-weight: bold;
    }
</style>

<table class="complex-table">
    <tr>
        <th rowspan="2">Product Category</th>
        <th colspan="2">Q1</th>
        <th colspan="2">Q2</th>
```

```
    </tr>
    <tr>
        <th>Units</th>
        <th>Revenue</th>
        <th>Units</th>
        <th>Revenue</th>
    </tr>
    <tr>
        <td rowspan="2" class="category-
cell">Electronics</td>
        <td>1,250</td>
        <td>$125,000</td>
        <td>1,400</td>
        <td>$140,000</td>
    </tr>
    <tr>
        <td colspan="4"><em>Includes smartphones,
tablets, and accessories</em></td>
    </tr>
    <tr>
        <td rowspan="2" class="category-
cell">Clothing</td>
        <td>2,100</td>
        <td>$84,000</td>
        <td>2,350</td>
        <td>$94,000</td>
    </tr>
    <tr>
        <td colspan="4"><em>Seasonal variations affect
quarterly performance</em></td>
    </tr>
</table>
```

Advanced Spanning Techniques

Here's a more complex example showing how spanning can be used to create sophisticated table layouts:

#html

```
<style>
    .schedule-table {
        border-collapse: collapse;
        width: 100%;
        font-family: Arial, sans-serif;
    }

    .schedule-table th,
    .schedule-table td {
        border: 1px solid #ddd;
        padding: 8px;
        text-align: center;
    }

    .schedule-table th {
        background-color: #4CAF50;
        color: white;
    }

    .time-slot {
        background-color: #f9f9f9;
        font-weight: bold;
    }
```

```
    .class-session {
        background-color: #e7f3ff;
    }

    .break-time {
        background-color: #fff2e7;
        font-style: italic;
    }
</style>

<table class="schedule-table">
    <tr>
        <th>Time</th>
        <th>Monday</th>
        <th>Tuesday</th>
        <th>Wednesday</th>
        <th>Thursday</th>
        <th>Friday</th>
    </tr>
    <tr>
        <td class="time-slot">9:00-10:00</td>
        <td class="class-session">Math 101</td>
        <td class="class-session">Physics</td>
        <td class="class-session">Math 101</td>
        <td class="class-session">Chemistry</td>
        <td class="class-session">Biology</td>
    </tr>
    <tr>
        <td class="time-slot">10:00-10:15</td>
        <td colspan="5" class="break-time">Break</td>
```

```
    </tr>
    <tr>
        <td class="time-slot">10:15-11:15</td>
        <td class="class-session">English</td>
        <td rowspan="2" class="class-session">Lab
Session<br>(2 hours)</td>
        <td class="class-session">English</td>
        <td class="class-session">History</td>
        <td rowspan="3" class="class-session">Project
Work<br>(3 hours)</td>
    </tr>
    <tr>
        <td class="time-slot">11:15-12:15</td>
        <td class="class-session">History</td>
        <td class="class-session">Art</td>
        <td class="class-session">Music</td>
    </tr>
    <tr>
        <td class="time-slot">12:15-1:00</td>
        <td colspan="3" class="break-time">Lunch
Break</td>
        <td class="break-time">Lunch</td>
    </tr>
</table>
```

Common Spanning Mistakes and Solutions

When working with spanning cells, it's important to understand how they affect the table structure. Here are common issues and their solutions:

#html

```html
<!-- Incorrect: Too many cells in a row -->
<table>
    <tr>
        <td colspan="2">Header</td>
        <td>Extra Cell</td> <!-- This creates an extra
column -->
        <td>Another Cell</td> <!-- This too -->
    </tr>
    <tr>
        <td>Cell 1</td>
        <td>Cell 2</td>
    </tr>
</table>

<!-- Correct: Proper cell count -->
<table>
    <tr>
        <td colspan="2">Header spans two columns</td>
    </tr>
    <tr>
        <td>Cell 1</td>
        <td>Cell 2</td>
    </tr>
</table>
```

Accessibility with Spanning Cells

When using spanning cells, maintain accessibility by providing appropriate headers and scope attributes:

#html

```
<table>
    <caption>Employee Performance by Department</caption>
    <tr>
        <th scope="col">Department</th>
        <th scope="colgroup" colspan="2">Q1
Performance</th>
        <th scope="colgroup" colspan="2">Q2
Performance</th>
    </tr>
    <tr>
        <th scope="col"></th>
        <th scope="col">Rating</th>
        <th scope="col">Bonus</th>
        <th scope="col">Rating</th>
        <th scope="col">Bonus</th>
    </tr>
    <tr>
        <th scope="rowgroup" rowspan="2">Sales</th>
        <td>4.2</td>
        <td>$2,000</td>
        <td>4.5</td>
        <td>$2,500</td>
    </tr>
    <tr>
        <td>4.0</td>
        <td>$1,800</td>
        <td>4.3</td>
        <td>$2,200</td>
    </tr>
</table>
```

Essential Tips

- Always use semantic table elements like `<thead>`, `<tbody>`, and `<tfoot>` to provide clear structure and improve accessibility for screen readers and other assistive technologies.
- Include meaningful captions using the `<caption>` element to describe the table's purpose and content, making it easier for all users to understand the data being presented.
- Apply the `scope` attribute to header cells to explicitly define whether they apply to columns, rows, or groups of cells, which significantly improves table navigation for users with disabilities.
- Design tables with responsive considerations in mind, using CSS media queries to modify table display on smaller screens, potentially converting to card layouts or simplified views.
- Keep table content concise and scannable by using consistent formatting, appropriate white space, and clear visual hierarchy through styling and typography choices.

Actionable Strategies

- Structure your tables with a clear hierarchy by placing the most important information in headers and organizing data logically from left to right and top to bottom.
- Implement consistent styling patterns across all tables in your website, including standard colors, fonts, spacing, and border treatments to maintain visual cohesion.
- Test table accessibility using screen readers and keyboard navigation to ensure all users can effectively access and understand your tabular data.
- Optimize table performance by avoiding overly complex nested structures and minimizing the use of inline styles in favor of external CSS stylesheets.
- Create reusable table templates and CSS classes that can be applied across different pages to maintain consistency and reduce development time.
- Plan for data scalability by designing tables that can accommodate varying amounts of content without breaking the layout or becoming difficult to read.

- Document your table structure and styling guidelines for other developers, including naming conventions for classes and proper usage of spanning attributes.

Chapter 9: Forms and Input Elements

9.1 Introduction to Forms

HTML forms represent one of the most crucial aspects of web development, serving as the primary mechanism for collecting user data and enabling interactive communication between websites and their visitors. Forms create a bridge between static web content and dynamic user engagement, allowing websites to gather information ranging from simple contact details to complex survey responses and application data.

Understanding the Purpose of Forms

Forms function as digital equivalents of paper forms, providing structured methods for users to input information that can be processed, stored, or transmitted to servers for further handling. Every time you log into a website, submit a contact form, make an online purchase, or participate in an online survey, you interact with HTML forms. These elements transform passive web browsing into active user participation.

The fundamental concept behind forms involves creating designated areas where users can enter various types of data through different input methods. This data collection process requires careful consideration of user experience, data validation, and security measures to ensure both functionality and protection of sensitive information.

Form Components and Structure

HTML forms consist of several interconnected components that work together to create a cohesive data collection system. The form container element serves as the wrapper that defines the boundaries of the form and specifies how the collected data should be handled. Within this container, various input elements provide different methods for users to enter information, from simple text fields to complex selection mechanisms.

Input elements come in numerous varieties, each designed for specific types of data collection. Text inputs handle general text entry, while specialized inputs like email fields provide built-in validation for specific data formats. Selection elements such as radio buttons and checkboxes offer predefined choices, while dropdown menus provide space-efficient options for longer lists of selections.

Form Accessibility and User Experience

Creating accessible forms requires attention to proper labeling, logical tab order, and clear visual hierarchy. Screen readers and other assistive technologies rely on properly structured forms to help users with disabilities navigate and complete form submissions successfully. This involves using semantic HTML elements, providing descriptive labels, and implementing appropriate keyboard navigation patterns.

User experience considerations extend beyond accessibility to include visual design, form length, error handling, and feedback mechanisms. Well-designed forms guide users through the completion process with clear instructions, appropriate field grouping, and helpful validation messages that prevent frustration and abandonment.

9.2 The `<form>` Tag and action Attribute

Basic Form Structure

The `<form>` element serves as the foundational container for all form-related elements, defining the scope and behavior of data collection mechanisms. This element acts as a wrapper that groups related input fields and specifies how the browser should handle the submitted data.

#html

```
<form action="/submit-form" method="POST">
    <!-- Form content goes here -->
</form>
```

The opening <form> tag establishes the beginning of a form section, while the closing </form> tag marks its end. All input elements, labels, and form controls must be placed between these tags to function correctly as part of the form submission process.

The action Attribute

The action attribute determines the destination URL where form data will be sent when users submit the form. This attribute accepts absolute URLs, relative paths, or can be left empty to submit data to the current page.

#html

```html
<!-- Absolute URL -->
<form action="https://example.com/process-form">
    <!-- Form elements -->
</form>

<!-- Relative path -->
<form action="/contact/submit">
    <!-- Form elements -->
</form>

<!-- Submit to current page -->
<form action="">
    <!-- Form elements -->
</form>
```

When the action attribute is omitted or left empty, the form data is submitted to the same URL that currently displays the form. This approach is commonly used when server-side scripts on the same page handle form processing.

HTTP Methods: GET vs POST

The `method` attribute specifies the HTTP method used to send form data to the server. The two primary methods are GET and POST, each serving different purposes and having distinct characteristics.

GET Method

The GET method appends form data to the URL as query parameters, making the submitted data visible in the browser's address bar. This method is suitable for search forms, filtering mechanisms, and other scenarios where data visibility and bookmarking are beneficial.

#html

```
<form action="/search" method="GET">
    <input type="text" name="query" placeholder="Search term">
    <input type="submit" value="Search">
</form>
```

When submitted, a GET form produces URLs like: `https://example.com/search?query=html+forms`

GET requests have length limitations imposed by browsers and servers, typically restricting URLs to around 2000 characters. This method should never be used for sensitive information like passwords or personal data, as the information becomes visible in browser history, server logs, and referrer headers.

POST Method

The POST method sends form data in the request body, keeping the information hidden from the URL. This method is appropriate for sensitive data, large amounts of information, and operations that modify server-side data.

#html

```
<form action="/login" method="POST">
    <input type="text" name="username"
placeholder="Username">
    <input type="password" name="password"
placeholder="Password">
    <input type="submit" value="Login">
</form>
```

POST requests can handle significantly larger amounts of data and provide better security for sensitive information. However, POST form submissions cannot be bookmarked in the same way as GET requests, and refreshing a POST submission typically triggers browser warnings about resubmitting data.

Additional Form Attributes

Target Attribute

The `target` attribute controls where the form response will be displayed, similar to link targets. Common values include `_self` (current window), `_blank` (new window), and specific frame or window names.

#html

```
<form action="/newsletter" method="POST" target="_blank">
    <input type="email" name="email" placeholder="Email
address">
    <input type="submit" value="Subscribe">
</form>
```

Enctype Attribute

The `enctype` attribute specifies how form data should be encoded before transmission to the server. The default value is `application/x-www-form-urlencoded`, suitable for most text-based forms.

#html

```
<!-- Default encoding for text data -->
<form action="/contact" method="POST"
enctype="application/x-www-form-urlencoded">
    <!-- Text inputs -->
</form>

<!-- Multipart encoding for file uploads -->
<form action="/upload" method="POST"
enctype="multipart/form-data">
    <input type="file" name="document">
    <input type="submit" value="Upload">
</form>
```

The `multipart/form-data` encoding is essential when forms include file upload inputs, as it allows binary data transmission alongside text data.

9.3 Text Fields and Password Fields

Basic Text Input Fields

Text input fields represent the most fundamental form elements, providing single-line areas where users can enter textual information. These versatile elements handle various types of text data, from names and addresses to search queries and comments.

#html

```
<form action="/profile" method="POST">
    <label for="firstName">First Name:</label>
    <input type="text" id="firstName" name="firstName"
placeholder="Enter your first name">


    <label for="lastName">Last Name:</label>
    <input type="text" id="lastName" name="lastName"
placeholder="Enter your last name">
</form>
```

The `type="text"` attribute explicitly declares the input as a text field, though this is the default type for input elements. The `name` attribute provides the identifier used when form data is submitted, while the `id` attribute enables proper label association and CSS/JavaScript targeting.

Input Attributes and Properties

Placeholder Text

The `placeholder` attribute displays helpful text inside empty input fields, providing users with examples or instructions about expected input format. This text disappears when users begin typing and reappears if the field becomes empty again.

#html

```
<input type="text" name="phone" placeholder="(555) 123-
4567">
<input type="text" name="website"
placeholder="https://www.example.com">
```

Placeholder text should complement, not replace, proper labels. Screen readers may not announce placeholder text consistently, making explicit labels essential for accessibility.

Value Attribute

The `value` attribute sets the initial content of input fields, useful for providing default values or pre-filling forms with known information.

#html

```html
<input type="text" name="country" value="United States">
<input type="text" name="language" value="English">
```

Maxlength and Minlength

These attributes control the character limits for text inputs, helping maintain data consistency and preventing excessively long entries.

#html

```html
<input type="text" name="username" maxlength="20"
minlength="3" placeholder="3-20 characters">
<input type="text" name="zipcode" maxlength="5"
placeholder="5-digit ZIP code">
```

Required Attribute

The `required` attribute makes fields mandatory, preventing form submission until users provide input for these fields.

#html

```html
<input type="text" name="email" required
placeholder="Email address (required)">
```

Readonly and Disabled States

The `readonly` attribute prevents user modification while keeping the field focusable and includable in form submissions. The `disabled` attribute completely prevents interaction and excludes the field from form submissions.

#html

```
<input type="text" name="orderNumber" value="ORD-12345"
readonly>
<input type="text" name="unavailableField" value="Not
available" disabled>
```

Specialized Text Input Types

HTML5 introduced specialized input types that provide enhanced functionality, validation, and user experience improvements over generic text fields.

Email Input Type

Email inputs provide built-in validation for email address formats and may display specialized keyboards on mobile devices.

#html

```
<label for="userEmail">Email Address:</label>
<input type="email" id="userEmail" name="userEmail"
required
       placeholder="user@example.com">
```

URL Input Type

URL inputs validate web addresses and often display specialized keyboards optimized for URL entry.

#html

```
<label for="website">Website:</label>
<input type="url" id="website" name="website"
       placeholder="https://www.example.com">
```

Tel Input Type

Telephone inputs may display numeric keypads on mobile devices, though they don't enforce specific formatting validation.

#html

```
<label for="phoneNumber">Phone Number:</label>
<input type="tel" id="phoneNumber" name="phoneNumber"
       placeholder="(555) 123-4567">
```

Search Input Type

Search inputs may display differently styled with features like clear buttons and are semantically identified as search fields.

#html

```
<label for="siteSearch">Search:</label>
<input type="search" id="siteSearch" name="siteSearch"
       placeholder="Search our website">
```

Password Fields

Password fields provide secure text input by hiding typed characters, displaying dots or asterisks instead of actual text. This visual obscuring protects sensitive information from casual observation.

#html

```
<form action="/login" method="POST">
    <label for="username">Username:</label>
    <input type="text" id="username" name="username"
required>

    <label for="password">Password:</label>
    <input type="password" id="password" name="password"
required>

    <input type="submit" value="Login">
</form>
```

Password Field Characteristics

Password fields behave similarly to text fields but with crucial security considerations. The browser masks the input visually, but the actual text is still accessible to JavaScript and transmitted in form submissions. This makes HTTPS encryption essential for forms containing password fields.

#html

```
<!-- Password confirmation field -->
<label for="newPassword">New Password:</label>
<input type="password" id="newPassword"
name="newPassword" required
       minlength="8">

<label for="confirmPassword">Confirm Password:</label>
```

```
<input type="password" id="confirmPassword"
name="confirmPassword" required
       minlength="8">
```

Security Considerations

Password fields should always be submitted over secure HTTPS connections to prevent interception during transmission. Additionally, proper server-side password hashing and validation are essential security measures beyond HTML implementation.

Many browsers offer password management features that can automatically generate, store, and fill password fields. The `autocomplete` attribute can provide hints about the password's purpose:

#html

```
<input type="password" name="currentPassword"
autocomplete="current-password">
<input type="password" name="newPassword"
autocomplete="new-password">
```

Text Areas for Multi-line Input

While not technically input elements, textarea elements provide multi-line text input capabilities for longer content like comments, messages, or descriptions.

#html

```
<label for="message">Message:</label>
<textarea id="message" name="message" rows="5" cols="40"
          placeholder="Enter your message
here..."></textarea>
```

The `rows` and `cols` attributes specify the visible dimensions, though CSS typically provides better control over textarea sizing. Like input fields, textareas support attributes like `maxlength`, `minlength`, `required`, and `placeholder`.

9.4 Radio Buttons and Checkboxes

Radio Buttons for Exclusive Selection

Radio buttons provide users with multiple options where only one selection is permitted. These circular input elements work in groups, with selecting one option automatically deselecting others in the same group. Radio buttons derive their name from old car radios where pressing one button would release others.

Basic Radio Button Implementation

Radio buttons share the same `name` attribute to form a group, while each option has a unique `value` attribute identifying the specific choice.

#html

```
<form action="/survey" method="POST">
    <fieldset>
        <legend>What is your preferred programming
language?</legend>

        <input type="radio" id="javascript"
name="language" value="javascript">
        <label for="javascript">JavaScript</label>

        <input type="radio" id="python" name="language"
value="python">
        <label for="python">Python</label>
```

```
        <input type="radio" id="java" name="language" value="java">
        <label for="java">Java</label>

        <input type="radio" id="csharp" name="language" value="csharp">
        <label for="csharp">C#</label>
    </fieldset>
</form>
```

The `fieldset` element groups related form controls, while the `legend` element provides a caption for the group. This semantic structure improves accessibility and provides visual grouping for better user understanding.

Pre-selecting Radio Options

The `checked` attribute pre-selects a specific radio button when the form loads. Only one radio button in a group should have the `checked` attribute.

#html

```html
<input type="radio" id="beginner" name="experience" value="beginner" checked>
<label for="beginner">Beginner</label>

<input type="radio" id="intermediate" name="experience" value="intermediate">
<label for="intermediate">Intermediate</label>

<input type="radio" id="advanced" name="experience" value="advanced">
<label for="advanced">Advanced</label>
```

Radio Button Styling and Accessibility

Proper labeling is crucial for radio button accessibility. Each radio button should have an associated label element connected through the `for` attribute and input's `id` attribute. This connection allows users to click labels to select radio buttons, increasing the clickable area and improving usability.

#html

```html
<!-- Method 1: Explicit association -->
<input type="radio" id="option1" name="choice" value="1">
<label for="option1">Option 1</label>

<!-- Method 2: Implicit association -->
<label>
    <input type="radio" name="choice" value="2">
    Option 2
</label>
```

Checkboxes for Multiple Selection

Checkboxes allow users to select multiple options from a list of choices. Unlike radio buttons, checkboxes operate independently, permitting zero, one, or multiple selections within a group.

Basic Checkbox Implementation

Each checkbox operates independently, requiring unique `name` attributes if individual processing is needed, or sharing names when grouping related options.

#html

```html
<form action="/preferences" method="POST">
```

```
    <fieldset>
        <legend>Select your interests:</legend>

        <input type="checkbox" id="webdev"
name="interests[]" value="web-development">
        <label for="webdev">Web Development</label>

        <input type="checkbox" id="mobile"
name="interests[]" value="mobile-development">
        <label for="mobile">Mobile Development</label>

        <input type="checkbox" id="ai" name="interests[]"
value="artificial-intelligence">
        <label for="ai">Artificial Intelligence</label>

        <input type="checkbox" id="cybersec"
name="interests[]" value="cybersecurity">
        <label for="cybersec">Cybersecurity</label>
    </fieldset>
</form>
```

The array notation `interests[]` in the name attribute helps server-side processing handle multiple selected values as an array.

Pre-selected Checkboxes

The `checked` attribute pre-selects checkboxes when the form loads. Multiple checkboxes can be pre-selected simultaneously.

#html

```
<input type="checkbox" id="newsletter"
name="subscriptions[]" value="newsletter" checked>
```

```
<label for="newsletter">Weekly Newsletter</label>


<input type="checkbox" id="updates"
name="subscriptions[]" value="updates" checked>
<label for="updates">Product Updates</label>


<input type="checkbox" id="promotions"
name="subscriptions[]" value="promotions">
<label for="promotions">Special Promotions</label>
```

Single Checkbox for Boolean Values

Individual checkboxes often represent boolean choices like agreement to terms, subscription preferences, or feature toggles.

#html

```
<input type="checkbox" id="terms" name="acceptTerms"
value="yes" required>
<label for="terms">I agree to the Terms of
Service</label>


<input type="checkbox" id="remember" name="rememberMe"
value="true">
<label for="remember">Remember me on this device</label>
```

Advanced Selection Patterns

Mixed Selection Groups

Complex forms may combine radio buttons and checkboxes to create sophisticated selection patterns that match real-world decision-making processes.

#html

```
<form action="/order" method="POST">
    <fieldset>
        <legend>Pizza Size (select one):</legend>
        <input type="radio" id="small" name="size"
value="small">
        <label for="small">Small ($12)</label>

        <input type="radio" id="medium" name="size"
value="medium" checked>
        <label for="medium">Medium ($16)</label>

        <input type="radio" id="large" name="size"
value="large">
        <label for="large">Large ($20)</label>
    </fieldset>

    <fieldset>
        <legend>Toppings (select any):</legend>
        <input type="checkbox" id="pepperoni"
name="toppings[]" value="pepperoni">
        <label for="pepperoni">Pepperoni (+$2)</label>

        <input type="checkbox" id="mushrooms"
name="toppings[]" value="mushrooms">
        <label for="mushrooms">Mushrooms (+$1)</label>

        <input type="checkbox" id="olives"
name="toppings[]" value="olives">
        <label for="olives">Black Olives (+$1)</label>
    </fieldset>
</form>
```

Dependent Selection Logic

Some forms require conditional logic where certain selections affect available options. While HTML alone cannot implement complex dependencies, proper structuring prepares forms for JavaScript enhancement.

#html

```
<fieldset>
    <legend>Shipping Method:</legend>
    <input type="radio" id="standard" name="shipping"
value="standard">
    <label for="standard">Standard Shipping (5-7
days)</label>

    <input type="radio" id="express" name="shipping"
value="express">
    <label for="express">Express Shipping (2-3
days)</label>

    <input type="radio" id="overnight" name="shipping"
value="overnight">
    <label for="overnight">Overnight Shipping</label>
</fieldset>

<fieldset>
    <legend>Additional Services:</legend>
    <input type="checkbox" id="insurance"
name="services[]" value="insurance">
    <label for="insurance">Shipping Insurance</label>
```

```
    <input type="checkbox" id="tracking"
name="services[]" value="tracking">
    <label for="tracking">Package Tracking</label>


    <input type="checkbox" id="signature"
name="services[]" value="signature">
    <label for="signature">Signature Required</label>
</fieldset>
```

Validation and Error Handling

Both radio buttons and checkboxes support the `required` attribute for validation. Radio button groups require selection of any option in the group, while individual checkboxes require their specific selection.

#html

```
<!-- Required radio group -->
<fieldset>
    <legend>Age Group (required):</legend>
    <input type="radio" id="under18" name="ageGroup"
value="under18" required>
    <label for="under18">Under 18</label>


    <input type="radio" id="adult" name="ageGroup"
value="adult" required>
    <label for="adult">18 or older</label>
</fieldset>


<!-- Required individual checkbox -->
<input type="checkbox" id="privacy" name="acceptPrivacy"
value="yes" required>
```

```
<label for="privacy">I accept the Privacy Policy
(required)</label>
```

9.5 Submit and Reset Buttons

Submit Buttons for Form Processing

Submit buttons trigger form submission, sending collected data to the specified action URL using the designated HTTP method. These buttons represent the primary call-to-action in forms, converting user input into actionable data transmission.

Basic Submit Button Implementation

The `type="submit"` attribute creates a button that submits the form when clicked. The button's text content or `value` attribute provides the visible label.

#html

```
<form action="/contact" method="POST">
    <label for="name">Name:</label>
    <input type="text" id="name" name="name" required>

    <label for="email">Email:</label>
    <input type="email" id="email" name="email" required>

    <label for="message">Message:</label>
    <textarea id="message" name="message"
required></textarea>

    <input type="submit" value="Send Message">
</form>
```

Alternative implementations use the `<button>` element with `type="submit"`, providing more flexibility for styling and content:

#html

```
<button type="submit">Send Message</button>
<button type="submit">
    <img src="send-icon.png" alt=""> Send Message
</button>
```

Multiple Submit Buttons

Forms can contain multiple submit buttons, each potentially having different values or triggering different server-side processing paths.

#html

```
<form action="/document" method="POST">
    <label for="title">Document Title:</label>
    <input type="text" id="title" name="title" required>

    <label for="content">Content:</label>
    <textarea id="content" name="content"
required></textarea>

    <input type="submit" name="action" value="Save
Draft">
    <input type="submit" name="action" value="Publish">
    <input type="submit" name="action" value="Save and
Preview">
</form>
```

The server-side code can determine which button was clicked by examining the submitted `action` parameter value.

Image Submit Buttons

Image inputs create graphical submit buttons using custom images instead of standard button appearances.

#html

```
<input type="image" src="submit-button.png" alt="Submit
Form"
       width="120" height="40">
```

Image submit buttons automatically submit the form when clicked and include the click coordinates in the submitted data, making them useful for image maps or precise click tracking.

Submit Button States and Accessibility

Submit buttons should provide clear indication of their purpose and current state. Disabled submit buttons prevent submission during processing or when validation requirements aren't met.

#html

```
<form action="/registration" method="POST" id="regForm">
    <label for="username">Username:</label>
    <input type="text" id="username" name="username"
required>

    <label for="password">Password:</label>
    <input type="password" id="password" name="password"
required>
```

```
    <input type="checkbox" id="terms" name="acceptTerms"
value="yes" required>
    <label for="terms">I accept the terms and
conditions</label>

    <button type="submit" id="submitBtn">Create
Account</button>
</form>
```

Accessible submit buttons include descriptive text that clearly indicates the action being performed. Generic labels like "Submit" should be avoided in favor of specific actions like "Send Message," "Create Account," or "Place Order."

Reset Buttons for Form Clearing

Reset buttons restore all form elements to their initial states, clearing user-entered data and returning to default values. While historically common, modern web design typically avoids reset buttons due to their potential for accidental activation and user frustration.

Basic Reset Button Implementation

The `type="reset"` attribute creates a button that clears form data when clicked.

#html

```
<form action="/feedback" method="POST">
    <label for="rating">Rating:</label>
    <select id="rating" name="rating">
        <option value="1">1 Star</option>
        <option value="2">2 Stars</option>
        <option value="3" selected>3 Stars</option>
        <option value="4">4 Stars</option>
```

```
        <option value="5">5 Stars</option>
    </select>

    <label for="comments">Comments:</label>
    <textarea id="comments" name="comments"></textarea>

    <input type="reset" value="Clear Form">
    <input type="submit" value="Submit Feedback">
</form>
```

Reset Button Behavior

Reset buttons return form elements to their initial HTML-defined states, not to empty states. Pre-selected options, default values, and checked attributes are restored to their original settings.

#html

```
<form>
    <input type="text" name="name" value="John Doe">
    <input type="radio" name="status" value="active"
checked>
    <label>Active</label>
    <input type="radio" name="status" value="inactive">
    <label>Inactive</label>

    <input type="reset" value="Reset to Defaults">
</form>
```

After user modification and subsequent reset button activation, the text field returns to "John Doe" and the "Active" radio button becomes selected again.

Alternative Button Types and Behaviors

Generic Buttons for Custom Functionality

Buttons with `type="button"` or no type attribute (when using `<button>` elements) don't trigger form submission, making them suitable for JavaScript-driven functionality.

#html

```
<form action="/calculator" method="POST">
    <label for="number1">First Number:</label>
    <input type="number" id="number1" name="number1">

    <label for="number2">Second Number:</label>
    <input type="number" id="number2" name="number2">

    <label for="result">Result:</label>
    <input type="text" id="result" name="result"
readonly>

    <button type="button"
onclick="calculate()">Calculate</button>
    <button type="submit">Save Result</button>
</form>
```

Form Validation and Submit Prevention

Modern forms often implement client-side validation that can prevent submission when validation criteria aren't met. This typically involves JavaScript functionality that checks form validity before allowing submission.

#html

```
<form action="/order" method="POST" onsubmit="return validateOrder()">
    <label for="quantity">Quantity:</label>
    <input type="number" id="quantity" name="quantity" min="1" max="10" required>

    <label for="email">Email:</label>
    <input type="email" id="email" name="email" required>

    <button type="submit">Place Order</button>
    <button type="button" onclick="previewOrder()">Preview Order</button>
</form>
```

Button Styling and User Experience

Submit and reset buttons benefit from clear visual hierarchy and consistent styling that indicates their relative importance. Submit buttons typically receive primary styling with prominent colors and positioning, while reset buttons use secondary styling to prevent accidental activation.

#html

```
<form action="/newsletter" method="POST">
    <label for="email">Email Address:</label>
    <input type="email" id="email" name="email" required>

    <div class="button-group">
        <button type="submit" class="btn-primary">Subscribe</button>
        <button type="reset" class="btn-secondary">Clear</button>
```

```
        <button type="button" class="btn-link"
onclick="showPreview()">Preview</button>
    </div>
</form>
```

Modern form design often positions submit buttons prominently while de-emphasizing or eliminating reset buttons entirely. When reset functionality is needed, it's often implemented as a less prominent link or secondary button with confirmation dialogs to prevent accidental data loss.

Essential Tips

- Always associate labels with form controls using the `for` attribute and corresponding `id` values to improve accessibility and increase clickable areas for better user experience.
- Use appropriate input types (`email`, `tel`, `url`, `number`) instead of generic text inputs to provide better validation, mobile keyboard optimization, and semantic meaning for assistive technologies.
- Implement proper form validation using both HTML5 attributes (`required`, `pattern`, `min`, `max`) and server-side validation to ensure data integrity and security while providing immediate user feedback.
- Group related form elements using `fieldset` and `legend` elements to create logical sections that improve both visual organization and screen reader navigation for complex forms.
- Provide clear, descriptive placeholder text and help instructions that guide users toward successful form completion without relying solely on placeholders for essential information.

Actionable Strategies

- Test forms across multiple devices and browsers to ensure consistent behavior, especially focusing on mobile responsiveness, touch targets, and keyboard navigation for comprehensive accessibility.

- Implement progressive enhancement by starting with functional HTML forms that work without JavaScript, then adding interactive features that enhance the user experience without breaking basic functionality.
- Use consistent naming conventions for form fields that make sense to both developers and server-side processing, avoiding special characters and using descriptive names that indicate the data purpose.
- Position submit buttons prominently and avoid reset buttons unless absolutely necessary, as they often cause user frustration and accidental data loss in modern web applications.
- Create forms with logical tab order that follows the visual flow of the page, ensuring keyboard users can navigate efficiently through all form controls in a predictable sequence.
- Implement client-side validation feedback that appears immediately when users complete fields, providing early error detection and correction opportunities before form submission attempts.
- Design form layouts that accommodate various content lengths and internationalization requirements, considering how different languages and cultural input patterns might affect form usability and layout.

Chapter 10: More Form Controls

Building on the foundation of basic form elements, this chapter expands your HTML toolkit with advanced form controls that enhance user interaction and data collection. These elements provide specialized input methods that make forms more intuitive, accessible, and user-friendly.

10.1 Dropdowns with <select>

The `<select>` element creates dropdown menus that allow users to choose from predefined options. This control saves screen space while providing multiple choices, making it ideal for situations where you need to present many options without overwhelming the interface.

Basic Select Structure

The `<select>` element works in conjunction with `<option>` elements to create dropdown lists:

#html

```
<form>
    <label for="country">Choose your country:</label>
    <select id="country" name="country">
        <option value="us">United States</option>
        <option value="ca">Canada</option>
        <option value="uk">United Kingdom</option>
        <option value="de">Germany</option>
        <option value="fr">France</option>
    </select>
</form>
```

Each `<option>` element represents a selectable choice. The `value` attribute defines what gets sent to the server when the form is submitted, while the text content between the opening and closing tags displays what users see in the dropdown.

Default Selection and Placeholder Options

You can pre-select an option using the `selected` attribute:

#html

```
<select id="language" name="language">
    <option value="">Select a language</option>
    <option value="en" selected>English</option>
    <option value="es">Spanish</option>
    <option value="fr">French</option>
    <option value="de">German</option>
</select>
```

The first option with an empty value serves as a placeholder, prompting users to make a selection. This approach helps prevent accidental submissions with unintended default values.

Multiple Selection Capability

The `multiple` attribute allows users to select multiple options simultaneously:

#html

```
<label for="skills">Select your programming
skills:</label>
<select id="skills" name="skills" multiple>
    <option value="html">HTML</option>
    <option value="css">CSS</option>
```

```
    <option value="javascript">JavaScript</option>
    <option value="python">Python</option>
    <option value="java">Java</option>
    <option value="php">PHP</option>
</select>
```

When using `multiple`, users can hold Ctrl (or Cmd on Mac) while clicking to select multiple options. The control displays as a list box rather than a dropdown, showing several options simultaneously.

Grouping Options with <optgroup>

For better organization of related options, use `<optgroup>` elements:

#html

```
<select id="food" name="food">
    <optgroup label="Fruits">
        <option value="apple">Apple</option>
        <option value="banana">Banana</option>
        <option value="orange">Orange</option>
    </optgroup>
    <optgroup label="Vegetables">
        <option value="carrot">Carrot</option>
        <option value="broccoli">Broccoli</option>
        <option value="spinach">Spinach</option>
    </optgroup>
</select>
```

The `<optgroup>` element creates visual separations within the dropdown, with the `label` attribute providing category headers that users cannot select.

Controlling Select Size and Appearance

The `size` attribute determines how many options display simultaneously:

#html

```
<select id="cities" name="cities" size="4">
    <option value="nyc">New York City</option>
    <option value="la">Los Angeles</option>
    <option value="chicago">Chicago</option>
    <option value="houston">Houston</option>
    <option value="phoenix">Phoenix</option>
    <option value="philadelphia">Philadelphia</option>
</select>
```

This creates a list box showing four options at once, with scroll bars appearing when more options exist.

10.2 Text Areas with `<textarea>`

The `<textarea>` element provides multi-line text input capabilities, essential for collecting longer text content like comments, descriptions, or messages.

Basic Textarea Implementation

Unlike input elements, `<textarea>` uses opening and closing tags with content between them:

#html

```
<form>
    <label for="comments">Your comments:</label>
```

```
    <textarea id="comments" name="comments" rows="4" cols="50">
Enter your comments here...
    </textarea>
</form>
```

The `rows` attribute specifies the visible height in text lines, while `cols` determines the width in characters. Default text appears between the opening and closing tags.

Controlling Textarea Dimensions

Modern web development often uses CSS for styling, but HTML attributes provide basic dimension control:

#html

```
<textarea id="description" name="description" rows="6" cols="60" style="width: 100%; max-width: 500px;">
</textarea>
```

Combining HTML attributes with CSS styles offers precise control over textarea appearance and behavior.

Restricting Text Input Length

The `maxlength` attribute limits the number of characters users can enter:

#html

```
<label for="tweet">Compose your tweet (280 characters max):</label>
```

```
<textarea id="tweet" name="tweet" rows="3" cols="50"
maxlength="280"></textarea>
```

This prevents users from entering more text than your application can handle, providing immediate feedback about character limits.

Placeholder Text and Required Fields

Placeholder text guides users about expected content:

#html

```
<textarea id="feedback" name="feedback" rows="5"
cols="40"
          placeholder="Please share your thoughts about
our service..."
          required></textarea>
```

The `required` attribute makes the field mandatory before form submission, while `placeholder` provides helpful hints without affecting form data.

Controlling Text Wrapping and Resizing

The `wrap` attribute controls how text wraps within the textarea:

#html

```
<textarea id="code" name="code" rows="10" cols="60"
wrap="off"></textarea>
```

Values include `soft` (default, wraps visually but doesn't insert line breaks), `hard` (inserts actual line breaks), and `off` (no wrapping).

Most browsers allow users to resize textareas by dragging the corner. Control this behavior with CSS:

#html

```
<textarea id="fixed-size" name="fixed-size" rows="4"
cols="50"
          style="resize: none;"></textarea>
```

10.3 Date and Time Inputs

HTML5 introduced specialized input types for handling dates and times, providing native calendar interfaces and validation.

Date Input Type

The `date` input type creates a date picker interface:

#html

```
<form>
    <label for="birthday">Date of birth:</label>
    <input type="date" id="birthday" name="birthday"
value="1990-01-01">

    <label for="appointment">Appointment date:</label>
    <input type="date" id="appointment"
name="appointment"
           min="2024-01-01" max="2024-12-31">
</form>
```

The `min` and `max` attributes restrict selectable dates, while `value` sets a default date. Dates use the ISO format (YYYY-MM-DD).

Time Input Type

The `time` input type handles time selection:

#html

```
<label for="meeting-time">Meeting time:</label>
<input type="time" id="meeting-time" name="meeting-time"
value="14:30">

<label for="alarm">Set alarm:</label>
<input type="time" id="alarm" name="alarm" min="06:00"
max="22:00" step="900">
```

The `step` attribute controls time intervals in seconds (900 seconds = 15 minutes). Time values use 24-hour format (HH:MM).

DateTime-Local Input Type

The `datetime-local` input combines date and time selection:

#html

```
<label for="event-start">Event start:</label>
<input type="datetime-local" id="event-start"
name="event-start"
       value="2024-06-01T09:00">

<label for="deadline">Project deadline:</label>
<input type="datetime-local" id="deadline"
name="deadline"
```

```
      min="2024-01-01T00:00" max="2024-12-31T23:59">
```

This input type provides comprehensive date and time selection in a single control, using the format YYYY-MM-DDTHH:MM.

Month and Week Input Types

For broader time period selection:

#html

```
<label for="birth-month">Birth month:</label>
<input type="month" id="birth-month" name="birth-month"
value="1990-05">

<label for="vacation-week">Vacation week:</label>
<input type="week" id="vacation-week" name="vacation-
week" value="2024-W25">
```

The `month` input uses YYYY-MM format, while `week` uses YYYY-WXX format where XX represents the week number.

Browser Compatibility and Fallbacks

Not all browsers support every date/time input type. Provide fallbacks for better compatibility:

#html

```
<label for="event-date">Event date:</label>
<input type="date" id="event-date" name="event-date"
       placeholder="MM/DD/YYYY" pattern="[0-9]{2}/[0-
9]{2}/[0-9]{4}">
```

The `placeholder` and `pattern` attributes help in browsers that don't support the `date` input type.

10.4 Range and Color Pickers

These specialized input types provide intuitive interfaces for selecting numerical ranges and colors.

Range Input Type

The `range` input creates a slider control for selecting numerical values:

#html

```html
<form>
    <label for="volume">Volume level:</label>
    <input type="range" id="volume" name="volume" min="0" max="100" value="50">
    <output for="volume">50</output>

    <label for="price-range">Price range ($):</label>
    <input type="range" id="price-range" name="price-range"
           min="0" max="1000" step="50" value="250">
</form>
```

The `min`, `max`, and `step` attributes control the range limits and increment values. The `<output>` element can display the current value dynamically with JavaScript.

Advanced Range Controls

Create more sophisticated range controls with additional attributes:

#html

```
<label for="opacity">Opacity level:</label>
<input type="range" id="opacity" name="opacity"
       min="0" max="1" step="0.1" value="0.5"
       list="opacity-values">
<datalist id="opacity-values">
    <option value="0" label="Transparent">
    <option value="0.25" label="25%">
    <option value="0.5" label="50%">
    <option value="0.75" label="75%">
    <option value="1" label="Opaque">
</datalist>
```

The `<datalist>` element provides tick marks and labels along the slider, helping users understand specific values.

Color Input Type

The `color` input type opens a color picker interface:

#html

```
<form>
    <label for="background-color">Choose background
color:</label>
    <input type="color" id="background-color"
name="background-color" value="#ffffff">

    <label for="text-color">Text color:</label>
```

```
    <input type="color" id="text-color" name="text-color"
value="#000000">

    <label for="theme-color">Theme color:</label>
    <input type="color" id="theme-color" name="theme-
color"
           value="#3366cc" list="theme-colors">
    <datalist id="theme-colors">
        <option value="#ff0000">Red</option>
        <option value="#00ff00">Green</option>
        <option value="#0000ff">Blue</option>
        <option value="#ffff00">Yellow</option>
    </datalist>
</form>
```

Color values use hexadecimal format (#RRGGBB). The `<datalist>` element can provide preset color options for quick selection.

Styling Range and Color Inputs

While these inputs have default browser styling, CSS can customize their appearance:

#html

```
<style>
input[type="range"] {
    width: 100%;
    margin: 10px 0;
}

input[type="color"] {
```

```
    width: 50px;
    height: 30px;
    border: none;
    border-radius: 5px;
}
</style>

<label for="custom-range">Custom styled range:</label>
<input type="range" id="custom-range" name="custom-range"
       min="0" max="100" value="75">
```

10.5 Fieldsets and Legends

Fieldsets group related form controls together, improving organization and accessibility.

Basic Fieldset Structure

The `<fieldset>` element creates visual and semantic groupings:

#html

```
<form>
    <fieldset>
        <legend>Personal Information</legend>
        <label for="first-name">First Name:</label>
        <input type="text" id="first-name" name="first-
name" required>

        <label for="last-name">Last Name:</label>
        <input type="text" id="last-name" name="last-
name" required>
```

```
        <label for="email">Email:</label>
        <input type="email" id="email" name="email"
required>
    </fieldset>

    <fieldset>
        <legend>Address Details</legend>
        <label for="street">Street Address:</label>
        <input type="text" id="street" name="street">

        <label for="city">City:</label>
        <input type="text" id="city" name="city">

        <label for="zip">ZIP Code:</label>
        <input type="text" id="zip" name="zip">
    </fieldset>
</form>
```

The `<legend>` element provides a caption for each fieldset, clearly identifying the purpose of grouped controls.

Disabling Entire Fieldsets

The `disabled` attribute can disable all controls within a fieldset:

#html

```
<fieldset disabled>
    <legend>Premium Features (Upgrade Required)</legend>
    <label for="premium-option1">Advanced
Analytics:</label>
```

```
    <input type="checkbox" id="premium-option1"
name="premium-option1">


    <label for="premium-option2">Priority
Support:</label>
    <input type="checkbox" id="premium-option2"
name="premium-option2">
</fieldset>
```

This provides a way to conditionally enable or disable entire sections of forms based on user permissions or subscription status.

Nested Fieldsets for Complex Forms

Complex forms benefit from nested fieldset structures:

#html

```
<form>
    <fieldset>
        <legend>Account Setup</legend>

        <fieldset>
            <legend>Login Credentials</legend>
            <label for="username">Username:</label>
            <input type="text" id="username"
name="username" required>

            <label for="password">Password:</label>
            <input type="password" id="password"
name="password" required>
        </fieldset>
```

```
        <fieldset>
            <legend>Security Questions</legend>
            <label for="security-question">Choose a security question:</label>
            <select id="security-question" name="security-question">
                <option value="pet">What was your first pet's name?</option>
                <option value="school">What elementary school did you attend?</option>
                <option value="city">In what city were you born?</option>
            </select>

            <label for="security-answer">Answer:</label>
            <input type="text" id="security-answer" name="security-answer" required>
        </fieldset>
    </fieldset>
</form>
```

Styling Fieldsets and Legends

CSS enhances the visual presentation of fieldsets:

#html

```
<style>
fieldset {
    border: 2px solid #ddd;
    border-radius: 8px;
    padding: 15px;
    margin: 20px 0;
```

```
}

legend {
    font-weight: bold;
    color: #333;
    padding: 0 10px;
}

fieldset:disabled {
    opacity: 0.6;
    background-color: #f5f5f5;
}
</style>

<fieldset>
    <legend>Styled Form Section</legend>
    <label for="sample-input">Sample Input:</label>
    <input type="text" id="sample-input" name="sample-
input">
</fieldset>
```

Accessibility Benefits of Fieldsets

Fieldsets significantly improve form accessibility by:

- Providing semantic structure that screen readers can navigate
- Creating logical groupings that help users understand form organization
- Allowing screen readers to announce legend content when users focus on controls within the fieldset
- Supporting keyboard navigation between form sections

#html

```
<form>
    <fieldset>
        <legend>Contact Preferences</legend>
        <p>How would you like us to contact you?</p>

        <input type="radio" id="contact-email"
name="contact-method" value="email">
        <label for="contact-email">Email</label>

        <input type="radio" id="contact-phone"
name="contact-method" value="phone">
        <label for="contact-phone">Phone</label>

        <input type="radio" id="contact-mail"
name="contact-method" value="mail">
        <label for="contact-mail">Postal Mail</label>
    </fieldset>
</form>
```

This structure helps screen reader users understand that all radio buttons relate to contact preferences, making form completion more intuitive.

Essential Tips

- Always provide clear labels and instructions for complex form controls to help users understand their purpose and how to use them effectively
- Test your forms across different browsers and devices, as support for HTML5 input types varies, and provide appropriate fallbacks for unsupported features
- Use the `autocomplete` attribute on form fields to help browsers and password managers fill forms automatically, improving user experience and form completion rates

- Consider the mobile experience when designing forms, as touch interfaces may require larger touch targets and different interaction patterns than desktop interfaces
- Implement proper form validation both on the client side using HTML5 validation attributes and on the server side to ensure data integrity and security

Actionable Strategies

- Group related form controls using fieldsets and legends to create logical sections that improve both visual organization and screen reader navigation
- Implement progressive disclosure by showing advanced options only when users need them, reducing initial form complexity while maintaining full functionality
- Use appropriate input types for different data formats (email, tel, url) to trigger correct mobile keyboards and enable built-in browser validation
- Provide real-time feedback for form validation errors and success states, helping users correct mistakes immediately rather than after form submission
- Create consistent styling and interaction patterns across all form elements to build user familiarity and reduce cognitive load during form completion
- Optimize form performance by minimizing the number of required fields and using smart defaults based on user context or previous interactions
- Test forms with actual users to identify pain points and usability issues that may not be apparent during development, then iterate based on feedback

Chapter 11: Semantic HTML Elements

11.1 What is Semantic HTML?

Semantic HTML represents a fundamental shift in how developers approach web markup, moving beyond the traditional focus on visual presentation to prioritize meaning and structure. This approach uses HTML elements that carry inherent meaning about the content they contain, making web pages more understandable for both human readers and automated systems.

Understanding the Core Concept

Semantic HTML elements describe the purpose and meaning of content rather than its appearance. Instead of using generic `<div>` and `<span>` elements for everything, semantic HTML provides specific tags that communicate the role of different content sections. These elements create a logical document structure that screen readers, search engines, and other automated tools can interpret accurately.

The concept extends beyond individual elements to encompass the entire document structure. A semantically structured page tells a story through its markup, with each element serving a specific purpose in the overall narrative of the content.

Historical Context and Evolution

HTML originally focused heavily on presentation, with elements like `<font>` and `<center>` controlling visual appearance directly within the markup. This approach created maintenance nightmares and accessibility barriers. The introduction of CSS separated presentation from content, but many developers continued using non-semantic elements like `<div>` for everything.

HTML5 revolutionized this landscape by introducing numerous semantic elements that describe content meaning. This evolution reflects the web's maturation from a document-sharing platform to a complex ecosystem of applications, services, and information systems.

The Semantic Advantage

Semantic HTML provides multiple layers of benefit. For developers, it creates self-documenting code that remains understandable months or years after creation. The markup itself communicates the intended structure and purpose of different content sections.

For users, particularly those using assistive technologies, semantic HTML provides crucial navigation aids. Screen readers can identify landmarks, skip to main content, and understand the relationship between different page sections. This creates a more accessible and usable experience for everyone.

Search engines rely heavily on semantic markup to understand content context and relevance. Proper semantic structure helps search algorithms identify key information, understand content hierarchy, and determine how different page sections relate to each other.

Common Non-Semantic Patterns to Avoid

Many developers fall into patterns that prioritize visual appearance over semantic meaning. Using `<div class="header">` instead of the semantic `<header>` element sacrifices meaning for no practical benefit. Similarly, creating fake headings with styled paragraphs or spans breaks the logical document outline that assistive technologies depend on.

Another common mistake involves using elements for their default styling rather than their semantic meaning. Using `<blockquote>` simply to indent text, or `<h1>` tags for large text without considering heading hierarchy, undermines the document's semantic structure.

#html

```
<!-- Non-semantic approach (avoid) -->
```

```
<div class="header">
  <div class="logo">Company Name</div>
  <div class="navigation">
    <div class="nav-item">Home</div>
    <div class="nav-item">About</div>
    <div class="nav-item">Contact</div>
  </div>
</div>

<!-- Semantic approach (preferred) -->
<header>
  <h1>Company Name</h1>
  <nav>
    <ul>
      <li><a href="/">Home</a></li>
      <li><a href="/about">About</a></li>
      <li><a href="/contact">Contact</a></li>
    </ul>
  </nav>
</header>
```

11.2 `<header>` and `<footer>`

The `<header>` and `<footer>` elements represent introductory and concluding content respectively, providing clear semantic boundaries for different content sections. These elements can appear multiple times within a single document, serving different contexts and scopes.

Understanding the `<header>` Element

The <header> element contains introductory content or navigational aids for its nearest ancestor sectioning element. This could be the document header, a section header, or an article header. The element typically includes headings, logos, navigation menus, search forms, and other introductory content.

Document-Level Headers

At the document level, the <header> typically contains the site's main branding, primary navigation, and global tools like search functionality. This header establishes the site's identity and provides primary navigation options for users.

#html

```
<header>
  <img src="logo.png" alt="TechNews Logo" class="site-
logo">
  <nav class="primary-navigation">
    <ul>
      <li><a href="/">Home</a></li>
      <li><a href="/tech">Technology</a></li>
      <li><a href="/business">Business</a></li>
      <li><a href="/science">Science</a></li>
    </ul>
  </nav>
  <form class="search-form" role="search">
    <input type="search" placeholder="Search
articles...">
    <button type="submit">Search</button>
  </form>
</header>
```

Section and Article Headers

Headers can also introduce specific content sections or articles. These contextual headers contain information relevant to their specific content area, such as section titles, publication dates, or author information.

#html

```html
<article>
  <header>
    <h2>Revolutionary Battery Technology
Breakthrough</h2>
    <p class="article-meta">
      Published on <time datetime="2024-03-15">March 15,
2024</time>
      by <span class="author">Dr. Sarah Chen</span>
    </p>
    <p class="article-summary">Scientists develop new
lithium-air battery with 10x capacity.</p>
  </header>

  <p>The main article content begins here...</p>
</article>
```

Header Content Guidelines

Headers should contain content that introduces or provides context for the following material. Avoid placing the main content itself within header elements. The header serves as a preview or introduction, not the primary content container.

Navigation elements within headers should relate to the content they introduce. Global navigation belongs in the document header, while section-specific navigation should appear in section headers.

Understanding the `<footer>` Element

The `<footer>` element represents concluding content for its nearest ancestor sectioning element. Like headers, footers can appear at multiple levels within a document, providing relevant closing information for different content scopes.

Document-Level Footers

Document footers typically contain site-wide information such as contact details, legal notices, social media links, and secondary navigation. This content remains consistent across multiple pages and provides essential site information.

#html

```
<footer class="site-footer">
  <div class="footer-content">
    <section class="contact-info">
      <h3>Contact Us</h3>
      <address>
        TechNews Media<br>
        123 Innovation Drive<br>
        Silicon Valley, CA 94000<br>
        <a href="tel:+1-555-0123">+1 (555) 012-
3456</a><br>
        <a
href="mailto:info@technews.example">info@technews.example
</a>
      </address>
    </section>
```

```
    <nav class="footer-navigation">
      <h3>Quick Links</h3>
      <ul>
        <li><a href="/privacy">Privacy Policy</a></li>
        <li><a href="/terms">Terms of Service</a></li>
        <li><a href="/careers">Careers</a></li>
        <li><a href="/advertise">Advertise</a></li>
      </ul>
    </nav>

    <section class="social-media">
      <h3>Follow Us</h3>
      <ul class="social-links">
        <li><a href="https://twitter.com/technews" aria-
label="Twitter">Twitter</a></li>
        <li><a
href="https://linkedin.com/company/technews" aria-
label="LinkedIn">LinkedIn</a></li>
        <li><a href="https://facebook.com/technews" aria-
label="Facebook">Facebook</a></li>
      </ul>
    </section>
  </div>

  <div class="copyright">
    <p>&copy; 2024 TechNews Media. All rights
reserved.</p>
  </div>
</footer>
```

Article and Section Footers

Footers can also conclude specific articles or sections, providing relevant closing information such as publication details, related links, or author biographies.

#html

```
<article>
  <header>
    <h2>The Future of Renewable Energy</h2>
  </header>

  <p>Article content goes here...</p>

  <footer class="article-footer">
    <div class="author-bio">
      <img src="author-photo.jpg" alt="Dr. Maria
Rodriguez">
      <div class="bio-text">
        <h4>Dr. Maria Rodriguez</h4>
        <p>Environmental scientist specializing in
renewable energy systems with over 15 years of research
experience.</p>
      </div>
    </div>

    <div class="article-tags">
      <span class="tag">Renewable Energy</span>
      <span class="tag">Solar Power</span>
      <span class="tag">Sustainability</span>
    </div>
```

```
    <div class="article-sharing">
      <h4>Share this article:</h4>
      <button class="share-button" data-
platform="twitter">Share on Twitter</button>
      <button class="share-button" data-
platform="linkedin">Share on LinkedIn</button>
    </div>
  </footer>
</article>
```

Best Practices for Headers and Footers

Headers and footers should contain content that naturally introduces or concludes their associated content. Avoid forcing unrelated content into these elements simply for styling purposes.

Multiple headers and footers within the same document should serve distinct purposes and relate to different content scopes. Each header or footer should provide value specific to its context.

Consider the user experience when designing header and footer content. Headers should help users understand what they're about to read, while footers should provide logical next steps or additional context.

11.3 `<article>` and `<section>`

The `<article>` and `<section>` elements provide semantic structure for organizing content into logical groups. These elements help create clear content hierarchies while providing semantic meaning that benefits both users and automated systems.

Understanding the <article> Element

The `<article>` element represents a complete, self-contained piece of content that could stand alone and be distributed independently. Articles should make sense when removed from their original context and viewed in isolation, such as in RSS feeds or content aggregation systems.

Characteristics of Article Content

Article content typically represents discrete pieces of information with clear boundaries. Blog posts, news articles, product descriptions, user comments, and forum posts all qualify as article content. The key criterion is independence - the content should provide complete value without requiring additional context from surrounding elements.

#html

```
<article class="blog-post">
  <header>
    <h1>Mastering CSS Grid Layout</h1>
    <p class="post-meta">
      Published <time datetime="2024-03-20">March 20, 2024</time>
      by <span class="author">Alex Thompson</span>
    </p>
  </header>

  <p>CSS Grid revolutionizes how developers approach layout design, providing powerful two-dimensional layout capabilities that surpass traditional methods.</p>

  <section>
    <h2>Getting Started with Grid</h2>
    <p>The foundation of CSS Grid lies in understanding the relationship between grid containers and grid items...</p>
```

```
    <pre><code>
.grid-container {
  display: grid;
  grid-template-columns: repeat(3, 1fr);
  grid-gap: 20px;
}
    </code></pre>
  </section>

  <section>
    <h2>Advanced Grid Techniques</h2>
    <p>Once you master basic grid concepts, advanced
techniques open up sophisticated layout
possibilities...</p>
  </section>

  <footer class="post-footer">
    <p>Tags: <span class="tag">CSS</span> <span
class="tag">Web Design</span> <span
class="tag">Layout</span></p>
    <div class="post-actions">
      <button class="like-button">Like (42)</button>
      <button class="share-button">Share</button>
    </div>
  </footer>
</article>
```

Nested Articles

Articles can contain other articles when the nested content represents related but independent pieces. Comment systems provide a common example, where each comment represents an independent article nested within the main article.

#html

```
<article class="main-article">
  <header>
    <h1>The Impact of Artificial Intelligence on
Education</h1>
    <p class="byline">By Dr. Jennifer Walsh</p>
  </header>

  <p>Artificial intelligence transforms educational
landscapes through personalized learning
experiences...</p>

  <section class="comments">
    <h2>Reader Comments</h2>

    <article class="comment">
      <header>
        <h3 class="commenter-name">Sarah Mitchell</h3>
        <time datetime="2024-03-21T10:30:00">March 21,
2024 at 10:30 AM</time>
      </header>
      <p>This article highlights crucial points about
AI's role in personalized education. I've seen similar
implementations in my district with remarkable
results.</p>
    </article>
```

```
    <article class="comment">
      <header>
        <h3 class="commenter-name">Professor David Chen</h3>
        <time datetime="2024-03-21T14:15:00">March 21, 2024 at 2:15 PM</time>
      </header>
      <p>While AI offers tremendous potential, we must also consider the ethical implications of data collection in educational settings.</p>
    </article>
  </section>
</article>
```

Understanding the `<section>` Element

The `<section>` element represents a distinct section of content with a common theme or purpose. Sections group related content together but don't necessarily represent independent, distributable units like articles do.

When to Use Sections

Sections work best for organizing content within larger structures. Chapter divisions in long articles, different product categories in catalogs, or thematic groupings in portfolios all represent appropriate section usage.

Each section should have a clear, identifiable theme that justifies its separation from surrounding content. If you can't articulate why content belongs in its own section, it might not need section markup.

#html

```
<article class="product-guide">
```

```
  <header>
    <h1>Complete Guide to Professional Cameras</h1>
    <p>Everything you need to know about choosing the
right camera for professional photography.</p>
  </header>

  <section class="camera-types">
    <h2>Types of Professional Cameras</h2>
    <p>Professional cameras fall into several distinct
categories, each optimized for specific use cases...</p>

    <section class="dslr-cameras">
      <h3>DSLR Cameras</h3>
      <p>Digital Single-Lens Reflex cameras offer
exceptional image quality and versatility...</p>

      <div class="camera-examples">
        <div class="camera-card">
          <h4>Canon EOS 5D Mark IV</h4>
          <p>Full-frame sensor with 30.4
megapixels...</p>
        </div>
      </div>
    </section>

    <section class="mirrorless-cameras">
      <h3>Mirrorless Cameras</h3>
      <p>Mirrorless systems provide DSLR-quality images
in more compact form factors...</p>
    </section>
  </section>
```

```
  <section class="buying-guide">
    <h2>How to Choose Your Camera</h2>
    <p>Selecting the right professional camera depends on several key factors...</p>

    <section class="budget-considerations">
      <h3>Budget Planning</h3>
      <p>Professional camera systems require significant investment beyond the camera body...</p>
    </section>
  </section>
</article>
```

Section Headings and Structure

Every section should include a heading that describes its content theme. This heading helps users and assistive technologies understand the section's purpose and navigate through the document structure effectively.

Sections create logical content hierarchies that screen readers can navigate. Users can jump between sections, get section overviews, and understand how different content pieces relate to each other.

Combining Articles and Sections

Articles and sections work together to create sophisticated content structures. Articles contain the main independent content pieces, while sections organize content within those articles into logical themes.

#html

```
<main>
  <article class="research-paper">
```

```
    <header>
      <h1>Climate Change Impacts on Arctic Wildlife</h1>
      <p class="paper-meta">Published in Journal of Environmental Science, Volume 45</p>
      <p class="authors">Dr. Elena Kowalski, Dr. James Arctic, Dr. Maria Fernandez</p>
    </header>

    <section class="abstract">
      <h2>Abstract</h2>
      <p>This study examines the effects of rising temperatures on Arctic wildlife populations over the past two decades...</p>
    </section>

    <section class="introduction">
      <h2>Introduction</h2>
      <p>Arctic ecosystems face unprecedented challenges as global temperatures continue to rise...</p>
    </section>

    <section class="methodology">
      <h2>Research Methodology</h2>
      <p>Our research employed a combination of satellite data analysis and field observations...</p>

      <section class="data-collection">
        <h3>Data Collection Process</h3>
        <p>Data collection occurred across three distinct phases...</p>
      </section>
    </section>
```

```
    <section class="results">
      <h2>Results and Analysis</h2>
      <p>Our findings reveal significant population
changes across multiple species...</p>
    </section>

    <section class="conclusions">
      <h2>Conclusions</h2>
      <p>The evidence clearly demonstrates the urgent
need for conservation action...</p>
    </section>
  </article>
</main>
```

Accessibility Considerations

Articles and sections provide crucial navigation landmarks for screen reader users. These elements create a logical document outline that assistive technologies can present to users, allowing them to understand content structure and navigate efficiently.

Proper heading hierarchies within articles and sections enhance this navigation experience. Each section should have an appropriate heading level that reflects its position in the document hierarchy.

11.4 `<aside>` and `<main>`

The `<aside>` and `<main>` elements serve complementary roles in defining content importance and relationship. These elements help distinguish primary content from supporting information, creating clearer page structures for both users and automated systems.

Understanding the <main> Element

The <main> element identifies the primary content of a document, representing the central topic or functionality that the page exists to provide. Each document should contain only one <main> element, positioned to encompass the core content while excluding repeated navigation, advertising, and subsidiary information.

Defining Main Content

Main content represents the unique, primary purpose of the page. For a blog post, the main content includes the article itself. For a product page, it encompasses the product information and purchase options. For a search results page, the main content consists of the search results and related functionality.

The main element should exclude content that appears across multiple pages, such as site headers, navigation menus, footer information, and advertising. These elements provide context and functionality but don't represent the page's primary purpose.

#html

```
<!DOCTYPE html>
<html lang="en">
<head>
  <title>Advanced JavaScript Techniques - DevTutorials</title>
</head>
<body>
  <header class="site-header">
    <h1>DevTutorials</h1>
    <nav class="primary-nav">
      <ul>
        <li><a href="/">Home</a></li>
```

```
        <li><a href="/tutorials">Tutorials</a></li>
        <li><a href="/articles">Articles</a></li>
        <li><a href="/about">About</a></li>
      </ul>
    </nav>
  </header>

  <main class="tutorial-content">
    <article class="tutorial">
      <header>
        <h1>Advanced JavaScript Techniques</h1>
        <p class="tutorial-meta">
          Duration: 45 minutes | Difficulty: Advanced |
          Updated: <time datetime="2024-03-18">March 18,
2024</time>
        </p>
      </header>

      <section class="tutorial-overview">
        <h2>What You'll Learn</h2>
        <ul>
          <li>Advanced closure patterns</li>
          <li>Prototype chain manipulation</li>
          <li>Asynchronous programming patterns</li>
          <li>Memory management optimization</li>
        </ul>
      </section>

      <section class="tutorial-content">
        <h2>Closure Patterns</h2>
```

```
        <p>Closures provide powerful mechanisms for data encapsulation and functional programming patterns...</p>

        <pre><code>
function createCounter() {
  let count = 0;
  return {
    increment: () => ++count,
    decrement: () => --count,
    getValue: () => count
  };
}

const counter = createCounter();
console.log(counter.increment()); // 1
console.log(counter.getValue());  // 1
        </code></pre>
      </section>

      <section class="practice-exercises">
        <h2>Practice Exercises</h2>
        <div class="exercise">
          <h3>Exercise 1: Module Pattern</h3>
          <p>Create a module that manages a shopping cart with private state...</p>
        </div>
      </section>
    </article>
  </main>

  <aside class="sidebar">
```

```
    <section class="related-tutorials">
      <h2>Related Tutorials</h2>
      <ul>
        <li><a href="/tutorials/javascript-
basics">JavaScript Basics</a></li>
        <li><a href="/tutorials/dom-manipulation">DOM
Manipulation</a></li>
        <li><a href="/tutorials/async-javascript">Async
JavaScript</a></li>
      </ul>
    </section>

    <section class="tutorial-resources">
      <h2>Additional Resources</h2>
      <ul>
        <li><a href="/downloads/code-
examples.zip">Download Code Examples</a></li>
        <li><a href="/reference/javascript-
api">JavaScript API Reference</a></li>
      </ul>
    </section>
  </aside>

  <footer class="site-footer">
    <p>&copy; 2024 DevTutorials. All rights reserved.</p>
  </footer>
</body>
</html>
```

Accessibility Benefits of Main

The `<main>` element provides a crucial landmark for screen reader users, allowing them to skip directly to the primary content without navigating through repetitive site elements. This functionality significantly improves the browsing experience for users with visual impairments.

Most screen readers provide keyboard shortcuts to jump directly to main content. By properly implementing the `<main>` element, developers ensure these navigation aids function correctly.

Understanding the `<aside>` Element

The `<aside>` element represents content that relates to the surrounding content but stands apart from it. This content could be removed without affecting the understanding or completeness of the main content. Asides provide supplementary information, context, or related resources.

Types of Aside Content

Aside content takes many forms depending on context. At the document level, asides typically contain sidebars with related links, advertisements, or supplementary information. Within articles, asides might include pull quotes, author biographies, or related statistics.

The key characteristic of aside content is its supplementary nature. Users should be able to understand and use the main content completely without reading the aside content.

Document-Level Asides

Document-level asides typically appear as sidebars containing related links, recent posts, advertising, or other supplementary site content. This content relates to the overall site or section but doesn't directly support the main content.

#html

```
<main class="blog-content">
  <article class="blog-post">
    <header>
      <h1>The Evolution of Web Development</h1>
      <p class="post-date">Published on <time datetime="2024-03-22">March 22, 2024</time></p>
    </header>

    <p>Web development has transformed dramatically over the past two decades...</p>

    <section class="historical-timeline">
      <h2>Key Milestones in Web Development</h2>
      <p>Understanding current web technologies requires examining their historical evolution...</p>
    </section>
  </article>
</main>

<aside class="site-sidebar">
  <section class="recent-posts">
    <h2>Recent Posts</h2>
    <ul>
      <li>
        <article class="sidebar-post">
          <h3><a href="/posts/css-grid-guide">Complete CSS Grid Guide</a></h3>
          <time datetime="2024-03-20">March 20, 2024</time>
        </article>
      </li>
```

```
      <li>
        <article class="sidebar-post">
          <h3><a href="/posts/javascript-
performance">JavaScript Performance Tips</a></h3>
          <time datetime="2024-03-18">March 18,
2024</time>
        </article>
      </li>
    </ul>
  </section>

  <section class="newsletter-signup">
    <h2>Stay Updated</h2>
    <p>Get weekly web development tips delivered to your
inbox.</p>
    <form class="newsletter-form">
      <input type="email" placeholder="Your email
address" required>
      <button type="submit">Subscribe</button>
    </form>
  </section>

  <section class="popular-tags">
    <h2>Popular Topics</h2>
    <ul class="tag-cloud">
      <li><a href="/tags/javascript"
class="tag">JavaScript</a></li>
      <li><a href="/tags/css" class="tag">CSS</a></li>
      <li><a href="/tags/html" class="tag">HTML</a></li>
      <li><a href="/tags/react"
class="tag">React</a></li>
    </ul>
```

```
  </section>
</aside>
```

Contextual Asides Within Content

Asides can also appear within main content to provide relevant but non-essential information. These contextual asides enhance understanding without being required for comprehension.

#html

```
<main>
  <article class="research-article">
    <header>
      <h1>Renewable Energy Adoption Trends</h1>
    </header>

    <p>Global renewable energy capacity has increased
exponentially over the past decade, driven by
technological advances and policy changes...</p>

    <aside class="statistic-callout">
      <h3>By the Numbers</h3>
      <ul>
        <li>Solar capacity increased 85% in 2023</li>
        <li>Wind power accounts for 12% of global
electricity</li>
        <li>Renewable investments reached $1.8
trillion</li>
      </ul>
    </aside>
```

```
    <p>The economic factors driving this transition
include decreasing technology costs and increasing
environmental awareness...</p>

    <section class="case-studies">
      <h2>Regional Case Studies</h2>

      <section class="europe-case">
        <h3>European Union Progress</h3>
        <p>The European Union has made significant
strides in renewable energy adoption...</p>

        <aside class="expert-quote">
          <blockquote>
            <p>"Europe's commitment to renewable energy
represents a fundamental shift in energy policy that
other regions are beginning to follow."</p>
            <cite>Dr. Anna Müller, European Energy Policy
Institute</cite>
          </blockquote>
        </aside>
      </section>
    </section>
  </article>
</main>
```

Best Practices for Main and Aside

The `<main>` element should encompass all content that directly serves the page's primary purpose. Avoid including navigation, advertising, or repeated elements that appear across multiple pages.

Use `<aside>` elements judiciously for content that genuinely supplements rather than distracts from the main content. Overuse of asides can fragment the user experience and make content harder to follow.

Consider the user journey when positioning aside content. Asides should enhance understanding or provide helpful resources without interrupting the natural flow of the main content.

Ensure that aside content remains accessible and doesn't interfere with the main content's usability. Users should be able to skip aside content entirely while still accessing all essential information.

11.5 Benefits for SEO and Accessibility

Semantic HTML elements provide substantial benefits for both search engine optimization and accessibility. These advantages stem from the elements' ability to communicate content meaning and structure to automated systems and assistive technologies.

Search Engine Optimization Benefits

Search engines rely increasingly on semantic HTML to understand content context, relevance, and structure. Properly implemented semantic elements help search algorithms identify key information, understand content relationships, and determine how different page sections contribute to the overall topic.

Content Structure Recognition

Search engines use semantic elements to identify content hierarchy and importance. The `<main>` element signals primary content that deserves the most indexing attention, while `<article>` elements identify discrete, valuable content pieces that might deserve individual ranking consideration.

Header elements (<h1> through <h6>) within semantic structures provide clear content outlines that search engines can follow. This hierarchical understanding helps algorithms identify key topics, subtopics, and supporting information.

#html

```
<!-- SEO-optimized semantic structure -->
<main>
  <article itemscope
itemtype="https://schema.org/Article">
    <header>
      <h1 itemprop="headline">Complete Guide to Organic
Gardening</h1>
      <p class="article-meta">
        Published <time datetime="2024-03-25"
itemprop="datePublished">March 25, 2024</time>
        by <span itemprop="author" itemscope
itemtype="https://schema.org/Person">
          <span itemprop="name">Sarah Green</span>
        </span>
      </p>
    </header>

    <section>
      <h2>Soil Preparation Fundamentals</h2>
      <p>Healthy soil forms the foundation of successful
organic gardening...</p>

      <section>
        <h3>Testing Soil pH</h3>
        <p>Understanding your soil's pH level is crucial
for plant health...</p>
      </section>
```

```
      <section>
        <h3>Composting Techniques</h3>
        <p>Composting transforms organic waste into
nutrient-rich soil amendments...</p>
      </section>
    </section>

    <section>
      <h2>Plant Selection Strategies</h2>
      <p>Choosing appropriate plants for your climate and
soil conditions...</p>
    </section>

    <aside class="related-info">
      <h3>Quick Reference</h3>
      <ul>
        <li>Best planting times by region</li>
        <li>Common organic fertilizers</li>
        <li>Natural pest control methods</li>
      </ul>
    </aside>
  </article>
</main>
```

Featured Snippets and Rich Results

Semantic HTML increases the likelihood of appearing in featured snippets and rich search results. Search engines can more easily extract relevant information from well-structured semantic content for display in special result formats.

Articles with clear semantic structure often qualify for article rich results, showing publication dates, author information, and other metadata directly in search results. This enhanced visibility can significantly improve click-through rates.

Content Relationship Understanding

Semantic elements help search engines understand how different content pieces relate to each other. The relationship between `<article>` and `<section>` elements, or between main content and `<aside>` supplementary information, provides context that improves content relevance assessment.

This relational understanding helps search engines determine which pages best answer specific user queries by considering not just keyword presence but content structure and meaning.

Accessibility Improvements

Semantic HTML provides crucial accessibility benefits by enabling assistive technologies to understand and navigate content effectively. These improvements benefit users with various disabilities while creating a better experience for all users.

Screen Reader Navigation

Screen readers use semantic elements to create navigation landmarks that users can access through keyboard shortcuts. The `<main>` element allows users to skip directly to primary content, while `<nav>` elements enable quick access to navigation menus.

Article and section elements create content outlines that screen reader users can navigate hierarchically. This capability allows users to understand content structure quickly and jump to relevant sections without reading everything sequentially.

#html

```
<!-- Accessibility-optimized semantic structure -->
<body>
  <a href="#main-content" class="skip-link">Skip to main
content</a>

  <header role="banner">
    <h1>TechReview Magazine</h1>
    <nav role="navigation" aria-label="Primary
navigation">
      <ul>
        <li><a href="/" aria-current="page">Home</a></li>
        <li><a href="/reviews">Reviews</a></li>


<li><a href="/news">News</a></li>
        <li><a href="/contact">Contact</a></li>
      </ul>
    </nav>
  </header>

  <main id="main-content" role="main">
    <article>
      <header>
        <h1>Latest Smartphone Camera Technology</h1>
        <p>Comprehensive review of cutting-edge mobile
photography features</p>
      </header>

      <section aria-labelledby="camera-specs">
```

```
        <h2 id="camera-specs">Technical
Specifications</h2>
        <p>Modern smartphone cameras incorporate advanced
computational photography...</p>
      </section>

      <section aria-labelledby="performance-analysis">
        <h2 id="performance-analysis">Performance
Analysis</h2>
        <p>Real-world testing reveals significant
improvements in low-light photography...</p>
      </section>
    </article>
  </main>

  <aside role="complementary" aria-label="Related
content">
    <h2>Related Reviews</h2>
    <nav aria-label="Related articles">
      <ul>
        <li><a href="/reviews/flagship-phones-2024">Best
Flagship Phones 2024</a></li>
        <li><a href="/reviews/camera-comparison">Camera
Comparison Guide</a></li>
      </ul>
    </nav>
  </aside>

  <footer role="contentinfo">
    <p>&copy; 2024 TechReview Magazine</p>
  </footer>
</body>
```

Keyboard Navigation Enhancement

Semantic elements improve keyboard navigation by creating logical tab orders and providing clear focus indicators. Users who cannot use pointing devices rely on keyboard navigation to access all interactive elements efficiently.

Proper semantic structure ensures that keyboard users can navigate through content in a logical order that matches the visual layout and content hierarchy. This predictable navigation pattern reduces cognitive load and improves usability.

Alternative Text and Context

Semantic HTML provides context that helps users understand the purpose and meaning of different content sections. This contextual information proves especially valuable for users with cognitive disabilities who benefit from clear content organization and predictable structures.

The combination of semantic elements with proper heading hierarchies creates content outlines that help all users understand complex information more effectively.

Technical Implementation Benefits

Beyond SEO and accessibility advantages, semantic HTML provides technical benefits that improve development workflows, code maintenance, and system integration capabilities.

Code Maintainability

Semantic HTML creates self-documenting code that remains understandable long after initial development. Future developers can quickly understand content structure and purpose without extensive documentation or comments.

This clarity reduces debugging time and simplifies content management system integration. Content creators can work with semantic structures more intuitively, requiring less technical knowledge to maintain content effectively.

CSS and JavaScript Integration

Semantic elements provide natural styling hooks that reduce dependence on arbitrary class names. CSS can target semantic elements directly, creating more maintainable stylesheets that adapt better to content changes.

JavaScript applications can leverage semantic structure for enhanced functionality. Event delegation becomes more predictable, and content manipulation scripts can work with meaningful element types rather than generic containers.

#css

```css
/* Semantic CSS targeting */
article header h1 {
  font-size: 2.5rem;
  margin-bottom: 1rem;
}

article section h2 {
  border-bottom: 2px solid #007acc;
  padding-bottom: 0.5rem;
}

aside nav ul {
  list-style: none;
  padding: 0;
}
```

```
main article + aside {
  margin-top: 2rem;
  border-top: 1px solid #eee;
}
```

Content Management System Benefits

Modern content management systems increasingly recognize and leverage semantic HTML structures. Proper semantic markup enables better content editing experiences, automated content organization, and improved content distribution capabilities.

Semantic structures also facilitate content syndication and API integration. Systems can extract meaningful content sections automatically, enabling content reuse across different platforms and contexts.

Performance Considerations

Semantic HTML contributes to better performance through improved caching strategies, reduced markup complexity, and enhanced content delivery optimization. These performance benefits compound over time as sites scale and traffic increases.

Reduced Markup Complexity

Semantic elements often require fewer nested containers and class attributes than non-semantic alternatives. This reduction in markup complexity leads to smaller HTML file sizes and faster rendering times.

The meaningful structure also enables more efficient CSS and JavaScript targeting, reducing the need for complex selectors that can impact rendering performance.

Enhanced Caching Strategies

Content delivery networks and caching systems can make more intelligent decisions about content caching when semantic structure clearly identifies different content types and update frequencies.

Articles, navigation elements, and supplementary content can receive different caching treatments based on their semantic roles, improving overall site performance for returning visitors.

Future-Proofing Benefits

Semantic HTML provides longevity advantages by aligning with web standards evolution and emerging technologies. As search engines and assistive technologies become more sophisticated, semantic markup ensures continued compatibility and enhanced functionality.

Emerging Technology Integration

Voice assistants, artificial intelligence systems, and other emerging technologies increasingly rely on semantic markup to understand and process web content. Proper semantic structure positions content for future technological developments.

Machine learning systems that extract and analyze web content work more effectively with semantic markup, enabling new possibilities for content discovery, analysis, and interaction.

Standards Evolution

Web standards continue evolving toward greater semantic meaning and accessibility. Early adoption of semantic HTML practices ensures compatibility with future standards and reduces technical debt accumulation.

The investment in semantic markup provides compound returns as browser capabilities expand and new semantic elements become available.

Essential Tips

- Always choose HTML elements based on meaning rather than appearance, using CSS for all visual styling to maintain proper semantic structure while achieving desired designs.
- Implement a single `<main>` element per page that contains only the primary content, excluding navigation, headers, footers, and sidebars to provide clear content boundaries for assistive technologies.
- Use `<article>` elements for content that could stand alone and be distributed independently, such as blog posts, news articles, or product descriptions that make complete sense out of context.
- Structure `<section>` elements with descriptive headings that create logical content hierarchies, helping both users and search engines understand how different content pieces relate to each other.
- Place supplementary content in `<aside>` elements only when it truly enhances but doesn't interrupt the main content flow, ensuring users can skip aside content without losing essential information.

Actionable Strategies

- Audit existing websites by converting generic `<div>` containers to appropriate semantic elements like `<header>`, `<nav>`, `<main>`, `<article>`, `<section>`, `<aside>`, and `<footer>` based on content purpose rather than visual layout.
- Create semantic HTML templates for common page types including blog posts, product pages, and landing pages, establishing consistent semantic patterns that development teams can reuse across projects.
- Test semantic structure accessibility using screen readers like NVDA or JAWS, verifying that users can navigate content efficiently through landmark jumping and heading navigation features.
- Implement structured data markup using Schema.org vocabulary within semantic HTML elements to enhance search engine understanding and enable rich snippet display in search results.

- Establish semantic HTML coding standards for development teams that specify when to use each semantic element, including examples and anti-patterns to avoid inconsistent implementation.
- Validate semantic structure using automated accessibility testing tools like axe-core or WAVE, integrating these checks into continuous integration pipelines to catch semantic errors before deployment.
- Monitor search engine performance improvements after implementing semantic HTML using Google Search Console and other SEO tools, tracking changes in featured snippet appearances, click-through rates, and content indexing efficiency.

Chapter 12: HTML Entities

HTML entities represent a fundamental aspect of web development that ensures proper display and interpretation of characters in web browsers. These special codes allow developers to include characters that would otherwise be impossible or problematic to display directly in HTML documents.

12.1 What Are HTML Entities?

Understanding the Foundation

HTML entities are special codes that represent characters in HTML documents. They begin with an ampersand (&) and end with a semicolon (;), with the entity name or number placed between these symbols. The browser interprets these codes and displays the corresponding character on the webpage.

The primary purpose of HTML entities stems from HTML's parsing mechanism. When browsers read HTML code, they interpret certain characters as markup instructions rather than content to display. For instance, the less-than symbol (<) signals the beginning of an HTML tag, making it impossible to display this character directly in content without confusing the browser's parser.

Syntax Structure

HTML entities follow two main syntax patterns:

Named Entities: These use descriptive names that relate to the character they represent. The format is `&entityname;` where entityname describes the character.

#html

```html
&lt; <!-- Less than symbol -->
&gt; <!-- Greater than symbol -->
&amp; <!-- Ampersand symbol -->
```

Numeric Entities: These use the character's Unicode code point in either decimal or hexadecimal format.

#html

```
&#60; <!-- Less than symbol in decimal -->
&#x3C; <!-- Less than symbol in hexadecimal -->
```

Historical Context and Development

HTML entities originated from SGML (Standard Generalized Markup Language), HTML's predecessor. Early web developers needed a method to include reserved characters in documents without breaking the markup structure. The entity system provided an elegant solution that maintained backward compatibility while expanding character support.

The HTML specification defines a comprehensive set of named entities, though browsers support thousands of Unicode characters through numeric entities. This dual approach ensures both human readability through named entities and complete Unicode support through numeric references.

Browser Processing

When browsers encounter HTML entities, they undergo a parsing process that converts the entity codes into their corresponding characters before rendering. This process occurs during the document parsing phase, before the browser applies CSS styling or executes JavaScript code.

#html

```
<!DOCTYPE html>
<html>
<head>
    <title>Entity Processing Example</title>
</head>
```

```html
<body>
    <p>The equation 5 &lt; 10 &amp; 10 &gt; 5 is always true.</p>
    <!-- Browser displays: The equation 5 < 10 & 10 > 5 is always true. -->
</body>
</html>
```

12.2 Common Entities: <, >, &

The Essential Three

Three HTML entities form the foundation of proper HTML coding: `<`, `>`, and `&`. These entities represent characters that have special meaning in HTML syntax and must be escaped to display properly as content.

Less Than Entity (<)

The less-than symbol (<) initiates HTML tags, making it impossible to display directly in content. The `<` entity resolves this conflict by providing a way to include the symbol without triggering tag parsing.

#html

```html
<p>To write HTML tags, use &lt;tagname&gt; syntax.</p>
<!-- Displays: To write HTML tags, use <tagname> syntax. -->


<p>Mathematical expressions: 5 &lt; 10 &lt; 15</p>
<!-- Displays: Mathematical expressions: 5 < 10 < 15 -->
```

Practical Applications:

Code documentation within HTML requires extensive use of `<` when explaining HTML syntax:

#html

```html
<div class="code-example">
    <p>Create a paragraph with &lt;p&gt;Your content here&lt;/p&gt;</p>
    <p>Add emphasis using &lt;em&gt;emphasized text&lt;/em&gt;</p>
    <p>Include links with &lt;a href="url"&gt;Link text&lt;/a&gt;</p>
</div>
```

Greater Than Entity (>)

While not always required, the `>` entity ensures consistency and prevents parsing issues in certain contexts. Modern browsers handle the greater-than symbol more gracefully than the less-than symbol, but using `>` maintains symmetry and prevents edge cases.

#html

```html
<p>Comparison operators: 10 &gt; 5 &gt; 2</p>
<!-- Displays: Comparison operators: 10 > 5 > 2 -->

<p>HTML closing tags end with &gt;</p>
<!-- Displays: HTML closing tags end with > -->
```

Advanced Usage Scenarios:

When creating educational content about HTML, proper entity usage enhances readability:

#html

```
<div class="tutorial-section">
    <h3>HTML Tag Structure</h3>
    <p>Every HTML element follows this pattern:</p>
    <p>&lt;opening-tag
attribute="value"&gt;Content&lt;/closing-tag&gt;</p>
    <p>Self-closing tags use this format:</p>
    <p>&lt;tag-name attribute="value" /&gt;</p>
</div>
```

Ampersand Entity (&)

The ampersand (&) initiates all HTML entities, creating a recursive problem when trying to display the symbol itself. The `&` entity solves this by providing a way to include ampersands in content without triggering entity parsing.

#html

```
<p>Johnson &amp; Associates LLC</p>
<!-- Displays: Johnson & Associates LLC -->

<p>Use &amp;lt; to display the less-than symbol</p>
<!-- Displays: Use &lt; to display the less-than symbol -
->
```

Complex Entity Combinations:

When explaining HTML entities themselves, multiple levels of escaping become necessary:

#html

```
<div class="entity-explanation">
```

```
    <p>To display &amp;lt; in your content, write
&amp;amp;lt; in your HTML.</p>
    <!-- Displays: To display &lt; in your content, write
&amp;lt; in your HTML. -->


    <p>The entity &amp;amp; represents the ampersand
character (&amp;).</p>
    <!-- Displays: The entity &amp; represents the
ampersand character (&). -->
</div>
```

Quotation Mark Entities

While not part of the essential three, quotation mark entities frequently accompany them in practice:

#html

```
<p>He said, &quot;HTML entities are &amp; essential &amp;
useful.&quot;</p>
<!-- Displays: He said, "HTML entities are & essential &
useful." -->


<p>The title attribute uses quotes: &lt;img
src=&quot;image.jpg&quot;
alt=&quot;Description&quot;&gt;</p>
<!-- Displays: The title attribute uses quotes: <img
src="image.jpg" alt="Description"> -->
```

12.3 Special Characters and Accents

International Character Support

HTML entities provide comprehensive support for international characters, accented letters, and special symbols that extend beyond basic ASCII characters. This support ensures proper display across different languages and regions.

Accented Latin Characters

European languages require various accented characters that HTML entities handle elegantly:

#html

```
<p>French: café, résumé, naïve, Français</p>
<p>Using entities: caf&eacute;, r&eacute;sum&eacute;, na&iuml;ve, Fran&ccedil;ais</p>

<p>Spanish: mañana, niño, señor, México</p>
<p>Using entities: ma&ntilde;ana, ni&ntilde;o, se&ntilde;or, M&eacute;xico</p>

<p>German: Müller, Größe, weiß, Bäcker</p>
<p>Using entities: M&uuml;ller, Gr&ouml;&szlig;e, wei&szlig;, B&auml;cker</p>
```

Comprehensive Accent Entity Table

Acute Accents:

#html

```
&aacute; &eacute; &iacute; &oacute; &uacute; <!-- á é í ó ú -->
&Aacute; &Eacute; &Iacute; &Oacute; &Uacute; <!-- Á É Í Ó Ú -->
```

Grave Accents:

#html

```
&agrave; &egrave; &igrave; &ograve; &ugrave; <!-- à è ì ò
ù -->
&Agrave; &Egrave; &Igrave; &Ograve; &Ugrave; <!-- À È Ì Ò
Ù -->
```

Circumflex Accents:

#html

```
&acirc; &ecirc; &icirc; &ocirc; &ucirc; <!-- â ê î ô û --
>
&Acirc; &Ecirc; &Icirc; &Ocirc; &Ucirc; <!-- Â Ê Î Ô Û --
>
```

Umlaut/Diaeresis:

#html

```
&auml; &euml; &iuml; &ouml; &uuml; <!-- ä ë ï ö ü -->
&Auml; &Euml; &Iuml; &Ouml; &Uuml; <!-- Ä Ë Ï Ö Ü -->
```

Special European Characters

Beyond accents, European languages include unique characters with dedicated entities:

#html

```
<p>Norwegian: &oslash; &Oslash; &aring; &Aring;</p> <!--
ø Ø å Å -->
<p>Danish: &aelig; &AElig;</p> <!-- æ Æ -->
<p>German: &szlig;</p> <!-- ß -->
<p>Spanish: &ntilde; &Ntilde;</p> <!-- ñ Ñ -->
<p>French: &ccedil; &Ccedil;</p> <!-- ç Ç -->
<p>Icelandic: &thorn; &THORN; &eth; &ETH;</p> <!-- þ Þ ð
Đ -->
```

Currency and Financial Symbols

Financial and currency symbols require special attention in international web development:

#html

```
<div class="currency-examples">
    <p>Euro: &euro; 100.50</p> <!-- € 100.50 -->
    <p>British Pound: &pound; 75.25</p> <!-- £ 75.25 -->
    <p>Japanese Yen: &yen; 1,500</p> <!-- ¥ 1,500 -->
    <p>US Dollar: $ 50.00</p> <!-- $ doesn't require an
entity -->
    <p>Cent: 99&cent;</p> <!-- 99¢ -->
    <p>Generic Currency: &curren;</p> <!-- ¤ -->
</div>
```

Mathematical and Scientific Symbols

Technical content often requires mathematical notation and scientific symbols:

#html

```
<div class="math-symbols">
    <p>Multiplication: 5 &times; 3 = 15</p> <!-- 5 × 3 =
15 -->
    <p>Division: 15 &divide; 3 = 5</p> <!-- 15 ÷ 3 = 5 --
>
    <p>Plus/Minus: &plusmn; 2.5</p> <!-- ± 2.5 -->
    <p>Degrees: 45&deg; angle</p> <!-- 45° angle -->
    <p>Fraction: &frac12; &frac14; &frac34;</p> <!-- ½ ¼
¾ -->
    <p>Superscript: E = mc&sup2;</p> <!-- E = mc² -->
    <p>Subscript: H&sub2;O</p> <!-- H₂O requires
different approach -->
    <p>Infinity: &infin;</p> <!-- ∞ -->
</div>
```

Punctuation and Typography

Professional typography requires attention to proper punctuation entities:

#html

```
<div class="typography-examples">
    <p>Em dash: The result&mdash;surprising to
everyone&mdash;was positive.</p>
    <p>En dash: Pages 15&ndash;30 contain the
analysis.</p>
    <p>Left single quote: &lsquo;Hello&rsquo;</p>
    <p>Left double quote: &ldquo;Professional
typography&rdquo;</p>
    <p>Ellipsis: To be continued&hellip;</p>
    <p>Non-breaking space: Mr. Smith (prevents line
break)</p>
    <p>Copyright: &copy; 2024 Company Name</p>
```

```
    <p>Trademark: Brand&trade;</p>
    <p>Registered: Company&reg;</p>
</div>
```

Practical Implementation Example

A complete multilingual webpage demonstrates proper entity usage:

#html

```
<!DOCTYPE html>
<html lang="en">
<head>
    <meta charset="UTF-8">
    <title>International Caf&eacute; Menu</title>
</head>
<body>
    <header>
        <h1>Caf&eacute; Internacional</h1>
        <p>Serving authentic cuisine since 1995
&copy;</p>
    </header>

    <main>
        <section class="menu-section">
            <h2>Beverage Menu</h2>
            <ul>
                <li>Caf&eacute; au Lait &mdash;
&euro;3.50</li>
                <li>Espa&ntilde;ol Caf&eacute; &mdash;
&euro;4.25</li>
```

```
                <li>T&eacute; Verde &mdash;
&euro;2.75</li>
                <li>Cappuccino &mdash; &euro;3.95</li>
            </ul>
        </section>

        <section class="contact-info">
            <h2>Contact Information</h2>
            <p>Address: 123 Rue de la Paix, 75001 Paris,
France</p>
            <p>Phone:
+33 1 42 96 87 65</p>
            <p>Email: info@cafe-international.fr</p>
        </section>
    </main>
</body>
</html>
```

12.4 Emoji Entities

Modern Web Communication

Emoji entities represent the evolution of web communication, allowing standardized emoji display across different platforms and devices. While modern browsers support direct emoji input, entities provide precise control and ensure consistent rendering.

Unicode Emoji Implementation

Emoji entities use Unicode code points to represent specific emoji characters:

```
#html
```

```
<p>Basic emotions: &#128512; &#128513; &#128514;
&#128515;</p>
<!-- Displays: 😀 😁 😂 😃 -->


<p>Hand gestures: &#128075; &#128076; &#128077;
&#128078;</p>
<!-- Displays: 👋 👌 👍 👎 -->


<p>Hearts: &#10084; &#128152; &#128153; &#128154;</p>
<!-- Displays: ❤ 💘 💙 💚 -->
```

Hexadecimal Emoji Notation

Hexadecimal format provides an alternative notation for emoji entities:

#html

```
<p>Weather: &#x2600; &#x2601; &#x2614; &#x26C4;</p>
<!-- Displays: ☀ ☁ ☔ ⛄ -->


<p>Transportation: &#x1F697; &#x1F699; &#x1F6B2;
&#x2708;</p>
<!-- Displays: 🚗 🚙 🚲 ✈ -->


<p>Food: &#x1F355; &#x1F354; &#x1F35F; &#x1F37F;</p>
<!-- Displays: 🍕 🍔 🍟 🍿 -->
```

Comprehensive Emoji Categories

Facial Expressions and Emotions:

#html

```
<div class="emoji-faces">
    <p>Happy: &#128512; &#128513; &#128514; &#128515;
&#128516;</p>
    <p>Sad: &#128532; &#128533; &#128534; &#128546;
&#128557;</p>
    <p>Surprised: &#128558; &#128559; &#128560; &#128561;
&#128562;</p>
    <p>Love: &#128525; &#128536; &#128537; &#128538;
&#128539;</p>
</div>
```

Hand Gestures and Body Parts:

#html

```
<div class="emoji-hands">
    <p>Pointing: &#128072; &#128073; &#128074;
&#128075;</p>
    <p>Approval: &#128076; &#128077; &#128078;
&#128079;</p>
    <p>Peace: &#9996; &#129304; &#129305; &#129306;</p>
    <p>Clapping: &#128079; &#128080; &#128591;</p>
</div>
```

Nature and Animals:

#html

```
<div class="emoji-nature">
    <p>Animals: &#128048; &#128049; &#128052;
&#128053;</p>
```

```
    <p>Plants: &#127802; &#127803; &#127804;
&#127805;</p>
    <p>Weather: &#127780; &#9729; &#9728; &#127783;</p>
    <p>Celestial: &#127773; &#127774; &#127775;
&#11088;</p>
</div>
```

Food and Beverages:

#html

```
<div class="emoji-food">
    <p>Fruits: &#127815; &#127816; &#127817;
&#127818;</p>
    <p>Meals: &#127828; &#127829; &#127830; &#127831;</p>
    <p>Drinks: &#127864; &#127865; &#127866;
&#127867;</p>
    <p>Desserts: &#127846; &#127847; &#127848;
&#127849;</p>
</div>
```

Practical Emoji Applications

Social Media Integration:

#html

```
<div class="social-post">
    <p>Just finished my morning workout! &#128170;
&#128513;</p>
    <p>Time for a healthy breakfast &#127859;
&#127864;</p>
    <p>Ready to tackle the day! &#128170; &#128293;</p>
```

```
    <div class="reactions">
        <button>&#128077; Like</button>
        <button>&#128514; Funny</button>
        <button>&#10084; Love</button>
    </div>
</div>
```

E-commerce Product Descriptions:

#html

```
<div class="product-listing">
    <h3>Premium Coffee Blend &#9749;</h3>
    <p>Start your morning right with our signature
blend!</p>
    <ul class="features">
        <li>&#127793; Organic certified</li>
        <li>&#127760; Fair trade sourced</li>
        <li>&#128293; Medium roast</li>
        <li>&#128077; Customer favorite</li>
    </ul>
    <p>Rating: &#11⭑;&#11088;&#11088;&#11088;&#11088;
(4.8/5)</p>
</div>
```

Event and Calendar Applications:

#html

```
<div class="event-calendar">
    <h3>Upcoming Events</h3>
    <div class="event">
```

```
        <p>&#127881; Company Party - Friday 8 PM</p>
        <p>&#127869; Birthday Celebration - Saturday 3
PM</p>
        <p>&#127944; Sports Tournament - Sunday 10 AM</p>
        <p>&#127891; Graduation Ceremony - Monday 6
PM</p>
    </div>
</div>
```

Cross-Platform Considerations

Different operating systems and browsers may render emoji differently. Using entities ensures consistent code, though visual appearance might vary:

#html

```
<div class="emoji-compatibility">
    <p>Standard approach: &#128512; &#128077;
&#10084;</p>
    <p class="fallback-text">
        Alternative text: [smile] [thumbs up] [heart]
    </p>
</div>


<style>
.emoji-compatibility {
    font-family: 'Apple Color Emoji', 'Segoe UI Emoji',
'Noto Color Emoji', sans-serif;
}
</style>
```

12.5 When and Why to Use Entities

Strategic Entity Implementation

Understanding when to use HTML entities versus direct character input requires consideration of multiple factors including browser compatibility, character encoding, content management, and maintenance requirements.

Mandatory Entity Usage Scenarios

Reserved HTML Characters: Certain characters must always use entities to prevent HTML parsing conflicts:

#html

```
<!-- Incorrect - Breaks HTML structure -->
<p>Use <div> tags for layout</p>

<!-- Correct - Uses entities -->
<p>Use &lt;div&gt; tags for layout</p>

<!-- Incorrect - Confuses entity parsing -->
<p>Johnson & Sons Company</p>

<!-- Correct - Escapes ampersand -->
<p>Johnson &amp; Sons Company</p>
```

Code Documentation and Tutorials: When explaining HTML, CSS, or JavaScript syntax within HTML documents:

#html

```
<div class="code-tutorial">
    <h3>HTML Form Structure</h3>
    <p>Basic form syntax:</p>
```

```
    <pre>
&lt;form action="submit.php" method="post"&gt;
    &lt;input type="text" name="username" required&gt;
    &lt;input type="password" name="password"
required&gt;
    &lt;button type="submit"&gt;Submit&lt;/button&gt;
&lt;/form&gt;
    </pre>
</div>
```

Character Encoding Considerations

UTF-8 vs Entity Trade-offs: Modern web development typically uses UTF-8 encoding, which supports direct Unicode character input. However, entities remain valuable in specific contexts:

#html

```
<!DOCTYPE html>
<html lang="en">
<head>
    <meta charset="UTF-8">
    <title>Encoding Comparison</title>
</head>
<body>
    <!-- Direct UTF-8 characters (modern approach) -->
    <p>Café résumé naïve</p>

    <!-- Entity approach (legacy compatibility) -->
    <p>Caf&eacute; r&eacute;sum&eacute; na&iuml;ve</p>

    <!-- Mixed approach for specific needs -->
```

```
    <p>Contact us: info@café-résumé.com</p>
    <p>HTML code: &lt;p&gt;Contact us: info@café-résumé.com&lt;/p&gt;</p>
</body>
</html>
```

Content Management System Integration

Database Storage Considerations: Different content management systems handle character encoding differently:

#html

```
<!-- CMS-safe entity approach -->
<article class="blog-post">
    <h1>Caf&eacute; Culture in Par&iacute;s</h1>
    <p>The tradition of caf&eacute; culture in Par&iacute;s dates back centuries&hellip;</p>
    <p>Prices typically range from &euro;2.50 to &euro;5.00 per cup.</p>
    <blockquote>
        &ldquo;Coffee is a language itself.&rdquo; &mdash; Jackie Chan
    </blockquote>
</article>
```

Email Template Development

Email clients have inconsistent character support, making entities essential for reliable rendering:

#html

```
<!DOCTYPE html PUBLIC "-//W3C//DTD XHTML 1.0
Transitional//EN"
    "http://www.w3.org/TR/xhtml1/DTD/xhtml1-
transitional.dtd">
<html xmlns="http://www.w3.org/1999/xhtml">
<head>
    <meta http-equiv="Content-Type" content="text/html;
charset=utf-8" />
    <title>Newsletter</title>
</head>
<body>
    <div class="email-content">
        <h1>Weekly Newsletter &#128231;</h1>
        <p>This week&rsquo;s highlights:</p>
        <ul>
            <li>New products &amp; services
&#127775;</li>
            <li>Customer testimonials &#128077;</li>
            <li>Upcoming events &#128197;</li>
        </ul>
        <p>Best regards,<br>
        The Team &#64; Company&trade;</p>
    </div>
</body>
</html>
```

SEO and Accessibility Implications

Search Engine Optimization: Search engines handle entities correctly, but direct characters often provide better readability in meta descriptions:

#html

```html
<head>
    <meta charset="UTF-8">
    <title>Café Résumé Services | Professional CV
Writing</title>
    <meta name="description" content="Professional résumé
writing services in París. Expert CV creation for café
industry professionals.">
    <!-- Entities in title could work but UTF-8 is
preferred -->
    <meta name="keywords" content="résumé, café, París,
professional, CV">
</head>
```

Screen Reader Compatibility: Screen readers handle both entities and direct characters, but consistency improves user experience:

#html

```html
<div class="accessibility-example">
    <p>Price: &euro;25.50 (twenty-five euros and fifty
cents)</p>
    <p>Temperature: 23&deg;C (twenty-three degrees
Celsius)</p>
    <p>Rating: &#11088;&#11088;&#11088;&#11088;&#9734;
(four out of five stars)</p>
</div>
```

Performance Considerations

File Size Impact: Entities increase HTML file size compared to direct UTF-8 characters:

#html

```html
<!-- Direct characters: 20 bytes -->
<p>Café résumé</p>

<!-- Entities: 28 bytes -->
<p>Caf&eacute; r&eacute;sum&eacute;</p>

<!-- Consider the trade-off for your specific use case --
>
```

Parsing Performance: Browsers parse entities slightly slower than direct characters, though the difference is negligible in most applications.

Legacy System Compatibility

Older Browser Support: Legacy browsers may not support full UTF-8 character sets, making entities necessary:

#html

```html
<!-- Legacy-compatible approach -->
<div class="legacy-support">
    <p>Espa&ntilde;ol: &iexcl;Hola! &iquest;C&oacute;mo
est&aacute;s?</p>
    <p>Fran&ccedil;ais: Caf&eacute; au lait co&ucirc;te
&euro;3.50</p>
    <p>Deutsch: M&uuml;nchen ist sch&ouml;n im
Fr&uuml;hling</p>
</div>
```

Decision Framework

When to Use Entities:

- HTML reserved characters (&, <, >, ")
- Code documentation and tutorials
- Email template development
- Legacy system compatibility requirements
- When encoding cannot be guaranteed
- Mathematical and scientific notation
- Copyright and trademark symbols

When to Use Direct Characters:

- Modern web applications with UTF-8 encoding
- Content management systems with proper encoding
- SEO-focused content
- User-generated content
- Performance-critical applications
- Mobile-first development

Hybrid Approach Example:

#html

```html
<!DOCTYPE html>
<html lang="en">
<head>
    <meta charset="UTF-8">
    <title>Modern Web Application</title>
</head>
<body>
    <!-- Direct characters for content -->
    <h1>Café International Menu</h1>
    <p>Specializing in authentic European cuisine since 1995</p>

    <!-- Entities for technical content -->
    <div class="code-example">
```

```
        <p>To create a heading, use: &lt;h1&gt;Your title&lt;/h1&gt;</p>
    </div>

    <!-- Entities for symbols -->
    <footer>
        <p>&copy; 2024 Café International. All rights reserved.</p>
        <p>Contact: info@cafe-international.com</p>
    </footer>
</body>
</html>
```

Essential Tips

- Always test entity rendering across different browsers and devices to ensure consistent display, especially when targeting international audiences or older browser versions.
- Use UTF-8 encoding in modern web development and reserve entities primarily for HTML reserved characters, mathematical symbols, and legacy system compatibility rather than standard accented characters.
- Maintain consistency in entity usage throughout your project by establishing coding standards that specify when to use entities versus direct characters based on your application's requirements.
- Implement proper fallback strategies for emoji entities since different operating systems and browsers may render them differently, potentially affecting user experience across platforms.
- Consider file size implications when using extensive entity sets, as they increase HTML document size compared to direct UTF-8 characters, which may impact page loading performance.

Actionable Strategies

- Create a comprehensive entity reference sheet for your development team that includes commonly used entities in your project domain, complete with both named and numeric formats for quick reference during coding.
- Establish automated testing procedures that verify entity rendering across your target browser matrix, ensuring that special characters display correctly in all supported environments before deployment.
- Develop content management system templates that automatically handle entity conversion for user-generated content, protecting against HTML injection while maintaining proper character display.
- Implement server-side validation that checks for unescaped HTML characters in user input and automatically converts them to appropriate entities before database storage or display.
- Configure your development environment with proper character encoding settings and editor plugins that highlight potential entity issues, reducing manual errors during the coding process.
- Design a content migration strategy for legacy systems that systematically converts between direct characters and entities based on your application's encoding capabilities and browser support requirements.
- Establish documentation standards that require entity usage examples in your project's style guide, ensuring consistent implementation across different team members and reducing confusion during code reviews.

Chapter 13: HTML Comments

HTML comments serve as invisible notes within your code, providing crucial documentation and explanations without affecting the visual presentation of your web pages. These powerful tools allow developers to communicate with themselves and their teammates, create temporary code storage, and maintain clean, organized codebases. Comments remain hidden from website visitors but become invaluable assets for anyone working with the source code.

13.1 Syntax for Comments

Understanding Comment Structure

HTML comments follow a specific syntax pattern that browsers recognize and ignore during rendering. The basic structure consists of opening and closing tags that encapsulate your comment text.

#html

```
<!-- This is a basic HTML comment -->
```

The comment begins with `<!--` and ends with `-->`. Everything between these markers becomes invisible to browsers and website visitors, though it remains visible in the source code.

Single-Line Comments

Single-line comments contain brief explanations or notes that fit on one line. These prove particularly useful for quick clarifications or temporary reminders.

#html

```
<!DOCTYPE html>
<html lang="en">
<head>
    <meta charset="UTF-8">
```

```html
    <!-- Page title for SEO optimization -->
    <title>My Website</title>
</head>
<body>
    <!-- Main navigation section -->
    <nav>
        <ul>
            <li><a href="#home">Home</a></li>
            <li><a href="#about">About</a></li>
            <!-- <li><a
href="#services">Services</a></li> -->
            <li><a href="#contact">Contact</a></li>
        </ul>
    </nav>
</body>
</html>
```

Multi-Line Comments

Multi-line comments span several lines and accommodate longer explanations, detailed instructions, or comprehensive documentation blocks.

#html

```html
<!--
    Header Section
    Contains the main navigation menu and logo
    Last updated: March 2024
    Author: John Developer

    TODO:
```

```
    - Add mobile responsive menu
    - Implement sticky header functionality
    - Update logo with new brand guidelines
-->
<header>
    <div class="logo">
        <img src="logo.png" alt="Company Logo">
    </div>
    <nav class="main-nav">
        <ul>
            <li><a href="#home">Home</a></li>
            <li><a href="#services">Services</a></li>
            <li><a href="#contact">Contact</a></li>
        </ul>
    </nav>
</header>
```

Nested Comment Considerations

HTML comments cannot contain other comments. Attempting to nest comments creates syntax errors and unexpected behavior.

#html

```
<!-- This is correct -->
<div class="container">
    <!-- Another correct comment -->
    <p>Content here</p>
</div>


<!--
```

```
This would cause problems:
<!-- Nested comment inside -->
This breaks the syntax
-->
```

Special Characters in Comments

Comments can contain most characters, including special symbols, but certain combinations require careful handling to avoid syntax conflicts.

#html

```html
<!--
Mathematical expressions: 2 + 2 = 4
Special symbols: @#$%^&*()
Arrows and comparisons: --> be careful with this
Question marks: What happens here?
-->
```

13.2 Using Comments in Code

Documentation and Code Explanation

Comments transform complex code sections into understandable documentation, helping current and future developers comprehend the purpose and functionality of specific elements.

#html

```html
<!DOCTYPE html>
<html lang="en">
<head>
    <meta charset="UTF-8">
```

```
    <meta name="viewport" content="width=device-width,
initial-scale=1.0">
    <!--
        Open Graph meta tags for social media sharing
        These tags control how the page appears when
shared on platforms
        like Facebook, Twitter, and LinkedIn
    -->
    <meta property="og:title" content="Professional Web
Development Services">
    <meta property="og:description" content="Expert web
development with modern technologies">
    <meta property="og:image"
content="https://example.com/preview-image.jpg">
    <meta property="og:url"
content="https://example.com">

    <title>Web Development Services</title>
</head>
<body>
    <!--
        Hero section with background video
        Video should be optimized for web (under 5MB)
        Fallback image provided for slower connections
    -->
    <section class="hero">
        <video autoplay muted loop poster="hero-
fallback.jpg">
            <source src="hero-video.mp4"
type="video/mp4">
            <source src="hero-video.webm"
type="video/webm">
        </video>
```

```
        <div class="hero-content">
            <h1>Professional Web Development</h1>
            <p>Creating digital experiences that drive
results</p>
            <!-- Call-to-action button with analytics
tracking -->
            <a href="#contact" class="cta-button" data-
track="hero-cta">Get Started</a>
        </div>
    </section>
</body>
</html>
```

Section Organization

Comments create clear boundaries between different sections of your HTML document, making navigation and maintenance significantly easier.

#html

```
<!DOCTYPE html>
<html lang="en">
<head>
    <!-- ========================================
         HEAD SECTION
         Contains meta information, styles, and scripts
         ======================================== -->
    <meta charset="UTF-8">
    <meta name="viewport" content="width=device-width,
initial-scale=1.0">
    <title>E-commerce Store</title>
    <link rel="stylesheet" href="styles.css">
```

```html
</head>
<body>
    <!-- ========================================
         HEADER SECTION
         Site branding and main navigation
         ======================================== -->
    <header>
        <div class="brand">
            <h1>Online Store</h1>
        </div>
        <nav>
            <ul>
                <li><a href="#products">Products</a></li>
                <li><a href="#about">About</a></li>
                <li><a href="#cart">Cart</a></li>
            </ul>
        </nav>
    </header>

    <!-- ========================================
         MAIN CONTENT AREA
         Product listings and featured items
         ======================================== -->
    <main>
        <!-- Featured products carousel -->
        <section class="featured">
            <h2>Featured Products</h2>
            <div class="product-grid">
                <!-- Individual product cards -->
                <div class="product-card">
```

```
                    <img src="product1.jpg" alt="Premium
Headphones">
                    <h3>Premium Headphones</h3>
                    <p class="price">$199.99</p>
                </div>
            </div>
        </section>
    </main>

    <!-- ========================================
         FOOTER SECTION
         Contact information and legal links
         ======================================== -->
    <footer>
        <div class="footer-content">
            <p>&copy; 2024 Online Store. All rights
reserved.</p>
        </div>
    </footer>
</body>
</html>
```

Variable and Dynamic Content Explanation

Comments help explain dynamic content areas, template variables, and server-side processing instructions.

#html

```
<!--
    User dashboard template
    Variables populated by server-side code:
```

```
    - {{username}}: Current user's display name
    - {{lastLogin}}: Last login timestamp
    - {{notificationCount}}: Unread notifications
-->
<div class="dashboard">
    <div class="welcome-section">
        <!-- Username populated from user session -->
        <h1>Welcome back, {{username}}!</h1>
        <!-- Last login info for security awareness -->
        <p class="last-login">Last login:
{{lastLogin}}</p>
    </div>

    <!-- Notification center -->
    <div class="notifications">
        <!-- Badge shows unread count, hidden if zero -->
        <h2>Notifications
            <span class="badge" style="display:
{{notificationCount > 0 ? 'inline' : 'none'}}">
                {{notificationCount}}
            </span>
        </h2>
    </div>
</div>
```

13.3 Hiding Code with Comments

Temporary Code Removal

Comments provide a non-destructive method for temporarily removing code elements during development, testing, or troubleshooting phases.

#html

```
<!DOCTYPE html>
<html lang="en">
<head>
    <meta charset="UTF-8">
    <title>Website Under Development</title>
</head>
<body>
    <header>
        <h1>My Website</h1>
        <nav>
            <ul>
                <li><a href="#home">Home</a></li>
                <li><a href="#about">About</a></li>
                <!-- Temporarily hiding services page
while under construction -->
                <!-- <li><a
href="#services">Services</a></li> -->
                <li><a href="#contact">Contact</a></li>
            </ul>
        </nav>
    </header>

    <main>
        <section id="home">
            <h2>Welcome to Our Site</h2>
            <p>This site is currently under
development.</p>
        </section>

        <!--
```

```
            Services section commented out until content
is ready
            Uncomment when service descriptions are
finalized
        -->
        <!--
        <section id="services">
            <h2>Our Services</h2>
            <div class="service-grid">
                <div class="service-item">
                    <h3>Web Design</h3>
                    <p>Custom website design services</p>
                </div>
                <div class="service-item">
                    <h3>Development</h3>
                    <p>Full-stack web development</p>
                </div>
            </div>
        </section>
        -->
    </main>
</body>
</html>
```

A/B Testing and Feature Flags

Comments facilitate A/B testing by allowing quick switching between different versions of content or layouts.

#html

```
<!-- Version A: Original hero section -->
```

```html
<section class="hero version-a">
    <h1>Transform Your Business Online</h1>
    <p>Professional web development services</p>
    <button class="cta-primary">Get Started
Today</button>
</section>

<!-- Version B: Alternative hero section for A/B testing
-->
<!--
<section class="hero version-b">
    <h1>Boost Your Online Presence</h1>
    <p>Expert digital solutions for modern businesses</p>
    <div class="cta-group">
        <button class="cta-primary">Start Free
Trial</button>
        <button class="cta-secondary">Learn More</button>
    </div>
</section>
-->

<!-- Form variations for conversion testing -->
<div class="contact-form">
    <!-- Standard form layout -->
    <form class="form-standard">
        <input type="text" placeholder="Full Name"
required>
        <input type="email" placeholder="Email Address"
required>
        <textarea placeholder="Your Message"></textarea>
        <button type="submit">Send Message</button>
    </form>
```

```
    <!-- Alternative compact form (currently disabled) --
>
    <!--
    <form class="form-compact">
        <div class="form-row">
            <input type="text" placeholder="Name"
required>
            <input type="email" placeholder="Email"
required>
        </div>
        <textarea placeholder="Message"></textarea>
        <button type="submit">Submit</button>
    </form>
    -->
</div>
```

Development Phase Management

Comments help manage different development phases, allowing developers to prepare future features while maintaining current functionality.

#html

```
<!DOCTYPE html>
<html lang="en">
<head>
    <meta charset="UTF-8">
    <title>E-commerce Platform</title>
    <!-- Phase 1 styles (currently active) -->
    <link rel="stylesheet" href="css/phase1.css">
```

```
    <!-- Phase 2 styles (for future release) -->
    <!-- <link rel="stylesheet" href="css/phase2.css"> --
>

    <!-- Phase 3 styles (advanced features) -->
    <!-- <link rel="stylesheet" href="css/phase3.css"> --
>
</head>
<body>
    <!-- Current navigation (Phase 1) -->
    <nav class="main-nav">
        <ul>
            <li><a href="#products">Products</a></li>
            <li><a href="#cart">Cart</a></li>
            <li><a href="#account">Account</a></li>
        </ul>
    </nav>

    <!-- Enhanced navigation for Phase 2 -->
    <!--
    <nav class="main-nav enhanced">
        <ul>
            <li><a href="#products">Products</a></li>
            <li><a href="#categories">Categories</a></li>
            <li><a href="#wishlist">Wishlist</a></li>
            <li><a href="#cart">Cart</a></li>
            <li><a href="#account">Account</a></li>
            <li><a href="#support">Support</a></li>
        </ul>
    </nav>
    -->
```

```
    <main>
        <section class="product-listing">
            <h2>Featured Products</h2>

            <!-- Basic product grid (Phase 1) -->
            <div class="product-grid">
                <div class="product-item">
                    <img src="product1.jpg" alt="Product
1">
                    <h3>Premium Headphones</h3>
                    <p class="price">$199.99</p>
                    <button class="add-to-cart">Add to
Cart</button>
                </div>
            </div>

            <!-- Advanced product grid with filters
(Phase 2) -->
            <!--
            <div class="product-grid-advanced">
                <aside class="filter-sidebar">
                    <h3>Filters</h3>
                    <div class="filter-group">
                        <label>Price Range</label>
                        <input type="range" min="0"
max="1000">
                    </div>
                    <div class="filter-group">
                        <label>Brand</label>
                        <select>
                            <option>All Brands</option>
```

```
                            <option>Brand A</option>
                            <option>Brand B</option>
                        </select>
                    </div>
                </aside>
                <div class="product-grid">
                    <!-- Enhanced product items with
ratings and reviews -->
                </div>
            </div>
            -->
        </section>
    </main>
</body>
</html>
```

13.4 Commenting for Collaboration

Team Communication Through Comments

Comments serve as a communication medium between team members, conveying important information about code decisions, requirements, and implementation details.

#html

```
<!DOCTYPE html>
<html lang="en">
<head>
    <!--
        Project: Corporate Website Redesign
        Started: January 2024
```

```
        Team Lead: Sarah Johnson
        Designers: Mike Chen, Lisa Rodriguez
        Developers: John Smith, Emma Wilson

        Browser Support Requirements:
        - Chrome 90+
        - Firefox 88+
        - Safari 14+
        - Edge 90+
    -->
    <meta charset="UTF-8">
    <meta name="viewport" content="width=device-width,
initial-scale=1.0">
    <title>Corporate Solutions Inc.</title>
</head>
<body>
    <!--
        DEVELOPER NOTE (John - March 15, 2024):
        Header structure modified per client feedback
        - Logo size increased by 20%
        - Navigation moved to right alignment
        - Added accessibility improvements per WCAG 2.1
AA standards

        DESIGNER NOTE (Mike - March 16, 2024):
        Colors updated to match new brand guidelines
        - Primary: #2C3E50
        - Secondary: #3498DB
        - Accent: #E74C3C
    -->
    <header class="site-header">
```

```
        <div class="container">
            <!-- Logo container - increased size per
client request -->
            <div class="logo-container">
                <img src="assets/logo-corporate.svg"
alt="Corporate Solutions Inc." width="180" height="60">
            </div>

            <!--
                Navigation Menu
                ACCESSIBILITY NOTE (Emma - March 17,
2024):
                Added ARIA labels and keyboard navigation
support
                Tested with screen readers: NVDA, JAWS
            -->
            <nav class="main-navigation"
role="navigation" aria-label="Main menu">
                <ul class="nav-list">
                    <li><a href="#home" aria-
current="page">Home</a></li>
                    <li><a
href="#services">Services</a></li>
                    <li><a href="#about">About
Us</a></li>
                    <li><a
href="#contact">Contact</a></li>
                </ul>
            </nav>
        </div>
    </header>

    <!--
```

```
        CRITICAL SECTION - DO NOT MODIFY WITHOUT APPROVAL
        Client specifically requested this hero layout
        Any changes must be approved by Sarah Johnson
(Team Lead)

        Performance Notes:
        - Hero image optimized to 85KB (was 340KB)
        - Lazy loading implemented for below-fold content
        - Critical CSS inlined for faster rendering
    -->
    <section class="hero-section">
        <div class="hero-content">
            <h1 class="hero-title">Innovative Business
Solutions</h1>
            <p class="hero-subtitle">Transforming
enterprises through technology</p>

            <!--
                CTA Button Analytics Tracking
                Google Analytics Event: hero_cta_click
                Hotjar Heatmap: Track clicks and user
interaction
                A/B Test: Button color variations
(running until March 30)
            -->
            <a href="#contact" class="cta-button" data-
ga-event="hero_cta_click" data-hotjar-track="cta-
primary">
                Get Started Today
            </a>
        </div>
    </section>
```

```
</body>
</html>
```

Code Review and Feedback Integration

Comments facilitate code review processes by providing context for reviewers and capturing feedback directly within the codebase.

#html

```
<!--
    CODE REVIEW FEEDBACK - March 20, 2024
    Reviewer: Senior Developer Alex Thompson

    Overall Assessment: Good structure, needs minor
optimizations

    Issues to Address:
    1. Add semantic HTML5 elements for better SEO
    2. Implement proper heading hierarchy
    3. Add loading attributes for images
    4. Consider implementing lazy loading for performance

    Approved with minor changes requested
-->

<!DOCTYPE html>
<html lang="en">
<head>
    <meta charset="UTF-8">
    <meta name="viewport" content="width=device-width,
initial-scale=1.0">
```

```
    <!--
        FEEDBACK IMPLEMENTED (John - March 21, 2024):
        Added proper meta description and keywords
        Improved social media meta tags
    -->
    <meta name="description" content="Professional
consulting services for business growth and digital
transformation">
    <meta name="keywords" content="business consulting,
digital transformation, strategic planning">
    <title>Business Consulting Services | Professional
Growth Solutions</title>
</head>
<body>
    <!--
        SEMANTIC HTML IMPROVEMENT (Response to Review
Point #1)
        Changed from generic divs to semantic HTML5
elements
        Benefits: Better SEO, improved accessibility,
cleaner structure
    -->
    <header role="banner">
        <nav role="navigation" aria-label="Primary
navigation">
            <ul>
                <li><a href="#home">Home</a></li>
                <li><a href="#services">Services</a></li>
                <li><a href="#about">About</a></li>
            </ul>
        </nav>
    </header>
```

```
    <main role="main">
        <!--
            HEADING HIERARCHY FIX (Response to Review
Point #2)
            Implemented proper H1 -> H2 -> H3 structure
            No heading levels skipped
        -->
        <section class="services-overview">
            <h1>Professional Consulting Services</h1>

            <article class="service-category">
                <h2>Strategic Planning</h2>
                <div class="service-details">
                    <h3>Market Analysis</h3>
                    <p>Comprehensive market research and
competitive analysis</p>

                    <h3>Growth Strategy</h3>
                    <p>Tailored strategies for business
expansion</p>
                </div>
            </article>

            <article class="service-category">
                <h2>Digital Transformation</h2>
                <div class="service-details">
                    <h3>Technology Assessment</h3>
                    <p>Evaluation of current systems and
infrastructure</p>

                    <!--
```

```
                        IMAGE OPTIMIZATION (Response to
Review Points #3 & #4)
                        Added loading="lazy" for
performance
                        Included width/height attributes
to prevent layout shift
                        Used modern image formats with
fallbacks
                    -->
                    <picture>
                        <source srcset="images/tech-
assessment.webp" type="image/webp">
                        <img src="images/tech-
assessment.jpg"
                             alt="Technology assessment
dashboard"
                             width="400"
                             height="300"
                             loading="lazy">
                    </picture>
                </div>
            </article>
        </section>
    </main>

    <!--
        PERFORMANCE MONITORING SECTION
        Added after code review for ongoing optimization
tracking

        TODO for next sprint:
        - Implement Google PageSpeed insights tracking
        - Add Core Web Vitals monitoring
```

```
        - Set up automated performance budgets
    -->
    <footer role="contentinfo">
        <div class="footer-content">
            <p>&copy; 2024 Business Consulting Services.
All rights reserved.</p>
        </div>
    </footer>
</body>
</html>
```

Documentation Standards and Guidelines

Comments establish and maintain documentation standards across team projects, ensuring consistency and quality throughout the development process.

#html

```
<!--

==========================================================================================
    PROJECT DOCUMENTATION STANDARDS

==========================================================================================

    File: index.html
    Project: E-learning Platform
    Version: 2.1.0
    Last Updated: March 2024
```

```
    COMMENTING CONVENTIONS:
    - Use section dividers (===) for major sections
    - Include author and date for significant changes
    - Document all external dependencies and integrations
    - Explain complex logic and business requirements
    - Include accessibility and SEO considerations

    NAMING CONVENTIONS:
    - CSS Classes: kebab-case (course-listing, user-
profile)
    - IDs: camelCase (courseDetails, userDashboard)
    - Images: descriptive names with dimensions (course-
thumbnail-300x200.jpg)

    BROWSER TESTING CHECKLIST:
    ☑ Chrome (latest 2 versions)
    ☑ Firefox (latest 2 versions)
    ☑ Safari (latest 2 versions)
    ☑ Edge (latest 2 versions)
    ☑ Mobile Chrome (Android)
    ☑ Mobile Safari (iOS)


=========================================================
====================
-->

<!DOCTYPE html>
<html lang="en">
<head>
    <!--
```

```
=========================================================================================
        DOCUMENT HEAD SECTION

=========================================================================================
        Contains meta information, stylesheets, and
scripts
        All external resources loaded from CDN for
performance
    -->
    <meta charset="UTF-8">
    <meta name="viewport" content="width=device-width,
initial-scale=1.0">

    <!--
        SEO Meta Tags
        Author: Marketing Team
        Updated: March 10, 2024
        Keywords researched using SEMrush and Google
Keyword Planner
    -->
    <meta name="description" content="Professional online
learning platform with courses in technology, business,
and creative skills">
    <meta name="keywords" content="online learning,
courses, education, professional development, skills
training">
    <meta name="author" content="EduTech Solutions">

    <!--
        Social Media Meta Tags (Open Graph)
```

```
        Used for social sharing on Facebook, LinkedIn,
Twitter
        Images sized according to platform requirements
    -->
    <meta property="og:title" content="EduTech Learning
Platform">
    <meta property="og:description" content="Master new
skills with our comprehensive online courses">
    <meta property="og:image"
content="https://cdn.edutech.com/social-preview-
1200x630.jpg">
    <meta property="og:url"
content="https://www.edutech.com">
    <meta property="og:type" content="website">

    <title>EduTech - Professional Online Learning
Platform</title>

    <!--
        External Stylesheets
        Loading order: Reset -> Base -> Components ->
Pages
        All stylesheets compressed and minified for
production
    -->
    <link rel="stylesheet"
href="https://cdn.edutech.com/css/reset.min.css">
    <link rel="stylesheet"
href="https://cdn.edutech.com/css/base.min.css">
    <link rel="stylesheet"
href="https://cdn.edutech.com/css/components.min.css">
    <link rel="stylesheet" href="css/homepage.css">
</head>
```

```
<body>
    <!--

=========================================================================
====================
        SITE HEADER SECTION

=========================================================================
====================
        Contains branding, navigation, and user account
access
        Sticky positioning implemented for improved UX

        Accessibility Features:
        - Skip navigation link for screen readers
        - ARIA labels for navigation elements
        - Keyboard navigation support
        - High contrast mode compatibility
    -->
    <a href="#main-content" class="skip-nav">Skip to main
content</a>

    <header class="site-header" role="banner">
        <div class="header-container">
            <!--
                Site Branding
                Logo optimized for retina displays
                Alternative text includes company name
for accessibility
            -->
            <div class="site-branding">
                <a href="/" class="logo-link" aria-
label="EduTech Learning Platform Home">
```

```
                    <img src="assets/logo-edutech.svg"
                         alt="EduTech Learning Platform"
                         width="160"
                         height="45"
                         class="site-logo">
                </a>
            </div>

            <!--
                Primary Navigation
                Dropdown menus implemented with ARIA for
accessibility
                Mobile-responsive hamburger menu
activated via CSS and JavaScript
            -->
            <nav class="primary-nav" role="navigation"
aria-label="Main navigation">
                <ul class="nav-menu">
                    <li class="nav-item">
                        <a href="#courses" class="nav-
link">Courses</a>
                        <!-- Mega menu for course
categories (hidden by default) -->
                        <div class="mega-menu" aria-
hidden="true">
                            <div class="menu-section">
                                <h3>Technology</h3>
                                <ul>
                                    <li><a
href="/courses/web-development">Web Development</a></li>
                        <li><a href="/courses/data-
science">Data Science</a></li>
```

```
                        <li><a href="/courses/digital-
marketing">Digital Marketing</a></li>
                        <li><a
href="/courses/business">Business Skills</a></li>
                    </ul>
                </div>

                <div class="link-group">
                    <h4 class="group-title">Company</h4>
                    <ul>
                        <li><a href="/about">About
Us</a></li>
                        <li><a
href="/careers">Careers</a></li>
                        <li><a
href="/contact">Contact</a></li>
                        <li><a
href="/press">Press</a></li>
                    </ul>
                </div>
            </div>

            <!--
                Copyright and Legal Information
                Updated annually or when legal
requirements change
                Links to privacy policy and terms of
service required by law
            -->
            <div class="footer-bottom">
                <p class="copyright">
                    &copy; 2024 EduTech Learning
Platform. All rights reserved.
```

```
                </p>
                <div class="legal-links">
                    <a href="/privacy-policy">Privacy
Policy</a>
                    <a href="/terms-of-service">Terms of
Service</a>
                    <a href="/cookie-policy">Cookie
Policy</a>
                </div>
            </div>
        </div>
    </footer>

    <!--

==========================================================
====================
        JAVASCRIPT AND ANALYTICS

==========================================================
====================
        External scripts loaded at end of body for
performance
        Analytics and tracking code for user behavior
analysis
    -->


    <!--
        Core JavaScript Functionality
        Minified for production, source maps available
for debugging
        Includes: Navigation, forms, lazy loading,
accessibility features
    -->
```

```
    <script src="https://cdn.edutech.com/js/core.min.js"
defer></script>

    <!--
        Analytics Integration
        Google Analytics 4 for user behavior tracking
        GDPR compliant with user consent management
    -->
    <script>
        // Analytics code commented out for development
        // Uncomment for production deployment
        /*

(function(w,d,s,l,i){w[l]=w[l]||[];w[l].push({'gtm.start'
:
        new Date().getTime(),event:'gtm.js'});var
f=d.getElementsByTagName(s)[0],

j=d.createElement(s),dl=l!='dataLayer'?'&l='+l:'';j.async
=true;j.src=

'https://www.googletagmanager.com/gtm.js?id='+i+dl;f.pare
ntNode.insertBefore(j,f);
        })(window,document,'script','dataLayer','GTM-
XXXXXXX');
        */
    </script>
</body>
</html>
```

Chapter 13.5: HTML Best Practices

Mastering HTML goes beyond simply learning tags and attributes. Professional web development requires understanding and implementing established best practices that ensure your code is maintainable, accessible, performant, and future-proof. This comprehensive guide covers essential practices that separate amateur code from professional-grade HTML.

Semantic HTML Structure

Understanding Semantic Elements

Semantic HTML forms the foundation of modern web development. Rather than relying on generic `<div>` and `<span>` elements with custom styling, semantic elements provide meaning and context to your content. This approach benefits search engines, screen readers, and other assistive technologies while making your code more readable and maintainable.

#html

```
<!-- Poor Practice: Generic containers -->
<div class="header">
  <div class="nav">
    <div class="nav-item">Home</div>
    <div class="nav-item">About</div>
  </div>
</div>
<div class="main-content">
  <div class="article">
    <div class="article-title">Understanding HTML5</div>
    <div class="article-content">Content here...</div>
  </div>
</div>

<!-- Best Practice: Semantic elements -->
<header>
  <nav>
```

```
    <ul>
      <li><a href="#home">Home</a></li>
      <li><a href="#about">About</a></li>
    </ul>
  </nav>
</header>
<main>
  <article>
    <h1>Understanding HTML5</h1>
    <p>Content here...</p>
  </article>
</main>
```

Proper Document Outline

Creating a logical document outline using heading elements (`h1` through `h6`) provides structure that benefits both users and search engines. Each page should have exactly one `h1` element, followed by a hierarchical arrangement of subsequent headings.

#html

```
<!DOCTYPE html>
<html lang="en">
<head>
  <meta charset="UTF-8">
  <meta name="viewport" content="width=device-width,
initial-scale=1.0">
  <title>Web Development Guide</title>
</head>
<body>
  <header>
    <h1>Complete Web Development Guide</h1>
```

```html
  </header>

  <main>
    <section>
      <h2>Frontend Development</h2>
      <article>
        <h3>HTML Fundamentals</h3>
        <h4>Semantic Elements</h4>
        <p>Content about semantic elements...</p>
        <h4>Accessibility Features</h4>
        <p>Content about accessibility...</p>
      </article>
      <article>
        <h3>CSS Styling</h3>
        <h4>Layout Techniques</h4>
        <p>Content about layouts...</p>
      </article>
    </section>

    <section>
      <h2>Backend Development</h2>
      <article>
        <h3>Server Technologies</h3>
        <p>Content about servers...</p>
      </article>
    </section>
  </main>
</body>
</html>
```

Content Sectioning Elements

Understanding when and how to use sectioning elements like <section>, <article>, <aside>, and <nav> creates meaningful content divisions. Each sectioning element should typically contain a heading element to establish its purpose within the document outline.

#html

```
<main>
  <section id="introduction">
    <h2>Introduction to Web Standards</h2>
    <p>Web standards ensure consistency across different browsers and devices.</p>
  </section>

  <section id="tutorials">
    <h2>Tutorial Collection</h2>

    <article>
      <h3>HTML Basics Tutorial</h3>
      <p>Learn the fundamentals of HTML markup.</p>
      <footer>
        <p>Published: <time datetime="2024-01-15">January 15, 2024</time></p>
      </footer>
    </article>

    <article>
      <h3>CSS Layout Tutorial</h3>
      <p>Master modern CSS layout techniques.</p>
      <footer>
        <p>Published: <time datetime="2024-01-20">January 20, 2024</time></p>
```

```
      </footer>
    </article>
  </section>

  <aside>
    <h2>Related Resources</h2>
    <ul>
      <li><a href="#">HTML Specification</a></li>
      <li><a href="#">Web Accessibility
Guidelines</a></li>
    </ul>
  </aside>
</main>
```

Code Organization and Structure

Consistent Indentation and Formatting

Maintaining consistent indentation and formatting makes your HTML code readable and professional. Choose either spaces or tabs for indentation and apply the same standard throughout your project. Most developers prefer two or four spaces for HTML indentation.

#html

```
<!-- Consistent formatting example -->
<!DOCTYPE html>
<html lang="en">
  <head>
    <meta charset="UTF-8">
    <meta name="viewport" content="width=device-width,
initial-scale=1.0">
    <title>Well-Formatted HTML</title>
```

```
    <link rel="stylesheet" href="styles.css">
  </head>
  <body>
    <header class="site-header">
      <nav class="main-navigation">
        <ul class="nav-list">
          <li class="nav-item">
            <a href="#home" class="nav-link">Home</a>
          </li>
          <li class="nav-item">
            <a href="#services" class="nav-
link">Services</a>
          </li>
          <li class="nav-item">
            <a href="#contact" class="nav-
link">Contact</a>
          </li>
        </ul>
      </nav>
    </header>

    <main class="main-content">
      <section class="hero-section">
        <h1 class="hero-title">Welcome to Our
Website</h1>
        <p class="hero-description">
          Discover amazing services and solutions
tailored to your needs.
        </p>
        <button class="cta-button" type="button">Get
Started</button>
      </section>
```

```
    </main>
  </body>
</html>
```

Meaningful Class and ID Names

Choose descriptive, purpose-driven names for classes and IDs rather than presentation-focused names. This approach makes your code more maintainable and allows for flexible styling changes without requiring HTML modifications.

#html

```
<!-- Poor naming practices -->
<div class="red-box">
  <p class="big-text">Important announcement</p>
  <button class="green-button">Click here</button>
</div>

<!-- Best practice naming -->
<div class="alert-message">
  <p class="announcement-title">Important
announcement</p>
  <button class="primary-action">Click here</button>
</div>

<!-- Component-based naming -->
<article class="blog-post">
  <header class="blog-post__header">
    <h2 class="blog-post__title">Article Title</h2>
    <time class="blog-post__date" datetime="2024-01-
15">January 15, 2024</time>
  </header>
```

```
  <div class="blog-post__content">
    <p class="blog-post__excerpt">Article excerpt
content...</p>
  </div>
  <footer class="blog-post__footer">
    <ul class="blog-post__tags">
      <li class="blog-post__tag">HTML</li>
      <li class="blog-post__tag">Web Development</li>
    </ul>
  </footer>
</article>
```

Comments and Documentation

Strategic use of comments helps explain complex sections, mark important divisions, and provide context for future modifications. However, avoid over-commenting obvious elements or using comments as a substitute for clear, semantic markup.

#html

```
<!-- Site Header - Contains main navigation and branding
-->
<header class="site-header" role="banner">
  <div class="header-container">
    <!-- Logo and site branding -->
    <div class="site-branding">
      <img src="logo.svg" alt="Company Name" class="site-
logo">
    </div>


    <!-- Main navigation menu -->
```

```
    <nav class="main-navigation" role="navigation" aria-
label="Main menu">
      <ul class="nav-menu">
        <li><a href="#home">Home</a></li>
        <li><a href="#services">Services</a></li>
        <li><a href="#about">About</a></li>
        <li><a href="#contact">Contact</a></li>
      </ul>
    </nav>
  </div>
</header>

<!-- Main content area -->
<main class="main-content" role="main">
  <!-- Hero section with call-to-action -->
  <section class="hero-section">
    <h1>Transform Your Business</h1>
    <p>Professional web solutions for modern
enterprises</p>
    <a href="#contact" class="cta-button">Get Started
Today</a>
  </section>

  <!-- Services overview -->
  <section class="services-overview">
    <h2>Our Services</h2>
    <!-- Service cards will be populated dynamically -->
    <div class="services-grid" id="services-container">
      <!-- Dynamic content insertion point -->
    </div>
  </section>
```

```
</main>
```

Accessibility Best Practices

Alternative Text for Images

Providing meaningful alternative text for images ensures content accessibility for users with visual impairments. The `alt` attribute should describe the image's content or function, not simply state that it's an image.

#html

```
<!-- Informative images -->
<img src="sales-chart-2024.png"
     alt="Sales increased 35% from January to December
2024, with peak performance in November">

<!-- Decorative images -->
<img src="decorative-border.png" alt=""
role="presentation">

<!-- Functional images (like buttons) -->
<button type="submit">
  <img src="search-icon.svg" alt="Search">
</button>

<!-- Complex images with detailed descriptions -->
<figure>
  <img src="complex-diagram.png"
       alt="Website architecture diagram showing user
interaction flow">
  <figcaption>
```

```
    <p>This diagram illustrates the complete user journey from initial page load
        through authentication, content browsing, and checkout processes.</p>
  </figcaption>
</figure>

<!-- Images with surrounding context -->
<article class="news-item">
  <h3>New Product Launch Announcement</h3>
  <img src="product-photo.jpg"
        alt="The new smartphone displaying its curved screen and metallic finish">
  <p>Our latest smartphone features advanced camera technology and extended battery life.</p>
</article>
```

Form Accessibility

Creating accessible forms involves proper labeling, grouping related elements, and providing clear instructions and error messages. Every form control should have an associated label, and complex forms should use fieldsets to group related information.

#html

```
<form class="contact-form" novalidate>
  <fieldset class="personal-info">
    <legend>Personal Information</legend>

    <div class="form-group">
      <label for="first-name">First Name <span class="required">*</span></label>
```

```
      <input type="text"
             id="first-name"
             name="firstName"
             required
             aria-describedby="first-name-error"
             class="form-control">
      <div id="first-name-error" class="error-message"
role="alert"></div>
    </div>

    <div class="form-group">
      <label for="email">Email Address <span
class="required">*</span></label>
      <input type="email"
             id="email"
             name="email"
             required
             aria-describedby="email-help email-error"
             class="form-control">
      <div id="email-help" class="help-text">
        We'll never share your email with third parties
      </div>
      <div id="email-error" class="error-message"
role="alert"></div>
    </div>
  </fieldset>

  <fieldset class="contact-preferences">
    <legend>Contact Preferences</legend>

    <div class="form-group">
```

```
      <span class="form-label">Preferred contact
method:</span>
      <div class="radio-group" role="radiogroup" aria-
labelledby="contact-method-label">
        <div class="radio-option">
          <input type="radio" id="contact-email"
name="contactMethod" value="email">
          <label for="contact-email">Email</label>
        </div>
        <div class="radio-option">
          <input type="radio" id="contact-phone"
name="contactMethod" value="phone">
          <label for="contact-phone">Phone</label>
        </div>
        <div class="radio-option">
          <input type="radio" id="contact-text"
name="contactMethod" value="text">
          <label for="contact-text">Text Message</label>
        </div>
      </div>
    </div>
  </fieldset>

  <div class="form-actions">
    <button type="submit" class="primary-button">Submit
Form</button>
    <button type="reset" class="secondary-button">Reset
Form</button>
  </div>
</form>
```

ARIA Attributes and Roles

ARIA (Accessible Rich Internet Applications) attributes provide additional semantic information to assistive technologies. Use ARIA attributes judiciously to enhance accessibility without over-engineering simple interactions.

#html

```
<!-- Navigation with ARIA landmarks -->
<nav role="navigation" aria-label="Main site navigation">
  <ul class="main-menu">
    <li><a href="#home" aria-current="page">Home</a></li>
    <li class="has-submenu">
      <a href="#services" aria-expanded="false" aria-
haspopup="true">Services</a>
      <ul class="submenu" aria-hidden="true">
        <li><a href="#web-design">Web Design</a></li>
        <li><a href="#development">Development</a></li>
        <li><a href="#consulting">Consulting</a></li>
      </ul>
    </li>
  </ul>
</nav>

<!-- Interactive elements with state information -->
<div class="tab-container">
  <ul class="tab-list" role="tablist" aria-label="Content
sections">
    <li role="none">
      <button role="tab"
              aria-selected="true"
              aria-controls="panel-overview"
              id="tab-overview"
              class="tab-button active">
```

```
        Overview
      </button>
    </li>
    <li role="none">
      <button role="tab"
              aria-selected="false"
              aria-controls="panel-details"
              id="tab-details"
              class="tab-button">
        Details
      </button>
    </li>
  </ul>

  <div role="tabpanel"
       id="panel-overview"
       aria-labelledby="tab-overview"
       class="tab-panel">
    <h3>Overview Content</h3>
    <p>General information about our services...</p>
  </div>

  <div role="tabpanel"
       id="panel-details"
       aria-labelledby="tab-details"
       class="tab-panel hidden"
       aria-hidden="true">
    <h3>Detailed Information</h3>
    <p>Comprehensive details about implementation...</p>
  </div>
</div>
```

```
<!-- Status and alert messages -->
<div class="form-status">
  <div id="success-message"
       class="alert alert-success"
       role="alert"
       aria-live="polite"
       style="display: none;">
    <h4>Form submitted successfully!</h4>
    <p>Thank you for your message. We'll respond within
24 hours.</p>
  </div>

  <div id="error-message"
       class="alert alert-error"
       role="alert"
       aria-live="assertive"
       style="display: none;">
    <h4>Form submission failed</h4>
    <p>Please correct the highlighted errors and try
again.</p>
  </div>
</div>
```

Performance Optimization

Optimized Loading Strategies

Implementing efficient loading strategies improves page performance and user experience. This includes optimizing images, using appropriate loading attributes, and strategically loading resources.

#html

```
<!DOCTYPE html>
<html lang="en">
<head>
  <meta charset="UTF-8">
  <meta name="viewport" content="width=device-width,
initial-scale=1.0">
  <title>Performance-Optimized Page</title>

  <!-- Critical CSS inlined for above-the-fold content --
>
  <style>
    /* Critical styles for immediate rendering */
    body { margin: 0; font-family: system-ui, sans-serif;
}
    .hero { height: 100vh; background: #f0f0f0; }
  </style>

  <!-- Preload critical resources -->
  <link rel="preload" href="fonts/main-font.woff2"
as="font" type="font/woff2" crossorigin>
  <link rel="preload" href="hero-image.webp" as="image">

  <!-- DNS prefetch for external resources -->
  <link rel="dns-prefetch" href="//analytics.google.com">
  <link rel="dns-prefetch" href="//fonts.googleapis.com">

  <!-- Non-critical CSS loaded asynchronously -->
  <link rel="preload" href="styles.css" as="style"
onload="this.onload=null;this.rel='stylesheet'">
  <noscript><link rel="stylesheet"
href="styles.css"></noscript>
```

```
</head>
<body>
  <!-- Above-the-fold content loads immediately -->
  <header class="site-header">
    <h1>Fast-Loading Website</h1>
    <nav>
      <ul>
        <li><a href="#home">Home</a></li>
        <li><a href="#about">About</a></li>
      </ul>
    </nav>
  </header>

  <!-- Hero section with optimized image loading -->
  <section class="hero">
    <picture>
      <source media="(min-width: 800px)"
              srcset="hero-large.webp 1200w, hero-
large.jpg 1200w"
              type="image/webp">
      <source media="(min-width: 400px)"
              srcset="hero-medium.webp 800w, hero-
medium.jpg 800w"
              type="image/webp">
      <img src="hero-small.jpg"
           srcset="hero-small.webp 400w, hero-small.jpg
400w"
           alt="Beautiful landscape showcasing our
services"
           loading="eager"
           decoding="async"
           class="hero-image">
```

```
    </picture>
    <div class="hero-content">
      <h2>Welcome to Our Service</h2>
      <p>Delivering excellence through innovative
solutions</p>
    </div>
  </section>

  <!-- Below-the-fold content with lazy loading -->
  <main class="main-content">
    <section class="services">
      <h2>Our Services</h2>
      <div class="service-grid">
        <article class="service-item">
          <img src="placeholder.jpg"
               data-src="service1.webp"
               alt="Web development service illustration"
               loading="lazy"
               decoding="async"
               class="service-image">
          <h3>Web Development</h3>
          <p>Custom websites built with modern
technologies</p>
        </article>

        <article class="service-item">
          <img src="placeholder.jpg"
               data-src="service2.webp"
               alt="Mobile app development service
illustration"
               loading="lazy"
```

```
                decoding="async"
                class="service-image">
           <h3>Mobile Apps</h3>
           <p>Native and cross-platform mobile
applications</p>
         </article>
       </div>
     </section>
  </main>

  <!-- Scripts loaded at the end for optimal performance
-->
  <script src="critical.js"></script>
  <script src="analytics.js" async defer></script>
</body>
</html>
```

Image Optimization Techniques

Modern image optimization involves choosing appropriate formats, implementing responsive images, and using efficient loading strategies. WebP format provides superior compression while maintaining quality, and proper `srcset` usage ensures optimal images for different device capabilities.

#html

```
<!-- Responsive images with multiple formats -->
<picture class="product-image">
  <!-- WebP format for supporting browsers -->
  <source media="(min-width: 1200px)"
          srcset="product-xl.webp 1200w, product-
xl@2x.webp 2400w"
          type="image/webp">
```

```
  <source media="(min-width: 800px)"
          srcset="product-lg.webp 800w, product-
lg@2x.webp 1600w"
          type="image/webp">
  <source media="(min-width: 400px)"
          srcset="product-md.webp 400w, product-
md@2x.webp 800w"
          type="image/webp">

  <!-- Fallback JPEG format -->
  <source media="(min-width: 1200px)"
          srcset="product-xl.jpg 1200w, product-xl@2x.jpg
2400w">
  <source media="(min-width: 800px)"
          srcset="product-lg.jpg 800w, product-lg@2x.jpg
1600w">
  <source media="(min-width: 400px)"
          srcset="product-md.jpg 400w, product-md@2x.jpg
800w">

  <!-- Default image for older browsers -->
  <img src="product-md.jpg"
       alt="Professional camera with advanced features
and sleek design"
       loading="lazy"
       decoding="async"
       width="400"
       height="300">
</picture>

<!-- Art direction with different crops for different
screen sizes -->
```

```
<picture class="banner-image">
  <!-- Desktop: landscape orientation -->
  <source media="(min-width: 1024px)"
          srcset="banner-desktop.webp"
          type="image/webp">
  <source media="(min-width: 1024px)"
          srcset="banner-desktop.jpg">

  <!-- Tablet: square crop -->
  <source media="(min-width: 768px)"
          srcset="banner-tablet.webp"
          type="image/webp">
  <source media="(min-width: 768px)"
          srcset="banner-tablet.jpg">

  <!-- Mobile: portrait crop focusing on subject -->
  <source srcset="banner-mobile.webp" type="image/webp">
  <img src="banner-mobile.jpg"
       alt="Team collaboration in modern office
environment"
       loading="lazy"
       width="320"
       height="400">
</picture>

<!-- Lazy loading implementation for image galleries -->
<div class="image-gallery">
  <div class="gallery-item">
    <img src="data:image/svg+xml,%3Csvg
xmlns='http://www.w3.org/2000/svg' width='300'
height='200'%3E%3Crect width='100%25' height='100%25'
fill='%23f0f0f0'/%3E%3C/svg%3E"
```

```
        data-src="gallery-image-1.webp"
        data-srcset="gallery-image-1-small.webp 300w,
gallery-image-1-large.webp 600w"
        alt="Architectural detail showcasing modern
design principles"
        loading="lazy"
        class="gallery-image">
  </div>

  <div class="gallery-item">
    <img src="data:image/svg+xml,%3Csvg
xmlns='http://www.w3.org/2000/svg' width='300'
height='200'%3E%3Crect width='100%25' height='100%25'
fill='%23f0f0f0'/%3E%3C/svg%3E"
        data-src="gallery-image-2.webp"
        data-srcset="gallery-image-2-small.webp 300w,
gallery-image-2-large.webp 600w"
        alt="Interior space demonstrating innovative
lighting solutions"
        loading="lazy"
        class="gallery-image">
  </div>
</div>
```

Cross-Browser Compatibility

Feature Detection and Fallbacks

Ensuring consistent functionality across different browsers requires implementing appropriate fallbacks and feature detection. Modern development practices focus on progressive enhancement rather than graceful degradation.

#html

```
<!DOCTYPE html>
<html lang="en">
<head>
  <meta charset="UTF-8">
  <meta name="viewport" content="width=device-width,
initial-scale=1.0">
  <title>Cross-Browser Compatible Page</title>

  <!-- CSS with fallbacks for older browsers -->
  <style>
    .feature-grid {
      /* Fallback for browsers without CSS Grid */
      display: block;

      /* CSS Grid for modern browsers */
      display: grid;
      grid-template-columns: repeat(auto-fit,
minmax(300px, 1fr));
      gap: 2rem;
    }

    .feature-item {
      /* Fallback styling */
      margin-bottom: 2rem;
      padding: 1rem;
      border: 1px solid #ddd;

      /* Modern styling with CSS custom properties */
      background: var(--card-background, #ffffff);
      border-radius: var(--border-radius, 8px);
```

```
      box-shadow: var(--card-shadow, 0 2px 4px 
rgba(0,0,0,0.1));
    }

    /* Progressive enhancement for modern browsers */
    @supports (display: grid) {
      .feature-item {
        margin-bottom: 0;
      }
    }

    /* CSS custom properties with fallbacks */
    :root {
      --primary-color: #007bff;
      --text-color: #333333;
      --background-color: #ffffff;
    }

    .primary-button {
      background-color: #007bff; /* Fallback */
      background-color: var(--primary-color);
      color: white;
      border: none;
      padding: 0.75rem 1.5rem;
      border-radius: 4px;
      cursor: pointer;
    }
  </style>
</head>
<body>
  <!-- HTML with fallbacks for form inputs -->
```

```
  <form class="contact-form" method="post"
action="/submit">
    <div class="form-group">
      <label for="user-email">Email Address:</label>
      <!-- HTML5 input with fallback -->
      <input type="email"
             id="user-email"
             name="email"
             pattern="[a-z0-9._%+-]+@[a-z0-9.-]+\.[a-
z]{2,}$"
             required
             placeholder="your@email.com"
             class="form-control">
      <!-- Fallback validation message for older browsers
-->
      <noscript>
        <small>Please enter a valid email address</small>
      </noscript>
    </div>

    <div class="form-group">
      <label for="birth-date">Date of Birth:</label>
      <!-- Date input with text fallback -->
      <input type="date"
             id="birth-date"
             name="birthDate"
             class="form-control">
      <!-- Instructions for browsers without date input
support -->
      <small class="form-help">Format: YYYY-MM-DD (e.g.,
1990-12-25)</small>
    </div>
```

```
    <div class="form-group">
      <label for="phone-number">Phone Number:</label>
      <!-- Tel input with pattern validation -->
      <input type="tel"
             id="phone-number"
             name="phone"
             pattern="[0-9]{3}-[0-9]{3}-[0-9]{4}"
             placeholder="123-456-7890"
             class="form-control">
    </div>

    <button type="submit" class="primary-button">Submit
Form</button>
  </form>

  <!-- Progressive enhancement script -->
  <script>
    // Feature detection for modern APIs
    if ('customElements' in window) {
      // Enhanced functionality for modern browsers
      console.log('Custom elements supported');
    }

    if ('IntersectionObserver' in window) {
      // Implement lazy loading for modern browsers
      const images = document.querySelectorAll('img[data-
src]');
      const observer = new IntersectionObserver((entries)
=> {
        entries.forEach(entry => {
```

```
          if (entry.isIntersecting) {
            const img = entry.target;
            img.src = img.dataset.src;
            observer.unobserve(img);
          }
        });
      });

      images.forEach(img => observer.observe(img));
    } else {
      // Fallback: load all images immediately
      const images = document.querySelectorAll('img[data-
src]');
      images.forEach(img => {
        img.src = img.dataset.src;
      });
    }
  </script>
</body>
</html>
```

Vendor Prefixes and Standards Compliance

While modern browsers have largely standardized CSS properties, understanding vendor prefixes and maintaining standards compliance ensures broader compatibility and future-proofing.

#html

```
<!DOCTYPE html>
<html lang="en">
<head>
```

```
  <meta charset="UTF-8">
  <meta name="viewport" content="width=device-width,
initial-scale=1.0">
  <title>Standards-Compliant Styling</title>

  <style>
    /* Modern CSS with appropriate fallbacks */
    .animated-element {
      /* Transform with vendor prefixes for older
browsers */
      -webkit-transform: translateX(0);
      -moz-transform: translateX(0);
      -ms-transform: translateX(0);
      transform: translateX(0);

      /* Transition with vendor prefixes */
      -webkit-transition: transform 0.3s ease;
      -moz-transition: transform 0.3s ease;
      -ms-transition: transform 0.3s ease;
      transition: transform 0.3s ease;
    }

    .animated-element:hover {
      -webkit-transform: translateX(10px);
      -moz-transform: translateX(10px);
      -ms-transform: translateX(10px);
      transform: translateX(10px);
    }

    /* Flexbox with fallbacks */
    .flex-container {
```

```
  /* Fallback for older browsers */
  display: block;

  /* Old flexbox syntax */
  display: -webkit-box;
  display: -webkit-flex;
  display: -moz-box;
  display: -ms-flexbox;

  /* Modern flexbox */
  display: flex;

  /* Flex direction with prefixes */
  -webkit-box-orient: horizontal;
  -webkit-box-direction: normal;
  -webkit-flex-direction: row;
  -moz-flex-direction: row;
  -ms-flex-direction: row;
  flex-direction: row;

  /* Justify content with prefixes */
  -webkit-box-pack: justify;
  -webkit-justify-content: space-between;
  -moz-justify-content: space-between;
  -ms-justify-content: space-between;
  justify-content: space-between;
}

/* CSS Grid with fallback */
.grid-container {
  /* Fallback layout */
```

```
      display: block;

      /* CSS Grid */
      display: -ms-grid;
      display: grid;

      /* Grid template columns */
      -ms-grid-columns: 1fr 2rem 1fr 2rem 1fr;
      grid-template-columns: repeat(3, 1fr);
      grid-gap: 2rem;
      gap: 2rem;
    }

    /* Custom properties with fallbacks */
    .themed-component {
      /* Fallback colors */
      background-color: #ffffff;
      color: #333333;
      border-color: #cccccc;

      /* CSS custom properties */
      background-color: var(--component-bg, #ffffff);
      color: var(--component-text, #333333);
      border-color: var(--component-border, #cccccc);
    }
  </style>
</head>
<body>
  <!-- Semantic HTML structure -->
  <header class="site-header">
    <h1>Cross-Browser Compatible Design</h1>
```

```
  </header>

  <main class="main-content">
    <section class="flex-container">
      <div class="animated-element">Hover for
animation</div>
      <div class="animated-element">Smooth
transitions</div>
      <div class="animated-element">Works
everywhere</div>
    </section>

    <section class="grid-container">
      <article class="themed-component">Grid Item
1</article>
      <article class="themed-component">Grid Item
2</article>
      <article class="themed-component">Grid Item
3</article>
    </section>
  </main>
</body>
</html>
```

Security Best Practices

Content Security and XSS Prevention

Implementing proper security measures protects users from malicious attacks and maintains data integrity. Content Security Policy (CSP) headers and careful handling of user input form the foundation of web security.

```
#html
```

```
<!DOCTYPE html>
<html lang="en">
<head>
  <meta charset="UTF-8">
  <meta name="viewport" content="width=device-width,
initial-scale=1.0">

  <!-- Content Security Policy -->
  <meta http-equiv="Content-Security-Policy"
        content="default-src 'self';
                 script-src 'self' 'unsafe-inline'
https://cdn.jsdelivr.net;
                 style-src 'self' 'unsafe-inline'
https://fonts.googleapis.com;
                 font-src 'self'
https://fonts.gstatic.com;
                 img-src 'self' data: https:;
                 connect-src 'self'
https://api.example.com;">

  <!-- Additional security headers -->
  <meta http-equiv="X-Content-Type-Options"
content="nosniff">
  <meta http-equiv="X-Frame-Options" content="DENY">
  <meta http-equiv="X-XSS-Protection" content="1;
mode=block">
  <meta http-equiv="Referrer-Policy" content="strict-
origin-when-cross-origin">


  <title>Secure Web Application</title>
</head>
<body>
```

```
  <!-- Form with proper security measures -->
  <form class="secure-form" method="post"
action="/api/submit">
    <!-- CSRF token (typically generated server-side) -->
    <input type="hidden" name="csrf_token"
value="abc123xyz789">

    <div class="form-group">
      <label for="username">Username:</label>
      <input type="text"
             id="username"
             name="username"
             maxlength="50"
             pattern="^[a-zA-Z0-9_-]{3,20}$"
             required
             autocomplete="username"
             class="form-control">
      <small class="form-help">3-20 characters, letters,
numbers, underscore, and hyphen only</small>
    </div>

    <div class="form-group">
      <label for="password">Password:</label>
      <input type="password"
             id="password"
             name="password"
             minlength="8"
             maxlength="128"
             required
             autocomplete="new-password"
             class="form-control">
```

```
      <small class="form-help">Minimum 8 characters
required</small>
    </div>

    <div class="form-group">
      <label for="email">Email:</label>
      <input type="email"
             id="email"
             name="email"
             maxlength="254"
             required
             autocomplete="email"
             class="form-control">
    </div>

    <!-- File upload with restrictions -->
    <div class="form-group">
      <label for="profile-image">Profile Image:</label>
      <input type="file"
             id="profile-image"
             name="profileImage"
             accept="image/jpeg,image/png,image/webp"
             class="form-control">
      <small class="form-help">JPEG, PNG, or WebP images
only. Maximum 5MB.</small>
    </div>

    <button type="submit" class="primary-button">Create
Account</button>
  </form>
```

```
  <!-- User-generated content display with proper
escaping -->
  <section class="user-content">
    <h2>User Comments</h2>
    <div class="comments-container">
      <!-- Server should HTML-encode all user content -->
      <article class="comment">
        <header class="comment-header">
          <strong class="comment-author">JohnDoe</strong>
          <time class="comment-time" datetime="2024-01-
15T10:30:00Z">January 15, 2024</time>
        </header>
        <div class="comment-content">
          <!-- All user content should be properly
escaped -->
          <p>This is a sample comment with &lt;script&gt;
tags properly escaped.</p>
        </div>
      </article>
    </div>
  </section>

  <!-- External links with security attributes -->
  <section class="external-links">
    <h2>External Resources</h2>
    <ul>
      <li>
        <a href="https://example.com"
           target="_blank"
           rel="noopener noreferrer"
           class="external-link">
          Visit Example Site
```

```
        </a>
      </li>
      <li>
        <a href="https://partner-site.com"
           target="_blank"
           rel="noopener noreferrer nofollow"
           class="external-link">
          Partner Website
        </a>
      </li>
    </ul>
  </section>
</body>
</html>
```

Input Validation and Sanitization

Client-side validation provides immediate feedback to users, but server-side validation remains essential for security. HTML5 form validation attributes offer built-in protection against common input issues.

#html

```
<form class="registration-form" method="post"
action="/register" novalidate>
  <fieldset class="account-info">
    <legend>Account Information</legend>

    <!-- Username with comprehensive validation -->
    <div class="form-group">
      <label for="reg-username">Choose Username:</label>
      <input type="text"
```

```
               id="reg-username"
               name="username"
               minlength="3"
               maxlength="20"
               pattern="^[a-zA-Z0-9][a-zA-Z0-9_.-]*[a-zA-
Z0-9]$"
               required
               aria-describedby="username-help username-
error"
               class="form-control">
        <div id="username-help" class="help-text">
          3-20 characters. Start and end with
letter/number. May contain underscore, period, hyphen.
        </div>
        <div id="username-error" class="error-message"
role="alert"></div>
      </div>

      <!-- Email with custom validation pattern -->
      <div class="form-group">
        <label for="reg-email">Email Address:</label>
        <input type="email"
               id="reg-email"
               name="email"
               maxlength="254"
               pattern="[a-z0-9._%+-]+@[a-z0-9.-]+\.[a-
z]{2,}$"
               required
               aria-describedby="email-help email-error"
               class="form-control">
        <div id="email-help" class="help-text">
```

```
        Enter a valid email address (e.g.,
user@example.com)
      </div>
      <div id="email-error" class="error-message"
role="alert"></div>
    </div>

    <!-- Password with strength requirements -->
    <div class="form-group">
      <label for="reg-password">Password:</label>
      <input type="password"
             id="reg-password"
             name="password"
             minlength="8"
             maxlength="128"
             pattern="^(?=.*[a-z])(?=.*[A-
Z])(?=.*\d)(?=.*[@$!%*?&])[A-Za-z\d@$!%*?&]{8,}$"
             required
             aria-describedby="password-help password-
error"
             class="form-control">
      <div id="password-help" class="help-text">
        Minimum 8 characters with at least one uppercase,
lowercase, number, and special character
      </div>
      <div id="password-error" class="error-message"
role="alert"></div>
    </div>

    <!-- Password confirmation -->
    <div class="form-group">
```

```
        <label for="confirm-password">Confirm
Password:</label>
        <input type="password"
               id="confirm-password"
               name="confirmPassword"
               minlength="8"
               maxlength="128"
               required
               aria-describedby="confirm-error"
               class="form-control">
        <div id="confirm-error" class="error-message"
role="alert"></div>
      </div>
    </fieldset>

    <fieldset class="personal-info">
      <legend>Personal Information</legend>

      <!-- Phone number with international format -->
      <div class="form-group">
        <label for="phone">Phone Number:</label>
        <input type="tel"
               id="phone"
               name="phone"
               pattern="^\+?[1-9]\d{1,14}$"
               maxlength="20"
               placeholder="+1234567890"
               aria-describedby="phone-help"
               class="form-control">
        <div id="phone-help" class="help-text">
```

```
        International format recommended (e.g.,
+1234567890)
      </div>
    </div>

    <!-- Date of birth with range validation -->
    <div class="form-group">
      <label for="birth-date">Date of Birth:</label>
      <input type="date"
             id="birth-date"
             name="birthDate"
             min="1900-01-01"
             max="2010-12-31"
             aria-describedby="birthdate-help"
             class="form-control">
      <div id="birthdate-help" class="help-text">
        Must be between 1900 and 2010
      </div>
    </div>

    <!-- URL with validation -->
    <div class="form-group">
      <label for="website">Personal Website
(Optional):</label>
      <input type="url"
             id="website"
             name="website"
             maxlength="2048"
             pattern="https?://.+"
             placeholder="https://example.com"
             aria-describedby="website-help"
```

```
              class="form-control">
        <div id="website-help" class="help-text">
          Must start with http:// or https://
        </div>
      </div>
    </fieldset>

    <!-- Agreement checkbox with required validation -->
    <div class="form-group checkbox-group">
      <input type="checkbox"
             id="terms-agreement"
             name="agreeTerms"
             required
             aria-describedby="terms-error"
             class="checkbox-input">
      <label for="terms-agreement" class="checkbox-label">
        I agree to the <a href="/terms" target="_blank"
rel="noopener">Terms of Service</a>
        and <a href="/privacy" target="_blank"
rel="noopener">Privacy Policy</a>
      </label>
      <div id="terms-error" class="error-message"
role="alert"></div>
    </div>

    <div class="form-actions">
      <button type="submit" class="primary-button">Create
Account</button>
      <button type="reset" class="secondary-button">Clear
Form</button>
    </div>
</form>
```

```
<!-- Client-side validation enhancement script -->
<script>
(function() {
  'use strict';

  const form = document.querySelector('.registration-
form');
  const passwordInput = document.getElementById('reg-
password');
  const confirmInput = document.getElementById('confirm-
password');

  // Custom validation for password confirmation
  function validatePasswordMatch() {
    const password = passwordInput.value;
    const confirm = confirmInput.value;

    if (confirm && password !== confirm) {
      confirmInput.setCustomValidity('Passwords do not
match');
      document.getElementById('confirm-
error').textContent = 'Passwords do not match';
    } else {
      confirmInput.setCustomValidity('');
      document.getElementById('confirm-
error').textContent = '';
    }
  }

  // Real-time password confirmation validation
```

```
  confirmInput.addEventListener('input',
validatePasswordMatch);
  passwordInput.addEventListener('input',
validatePasswordMatch);

  // Form submission with comprehensive validation
  form.addEventListener('submit', function(event) {
    event.preventDefault();

    // Clear previous error messages
    const errorElements = form.querySelectorAll('.error-
message');
    errorElements.forEach(el => el.textContent = '');

    // Validate all required fields
    const isValid = form.checkValidity();

    if (isValid) {
      // Additional custom validations
      validatePasswordMatch();

      if (form.checkValidity()) {
        // Form is valid, proceed with submission
        console.log('Form is valid and ready for
submission');
        // form.submit(); // Uncomment for actual
submission
      }
    } else {
      // Display validation errors
      const invalidFields =
form.querySelectorAll(':invalid');
```

```
      invalidFields.forEach(field => {
        const errorElement =
document.getElementById(field.getAttribute('aria-
describedby').split(' ').find(id =>
id.includes('error')));
        if (errorElement) {
          errorElement.textContent =
field.validationMessage;
        }
      });
    }
  });
})();
</script>
```

Maintainability and Documentation

Code Comments and Structure

Strategic commenting and consistent code organization facilitate long-term maintenance and team collaboration. Comments should explain the "why" rather than the "what" of your code.

#html

```
<!DOCTYPE html>
<html lang="en">
<head>
  <meta charset="UTF-8">
  <meta name="viewport" content="width=device-width,
initial-scale=1.0">
  <title>Well-Documented HTML Structure</title>
```

```
  <!--
    Critical CSS loaded inline for above-the-fold content
    This reduces render-blocking and improves initial
page load performance
  -->
  <style>
    /* Base styles that prevent layout shift during font
loading */
    body {
      font-family: system-ui, -apple-system, sans-serif;
      line-height: 1.6;
      margin: 0;
      padding: 0;
    }
  </style>

  <!-- Preload critical resources identified through
performance auditing -->
  <link rel="preload" href="fonts/primary-font.woff2"
as="font" type="font/woff2" crossorigin>
  <link rel="preload" href="css/critical.css" as="style">
</head>
<body>
  <!--
    Site Header - Contains branding and primary
navigation
    Uses semantic landmarks for accessibility and SEO
  -->
  <header class="site-header" role="banner">
    <!-- Skip link for keyboard navigation accessibility
-->
```

```
    <a href="#main-content" class="skip-link">Skip to
main content</a>

    <div class="header-container">
      <!-- Company branding section -->
      <div class="site-branding">
        <a href="/" aria-label="Return to homepage">
          <img src="logo.svg" alt="Company Name"
class="site-logo" width="120" height="40">
        </a>
      </div>

      <!--
        Primary navigation menu
        Uses ARIA attributes for enhanced accessibility
        Mobile-first responsive design approach
      -->
      <nav class="primary-navigation" role="navigation"
aria-label="Main navigation">
        <!-- Mobile menu toggle (hidden by default, shown
on mobile) -->
        <button class="menu-toggle"
                aria-expanded="false"
                aria-controls="main-menu"
                aria-label="Toggle navigation menu">
          <span class="menu-icon"></span>
        </button>

        <ul class="main-menu" id="main-menu">
          <li class="menu-item">
            <a href="/" class="menu-link" aria-
current="page">Home</a>
```

```
          </li>
          <li class="menu-item menu-item--has-dropdown">
            <a href="/services"
               class="menu-link"
               aria-expanded="false"
               aria-haspopup="true">Services</a>
            <!-- Dropdown submenu for service categories
-->
            <ul class="submenu" aria-hidden="true">
              <li><a href="/services/web-design"
class="submenu-link">Web Design</a></li>
              <li><a href="/services/development"
class="submenu-link">Development</a></li>
              <li><a href="/services/consulting"
class="submenu-link">Consulting</a></li>
            </ul>
          </li>
          <li class="menu-item">
            <a href="/about" class="menu-link">About</a>
          </li>
          <li class="menu-item">
            <a href="/contact" class="menu-
link">Contact</a>
          </li>
        </ul>
      </nav>
    </div>
  </header>

  <!--
    Main content area - Contains primary page content
    ID used for skip link target and main landmark
```

```
  -->
  <main class="main-content" id="main-content"
role="main">
    <!--
      Hero section - Primary call-to-action area
      Designed for maximum visual impact and conversion
    -->
    <section class="hero-section" aria-labelledby="hero-
title">
      <div class="hero-container">
        <div class="hero-content">
          <h1 id="hero-title" class="hero-title">
            Transform Your Digital Presence
          </h1>
          <p class="hero-description">
            Professional web solutions that drive results
and exceed expectations.
            Partner with us to create exceptional digital
experiences.
          </p>
          <!-- Primary call-to-action button -->
          <div class="hero-actions">
            <a href="/contact" class="cta-button cta-
button--primary">
              Get Started Today
            </a>
            <a href="/portfolio" class="cta-button cta-
button--secondary">
              View Our Work
            </a>
          </div>
        </div>
```

```
        <!-- Hero image with optimized loading strategy -
->
        <div class="hero-media">
          <picture class="hero-image">
            <!-- Different image crops for different
screen sizes -->
            <source media="(min-width: 1024px)"
                    srcset="hero-desktop.webp 1200w,
hero-desktop@2x.webp 2400w"
                    type="image/webp">
            <source media="(min-width: 768px)"
                    srcset="hero-tablet.webp 800w, hero-
tablet@2x.webp 1600w"
                    type="image/webp">
            <img src="hero-mobile.jpg"
                 srcset="hero-mobile.webp 400w, hero-
mobile@2x.webp 800w"
                 alt="Professional team collaborating on
innovative web solutions"
                 loading="eager"
                 decoding="async"
                 width="400"
                 height="300"
                 class="hero-img">
          </picture>
        </div>
      </div>
    </section>

    <!--
      Services overview section
```

```
      Grid layout with responsive cards showcasing main
service offerings
    -->
    <section class="services-section" aria-
labelledby="services-title">
      <div class="section-container">
        <header class="section-header">
          <h2 id="services-title" class="section-
title">Our Services</h2>
          <p class="section-description">
            Comprehensive digital solutions tailored to
your business needs
          </p>
        </header>

        <!-- Services grid - Uses CSS Grid with fallback
support -->
        <div class="services-grid">
          <!-- Individual service cards -->
          <article class="service-card">
            <div class="service-icon">
              <img src="icons/web-design.svg"
                   alt=""
                   role="presentation"
                   width="48"
                   height="48">
            </div>
            <h3 class="service-title">Web Design</h3>
            <p class="service-description">
              Create stunning, user-focused designs that
convert visitors into customers.
            </p>
```

```
            <a href="/services/web-design"
class="service-link">
              Learn More <span class="visually-
hidden">about Web Design</span>
            </a>
          </article>

          <article class="service-card">
            <div class="service-icon">
              <img src="icons/development.svg"
                   alt=""
                   role="presentation"
                   width="48"
                   height="48">
            </div>
            <h3 class="service-title">Development</h3>
            <p class="service-description">
              Build robust, scalable applications using
modern technologies and best practices.
            </p>
            <a href="/services/development"
class="service-link">
              Learn More <span class="visually-
hidden">about Development</span>
            </a>
          </article>

          <article class="service-card">
            <div class="service-icon">
              <img src="icons/consulting.svg"
                   alt=""
                   role="presentation"
```

```
                    width="48"
                    height="48">
             </div>
             <h3 class="service-title">Consulting</h3>
             <p class="service-description">
               Strategic guidance to optimize your digital
presence and business processes.
             </p>
             <a href="/services/consulting"
class="service-link">
               Learn More <span class="visually-
hidden">about Consulting</span>
             </a>
           </article>
         </div>
       </div>
     </section>
   </main>

   <!--
     Site Footer - Contains secondary navigation, contact
info, and legal links
     Uses semantic structure for better accessibility and
SEO
   -->
   <footer class="site-footer" role="contentinfo">
     <div class="footer-container">
       <!-- Footer content organized in logical sections -
->
       <div class="footer-content">
         <!-- Company information section -->
```

```
        <div class="footer-section footer-section--
company">
          <h3 class="footer-title">Company Name</h3>
          <p class="footer-description">
            Creating exceptional digital experiences
since 2010.
            Your success is our mission.
          </p>
          <!-- Social media links with proper
accessibility -->
          <ul class="social-links" aria-label="Follow us
on social media">
            <li>
              <a href="https://twitter.com/company"
                 target="_blank"
                 rel="noopener noreferrer"
                 aria-label="Follow us on Twitter">
                <img src="icons/twitter.svg"
alt="Twitter" width="24" height="24">
              </a>
            </li>
            <li>
              <a
href="https://linkedin.com/company/company"
                 target="_blank"
                 rel="noopener noreferrer"
                 aria-label="Connect with us on
LinkedIn">
                <img src="icons/linkedin.svg"
alt="LinkedIn" width="24" height="24">
              </a>
            </li>
          </ul>
```

```
        </div>

        <!-- Quick Links section -->
        <div class="footer-section footer-section--
links">
          <h3 class="footer-title">Quick Links</h3>
          <ul class="footer-links">
            <li><a href="/about" class="footer-
link">About Us</a></li>
            <li><a href="/services" class="footer-
link">Services</a></li>
            <li><a href="/portfolio" class="footer-
link">Portfolio</a></li>
            <li><a href="/blog" class="footer-
link">Blog</a></li>
            <li><a href="/contact" class="footer-
link">Contact</a></li>
          </ul>
        </div>

        <!-- Contact information section -->
        <div class="footer-section footer-section--
contact">
          <h3 class="footer-title">Contact Info</h3>
          <address class="contact-info">
            <p>
              <strong>Email:</strong>
              <a href="mailto:info@company.com"
class="contact-link">info@company.com</a>
            </p>
            <p>
              <strong>Phone:</strong>
```

```
              <a href="tel:+1234567890" class="contact-
link">+1 (234) 567-8900</a>
            </p>
            <p>
              <strong>Address:</strong><br>
              123 Business Street<br>
              City, State 12345
            </p>
          </address>
        </div>
      </div>

      <!-- Footer bottom section with legal information -
->
      <div class="footer-bottom">
        <p class="copyright">
          &copy; 2024 Company Name. All rights reserved.
        </p>
        <ul class="legal-links">
          <li><a href="/privacy" class="legal-
link">Privacy Policy</a></li>
          <li><a href="/terms" class="legal-link">Terms
of Service</a></li>
          <li><a href="/accessibility" class="legal-
link">Accessibility</a></li>
        </ul>
      </div>
    </div>
  </footer>

  <!--
```

```
    JavaScript files loaded at the end for optimal
performance
    Critical scripts loaded first, followed by
enhancement scripts
  -->
  <script src="js/critical.js"></script>
  <script src="js/navigation.js" defer></script>
  <script src="js/analytics.js" async></script>
</body>
</html>
```

Version Control Integration

Organizing HTML files for effective version control requires consistent naming conventions, logical file structure, and clear commit practices. This approach facilitates team collaboration and project maintenance.

#html

```
<!--
  File: templates/base.html
  Purpose: Base template for consistent page structure
  Last Modified: 2024-01-15
  Dependencies: css/critical.css, js/base.js
-->
<!DOCTYPE html>
<html lang="en">
<head>
  <meta charset="UTF-8">
  <meta name="viewport" content="width=device-width,
initial-scale=1.0">
```

```
  <!-- Page-specific meta information (to be customized
per page) -->
  <title>{% block title %}Default Page Title{% endblock
%}</title>
  <meta name="description" content="{% block description
%}Default description{% endblock %}">

  <!-- Canonical URL for SEO -->
  <link rel="canonical" href="{% block canonical %}{%
endblock %}">

  <!-- Base stylesheets loaded for all pages -->
  <link rel="stylesheet" href="/css/base.css">
  <link rel="stylesheet" href="/css/components.css">

  <!-- Page-specific stylesheets -->
  {% block styles %}{% endblock %}
</head>
<body class="{% block body_class %}{% endblock %}">
  <!-- Consistent header across all pages -->
  <header class="site-header">
    <!-- Header content from separate include file -->
    {% include 'partials/header.html' %}
  </header>

  <!-- Main content area - customizable per page -->
  <main class="main-content">
    {% block content %}
    <section class="default-content">
      <h1>Page Content</h1>
      <p>This is the default content area.</p>
    </section>
```

```
    {% endblock %}
  </main>

  <!-- Consistent footer across all pages -->
  <footer class="site-footer">
    {% include 'partials/footer.html' %}
  </footer>

  <!-- Base JavaScript files -->
  <script src="/js/base.js"></script>

  <!-- Page-specific JavaScript -->
  {% block scripts %}{% endblock %}
</body>
</html>
```

Essential Tips

- **Master semantic HTML before styling**: Focus on creating meaningful document structure using appropriate semantic elements before adding visual styling. This foundation improves accessibility, SEO, and code maintainability while making your content more future-proof.
- **Implement progressive enhancement consistently**: Build your base functionality in HTML, enhance with CSS for presentation, and add JavaScript for interactive features. This approach ensures your content remains accessible even when stylesheets or scripts fail to load.
- **Optimize for performance from the beginning**: Consider loading performance during development rather than as an afterthought. Use appropriate image formats, implement lazy loading for below-the-fold content, and minimize render-blocking resources to create fast-loading experiences.
- **Test accessibility throughout development**: Regularly validate your HTML with screen readers, keyboard navigation, and accessibility testing

tools. Building accessible features from the start is more efficient than retrofitting accessibility later in the development process.

- **Maintain consistent coding standards**: Establish and follow consistent indentation, naming conventions, and code organization patterns. This consistency reduces cognitive load during development and makes collaboration with team members more effective.

Actionable Strategies

- **Create a comprehensive HTML style guide** that documents your team's coding standards, including indentation preferences, naming conventions, comment styles, and file organization patterns. Reference this guide during code reviews and onboarding new team members.
- **Implement automated validation workflows** using HTML validators, accessibility checkers, and linting tools in your development process. Set up continuous integration checks that prevent invalid or inaccessible code from reaching production environments.
- **Build a reusable component library** starting with common patterns like navigation menus, form elements, and content cards. Document each component's purpose, usage guidelines, and accessibility requirements to promote consistency across projects.
- **Establish performance budgets and monitoring** by setting measurable targets for page load times, file sizes, and Core Web Vitals metrics. Use automated testing tools to track performance regressions and ensure optimizations remain effective over time.
- **Conduct regular accessibility audits** using both automated tools and manual testing with screen readers and keyboard navigation. Create checklists for common accessibility issues and integrate these checks into your quality assurance processes.
- **Document browser support requirements** and create testing matrices for your target audiences. Establish fallback strategies for unsupported features and maintain updated lists of required polyfills or alternative approaches for legacy browser support.
- **Implement security-first development practices** by creating templates with proper Content Security Policy headers, input validation patterns, and secure coding guidelines. Regularly review and update these security measures to address emerging threats and vulnerabilities.

Chapter 14: File Paths and URLs

File paths and URLs form the backbone of web navigation and resource management in HTML. Understanding how to properly structure and reference files determines whether your website functions seamlessly or breaks with missing links and images. This chapter provides comprehensive coverage of path structures, linking techniques, and troubleshooting methods that every web developer must master.

14.1 Relative vs. Absolute Paths

Understanding Path Types

Web development relies on two fundamental path types: relative and absolute paths. Each serves distinct purposes and understanding their differences prevents common navigation errors that plague beginner websites.

Absolute Paths specify the complete location of a resource from the root directory or domain. These paths remain constant regardless of the current page location, making them reliable but less flexible for local development and site migrations.

Relative Paths describe resource locations in relation to the current file's position. These paths adapt based on the current directory, offering flexibility during development and making websites more portable across different environments.

Absolute Path Structure

Absolute paths in web development take several forms depending on context and requirements.

Full URL Absolute Paths include the complete web address:

```
#html
```

```
<a href="https://www.example.com/about/team.html">Our
Team</a>

<img src="https://cdn.example.com/images/logo.png"
alt="Company Logo">
```

Root-Relative Absolute Paths start from the website's root directory using a forward slash:

#html

```
<a href="/about/team.html">Our Team</a>
<img src="/images/logo.png" alt="Company Logo">
<link rel="stylesheet" href="/css/styles.css">
```

Protocol-Relative Absolute Paths adapt to the current protocol (HTTP or HTTPS):

#html

```
<script src="//cdn.example.com/js/library.js"></script>
<img src="//images.example.com/photo.jpg" alt="Sample
Photo">
```

Relative Path Navigation

Relative paths use special notation to navigate directory structures efficiently.

Same Directory References link to files in the current folder:

#html

```
<a href="contact.html">Contact Us</a>
<img src="banner.jpg" alt="Page Banner">
```

Parent Directory Navigation uses double dots to move up one level:

#html

```html
<a href="../index.html">Home</a>
<img src="../images/logo.png" alt="Logo">
<link rel="stylesheet" href="../css/main.css">
```

Subdirectory Access navigates down into child folders:

#html

```html
<a href="products/catalog.html">Product Catalog</a>
<img src="gallery/photo1.jpg" alt="Gallery Image">
```

Complex Navigation Examples combine multiple directory movements:

#html

```html
<!-- From /products/electronics/phones.html to
/about/team.html -->
<a href="../../about/team.html">About Our Team</a>

<!-- From /blog/2024/january/post.html to
/images/header.jpg -->
<img src="../../../images/header.jpg" alt="Header Image">
```

Choosing Between Path Types

Use Absolute Paths When:

- Linking to external websites

- Referencing CDN resources
- Creating consistent navigation across deep directory structures
- Building APIs or web services that require fixed endpoints

Use Relative Paths When:

- Developing locally before deployment
- Creating portable website structures
- Linking between pages in the same section
- Building websites that may change domains or subdirectories

14.2 Linking to Other Pages

Basic Hyperlink Structure

HTML hyperlinks connect web pages through the anchor element, creating the web's interconnected nature. Proper link construction ensures smooth user navigation and maintains website functionality.

Standard Link Syntax:

#html

```
<a href="destination.html">Link Text</a>
```

Internal Page Linking Examples:

#html

```
<!-- Same directory -->
<a href="about.html">About Us</a>
<a href="services.html">Our Services</a>

<!-- Subdirectory navigation -->
```

```
<a href="products/laptops.html">Laptop Collection</a>
<a href="blog/latest-news.html">Latest News</a>

<!-- Parent directory navigation -->
<a href="../contact.html">Contact Information</a>
<a href="../portfolio/web-design.html">Web Design
Portfolio</a>
```

Advanced Linking Techniques

Opening Links in New Windows or Tabs:

#html

```
<a href="external-site.html" target="_blank">Open in New
Tab</a>
<a href="document.pdf" target="_blank"
rel="noopener">View PDF</a>
```

Email and Phone Links:

#html

```
<a href="mailto:contact@example.com">Send Email</a>
<a href="tel:+1234567890">Call Us</a>
<a href="sms:+1234567890">Send SMS</a>
```

Download Links:

#html

```
<a href="files/brochure.pdf" download>Download
Brochure</a>
```

```
<a href="images/photo.jpg" download="vacation-
photo.jpg">Save Photo</a>
```

Section and Anchor Linking

Creating Internal Page Anchors:

#html

```
<h2 id="services">Our Services</h2>
<h3 id="web-design">Web Design</h3>
<h3 id="seo">Search Engine Optimization</h3>
```

Linking to Page Sections:

#html

```
<!-- Same page section links -->
<a href="#services">Jump to Services</a>
<a href="#web-design">Web Design Section</a>

<!-- Other page section links -->
<a href="about.html#team">Meet Our Team</a>
<a href="../portfolio.html#recent-work">Recent
Projects</a>
```

Smooth Scrolling Implementation:

#html

```
<style>
html {
```

```
    scroll-behavior: smooth;
}
</style>

<a href="#top">Back to Top</a>
```

Navigation Menu Construction

Horizontal Navigation Bar:

#html

```
<nav>
    <ul class="main-nav">
        <li><a href="index.html">Home</a></li>
        <li><a href="about.html">About</a></li>
        <li><a
href="services/index.html">Services</a></li>
        <li><a
href="portfolio/index.html">Portfolio</a></li>
        <li><a href="contact.html">Contact</a></li>
    </ul>
</nav>
```

Dropdown Menu Structure:

#html

```
<nav>
    <ul class="dropdown-nav">
        <li>
            <a href="services/index.html">Services</a>
```

```
            <ul class="dropdown">
                <li><a href="services/web-
design.html">Web Design</a></li>
                <li><a href="services/seo.html">SEO
Services</a></li>
                <li><a
href="services/marketing.html">Digital Marketing</a></li>
            </ul>
        </li>
    </ul>
</nav>
```

14.3 Image and Resource Locations

Image Path Management

Images require careful path management to display correctly across different pages and directory levels. Understanding image organization prevents broken visuals that damage user experience.

Basic Image Referencing:

#html

```
<!-- Same directory -->
<img src="logo.png" alt="Company Logo">

<!-- Images subdirectory -->
<img src="images/banner.jpg" alt="Website Banner">

<!-- Nested directory structure -->
<img src="assets/images/gallery/photo1.jpg" alt="Gallery
Photo">
```

```
```

Responsive Image Implementation:

#html

```html
<img src="images/hero-mobile.jpg"
     srcset="images/hero-mobile.jpg 480w,
             images/hero-tablet.jpg 768w,
             images/hero-desktop.jpg 1200w"
     sizes="(max-width: 480px) 100vw,
            (max-width: 768px) 100vw,
            1200px"
     alt="Hero Image">
```

CSS Resource Linking

External Stylesheet References:

#html

```html
<!-- Same directory -->
<link rel="stylesheet" href="styles.css">

<!-- CSS subdirectory -->
<link rel="stylesheet" href="css/main.css">

<!-- Framework references -->
<link rel="stylesheet" href="css/bootstrap.min.css">
<link rel="stylesheet" href="css/custom.css">
```

CSS Background Image Paths:

#css

```
/* From CSS file in /css/ directory */
.hero-section {
    background-image: url('../images/hero-bg.jpg');
}

.card {
    background-image: url('../assets/patterns/subtle-
pattern.png');
}

/* Absolute path reference */
.header {
    background-image: url('/images/header-bg.jpg');
}
```

JavaScript Resource Management

Script File Organization:

#html

```
<!-- Local JavaScript files -->
<script src="js/main.js"></script>
<script src="js/utils/helpers.js"></script>

<!-- External library references -->
<script src="https://code.jquery.com/jquery-
3.6.0.min.js"></script>
<script src="js/plugins/slider.js"></script>
```

Module Script Loading:

#html

```
<script type="module" src="js/app.js"></script>
<script type="module">
    import { initializeApp } from './js/modules/app.js';
    initializeApp();
</script>
```

Font Resource Integration

Web Font Implementation:

#html

```
<!-- Google Fonts -->
<link
href="https://fonts.googleapis.com/css2?family=Inter:wght
@300;400;600&display=swap" rel="stylesheet">

<!-- Local font files -->
<style>
@font-face {
    font-family: 'CustomFont';
    src: url('fonts/custom-font.woff2') format('woff2'),
         url('fonts/custom-font.woff') format('woff');
    font-weight: normal;
    font-style: normal;
}
</style>
```

Media Resource Organization

Video File References:

#html

```
<video controls>
    <source src="videos/presentation.mp4"
type="video/mp4">
    <source src="videos/presentation.webm"
type="video/webm">
    Your browser does not support the video tag.
</video>
```

Audio File Integration:

#html

```
<audio controls>
    <source src="audio/podcast.mp3" type="audio/mpeg">
    <source src="audio/podcast.ogg" type="audio/ogg">
    Your browser does not support the audio tag.
</audio>
```

14.4 Using Folder Structures

Standard Website Organization

Proper folder structure creates maintainable websites that scale efficiently. Industry-standard organization patterns help developers navigate projects and collaborate effectively.

Basic Website Structure:

```
website-root/
├── index.html
├── about.html
├── contact.html
├── css/
│   ├── main.css
│   ├── responsive.css
│   └── components/
│       ├── navigation.css
│       └── forms.css
├── js/
│   ├── main.js
│   ├── utils.js
│   └── modules/
│       ├── slider.js
│       └── form-validation.js
├── images/
│   ├── logo.png
│   ├── banner.jpg
│   └── gallery/
│       ├── photo1.jpg
│       └── photo2.jpg
├── fonts/
│   ├── custom-font.woff2
│   └── custom-font.woff
└── documents/
    ├── brochure.pdf
    └── terms.pdf
```

Advanced Project Structure:

```
project-root/
├── src/
│   ├── pages/
│   │   ├── home/
│   │   │   ├── index.html
│   │   │   └── home.css
│   │   ├── about/
│   │   │   ├── index.html
│   │   │   ├── team.html
│   │   │   └── about.css
│   │   └── services/
│   │       ├── index.html
│   │       ├── web-design.html
│   │       └── services.css
│   ├── assets/
│   │   ├── css/
│   │   │   ├── base/
│   │   │   ├── components/
│   │   │   └── layouts/
│   │   ├── js/
│   │   │   ├── components/
│   │   │   └── utilities/
│   │   ├── images/
│   │   │   ├── icons/
│   │   │   ├── backgrounds/
│   │   │   └── content/
│   │   └── fonts/
│   └── includes/
│       ├── header.html
│       ├── footer.html
│       └── navigation.html
│
```

```
└── dist/
    └── (compiled/optimized files)
```

Navigation Between Directories

Multi-Level Directory Navigation:

#html

```html
<!-- From /pages/about/team.html -->
<a href="../index.html">About Home</a>
<a href="../../index.html">Site Home</a>
<a href="../services/web-design.html">Web Design
Services</a>

<!-- Resource references from nested pages -->
<link rel="stylesheet" href="../../assets/css/main.css">
<script src="../../assets/js/main.js"></script>
<img src="../../assets/images/logo.png" alt="Logo">
```

Template-Based Navigation:

#html

```html
<!-- Consistent navigation across all pages -->
<nav class="main-navigation">
    <a href="/index.html">Home</a>
    <a href="/about/index.html">About</a>
    <a href="/services/index.html">Services</a>
    <a href="/portfolio/index.html">Portfolio</a>
    <a href="/blog/index.html">Blog</a>
    <a href="/contact.html">Contact</a>
```

```
</nav>
```

Content Organization Strategies

Section-Based Organization:

```
website/
├── home/
│   └── index.html
├── about/
│   ├── index.html
│   ├── team.html
│   ├── history.html
│   └── careers.html
├── services/
│   ├── index.html
│   ├── web-design/
│   │   ├── index.html
│   │   ├── portfolio.html
│   │   └── pricing.html
│   └── seo/
│       ├── index.html
│       └── case-studies.html
└── shared/
    ├── css/
    ├── js/
    └── images/
```

Feature-Based Organization:

```
#html
```

```html
<!-- Component-style linking -->
<link rel="stylesheet"
href="/components/header/header.css">
<link rel="stylesheet" href="/components/hero/hero.css">
<link rel="stylesheet"
href="/components/footer/footer.css">

<script src="/components/slider/slider.js"></script>
<script src="/components/modal/modal.js"></script>
```

Asset Management Best Practices

Versioned Asset References:

#html

```html
<link rel="stylesheet" href="css/main.css?v=1.2.0">
<script src="js/app.js?v=2.1.5"></script>
```

Environment-Specific Paths:

#html

```html
<!-- Development environment -->
<link rel="stylesheet" href="/dev/css/main.css">

<!-- Production environment -->
<link rel="stylesheet" href="/dist/css/main.min.css">
```

14.5 Troubleshooting Broken Links

Common Link Problems

Broken links frustrate users and damage website credibility. Understanding common causes enables quick identification and resolution of navigation issues.

Case Sensitivity Issues:

#html

```html
<!-- Incorrect - file is actually "About.html" -->
<a href="about.html">About Us</a>

<!-- Correct -->
<a href="About.html">About Us</a>
```

File Extension Problems:

#html

```html
<!-- Missing extension -->
<a href="contact">Contact</a>

<!-- Correct -->
<a href="contact.html">Contact</a>
```

Space and Special Character Issues:

#html

```html
<!-- Problematic file names -->
<a href="our services.html">Services</a> <!-- Space in filename -->
<a href="about&us.html">About</a> <!-- Special character -->
```

```html
<!-- Better file naming -->
<a href="our-services.html">Services</a>
<a href="about-us.html">About</a>
```

Debugging Techniques

Browser Developer Tools Method:

- Open browser Developer Tools (F12)
- Navigate to Console tab
- Look for 404 errors indicating missing files
- Check Network tab for failed resource requests

Manual Link Verification:

#html

```html
<!-- Test each link systematically -->
<nav>
    <a href="index.html">Home</a> <!-- ✓ Verify file exists -->
    <a href="about.html">About</a> <!-- ✓ Check spelling -->
    <a href="services/index.html">Services</a> <!-- ✓ Confirm directory -->
    <a href="contact.html">Contact</a> <!-- ✓ Test functionality -->
</nav>
```

Relative Path Verification:

#html

```html
<!-- From /blog/2024/january/post.html -->
<!-- Verify each step of navigation -->
<a href="../../../index.html">Home</a>
<!-- ../ = january → 2024 -->
<!-- ../ = 2024 → blog -->
<!-- ../ = blog → root -->
```

Link Validation Methods

HTML Link Checker Tools:

#html

```html
<!-- Add validation comments for complex links -->
<!-- Link verified: 2024-01-15 -->
<a href="../../resources/documents/manual.pdf">User
Manual</a>

<!-- External link - check periodically -->
<a href="https://partner-
site.com/integration">Integration Guide</a>
```

Automated Testing Approach:

#javascript

```javascript
// Simple link checker script
function checkLinks() {
    const links = document.querySelectorAll('a[href]');
    links.forEach(link => {
        fetch(link.href)
```

```
            .then(response => {
                if (!response.ok) {
                    console.error(`Broken link:
${link.href}`);
                }
            })
            .catch(error => {
                console.error(`Link error: ${link.href}`,
error);
            });
    });
}
```

Fixing Common Issues

Correcting Path Problems:

#html

```
<!-- Problem: Image not displaying from nested page -->
<!-- From /products/electronics/smartphones.html -->
<img src="images/phone.jpg" alt="Phone"> <!-- ✗ Wrong
path -->

<!-- Solution: Correct relative path -->
<img src="../../images/products/phone.jpg" alt="Phone">
<!-- ✅ Correct -->

<!-- Alternative: Use absolute path -->
<img src="/images/products/phone.jpg" alt="Phone"> <!--
✅ Also correct -->
```

Resolving Directory Structure Issues:

#html

```
<!-- Before restructuring -->
<a href="about.html">About</a>
<a href="services.html">Services</a>

<!-- After moving files to directories -->
<a href="about/index.html">About</a>
<a href="services/index.html">Services</a>
```

Handling Missing Files:

#html

```
<!-- Create fallback options -->
<img src="images/product.jpg"
     onerror="this.src='images/placeholder.jpg'"
     alt="Product Image">

<!-- Provide alternative links -->
<a href="contact.html">Contact Us</a>
<small>Having trouble? <a
href="mailto:help@example.com">Email us
directly</a></small>
```

Prevention Strategies

Consistent Naming Conventions:

#html

```
<!-- Use lowercase, hyphen-separated names -->
<a href="about-us.html">About Us</a>
<a href="our-services.html">Our Services</a>
<a href="contact-information.html">Contact
Information</a>
```

Documentation and Comments:

#html

```
<!-- Navigation last updated: 2024-01-15 -->
<nav>
    <!-- Main site sections -->
    <a href="index.html">Home</a>
    <a href="about/index.html">About</a>

    <!-- Service categories -->
    <a href="services/web-design.html">Web Design</a>
    <a href="services/seo.html">SEO Services</a>
</nav>
```

Testing Workflow:

#html

```
<!-- Regular testing checklist -->
<!-- ✓ All internal links functional -->
<!-- ✓ External links current -->
<!-- ✓ Images displaying correctly -->
```

```
<!-- ✓ CSS and JS files loading -->
<!-- ✓ Mobile navigation working -->
```

Essential Tips

- Always use forward slashes in web paths, even on Windows systems, as web servers expect forward slash notation regardless of the operating system.
- Create a consistent folder structure from project start and document it for team members to prevent confusion and maintain organization throughout development.
- Test your website from different directory levels to ensure relative paths work correctly across all pages, especially when moving from shallow to deep directory structures.
- Use descriptive file and folder names without spaces or special characters to avoid encoding issues and make paths more predictable and memorable.
- Keep a master list of all external links and check them periodically, as external websites change URLs frequently and can break your site's functionality.

Actionable Strategies

- Implement a root-relative path strategy for main navigation elements to ensure consistency across all pages regardless of their directory depth or location.
- Create a standardized folder structure template that you can reuse across projects, including dedicated directories for CSS, JavaScript, images, and documents.
- Build a simple link checking routine into your development workflow by manually testing all links before publishing and using browser developer tools to identify issues.
- Establish clear naming conventions for files and directories at project start, using lowercase letters, hyphens instead of spaces, and descriptive names that indicate content purpose.

- Set up your development environment to mirror your production server structure as closely as possible to catch path-related issues before deployment.
- Use placeholder images and fallback resources for development to prevent broken image icons from appearing while content is being created and organized.
- Create a comprehensive site map document that shows all file locations and their relationships, making it easier to construct correct paths and troubleshoot navigation issues.

Chapter 15: Introduction to CSS in HTML

15.1 What is CSS?

Understanding the Foundation of Web Styling

CSS, which stands for Cascading Style Sheets, represents one of the most fundamental technologies for creating visually appealing and professionally designed websites. This powerful styling language works hand-in-hand with HTML to transform plain, unstyled markup into dynamic, engaging web experiences that capture user attention and enhance usability.

CSS operates as a separate layer from HTML, allowing developers to maintain clean separation between content structure and visual presentation. This separation proves invaluable for maintaining large websites, as it enables developers to make sweeping design changes without touching the underlying HTML structure.

The Power of Cascading

The "cascading" nature of CSS refers to how styles flow down through the document hierarchy and how conflicting styles are resolved. When multiple CSS rules apply to the same element, the browser follows specific rules to determine which styles take precedence. This cascading behavior creates a sophisticated system for managing complex styling scenarios.

The cascade follows three primary principles: specificity, inheritance, and source order. Specificity determines which rule wins when multiple rules target the same element, with more specific selectors taking precedence over general ones. Inheritance allows certain properties to pass from parent elements to their children, creating consistency throughout the document. Source order means that when rules have equal specificity, the last one declared takes effect.

CSS Syntax Structure

CSS follows a straightforward syntax pattern consisting of selectors, properties, and values. A CSS rule begins with a selector that identifies which HTML elements should receive the styling. The selector is followed by curly braces containing one or more property-value pairs, each ending with a semicolon.

#css

```
selector {
    property: value;
    another-property: another-value;
}
```

This clean, readable syntax makes CSS accessible to beginners while remaining powerful enough for complex design requirements.

The Role of CSS in Modern Web Development

CSS has evolved significantly since its introduction, now encompassing advanced features like animations, transitions, flexbox layouts, grid systems, and responsive design capabilities. Modern CSS enables developers to create sophisticated layouts that adapt seamlessly across different devices and screen sizes without requiring JavaScript intervention.

The language continues expanding with new features regularly added to enhance developer productivity and user experience. Features like CSS Grid and Flexbox have revolutionized layout design, while CSS Custom Properties (variables) have brought programming-like capabilities to stylesheets.

15.2 Inline CSS

Direct Element Styling

Inline CSS represents the most direct method for applying styles to HTML elements by placing CSS properties directly within the HTML tag using the style attribute. This approach creates an immediate connection between the

HTML element and its visual appearance, making it useful for quick styling decisions and one-off customizations.

#html

```
<p style="color: blue; font-size: 18px; font-weight: bold;">
    This paragraph has inline styles applied directly.
</p>
```

Advantages of Inline CSS

Inline CSS offers several distinct advantages in specific scenarios. The most significant benefit is its high specificity, which means inline styles will override almost all other CSS rules, making them ideal for testing purposes or when you need to ensure a particular style applies regardless of other stylesheets.

The immediate visual feedback provided by inline CSS makes it excellent for rapid prototyping and experimentation. Developers can quickly test different styling options without creating separate CSS files or switching between multiple documents.

#html

```
<div style="background-color: #f0f0f0; padding: 20px; border-radius: 10px; box-shadow: 0 2px 5px rgba(0,0,0,0.1);">
    <h2 style="color: #333; margin-bottom: 15px;">Styled Container</h2>
    <p style="line-height: 1.6; color: #666;">
        This content demonstrates multiple inline styles working together.
    </p>
</div>
```

Limitations and Considerations

Despite its usefulness in certain situations, inline CSS comes with significant limitations that make it unsuitable for larger projects. The primary concern is maintainability – when styles are scattered throughout HTML documents, making consistent changes becomes extremely difficult and time-consuming.

Inline CSS also increases HTML file size and reduces loading performance, as the same styles may be repeated across multiple elements. This repetition violates the DRY (Don't Repeat Yourself) principle of programming and leads to bloated code.

Best Practices for Inline CSS Usage

When using inline CSS, focus on temporary styling needs, email templates (where external stylesheets may not be supported), and specific overrides that won't be reused elsewhere. Avoid using inline CSS for styles that might be applied to multiple elements or that represent design patterns used throughout the site.

#html

```
<!-- Good use case: Temporary testing -->
<button style="background-color: red;">Test
Button</button>


<!-- Poor use case: Repeated styling -->
<p style="font-family: Arial; color: #333; line-height:
1.5;">Paragraph 1</p>
<p style="font-family: Arial; color: #333; line-height:
1.5;">Paragraph 2</p>
<p style="font-family: Arial; color: #333; line-height:
1.5;">Paragraph 3</p>
```

15.3 Internal CSS

Document-Level Styling

Internal CSS, also known as embedded CSS, involves placing CSS rules within the HTML document itself using the `<style>` element in the document's head section. This approach provides a middle ground between inline CSS and external stylesheets, offering better organization than inline styles while keeping everything contained within a single file.

#html

```
<!DOCTYPE html>
<html lang="en">
<head>
    <meta charset="UTF-8">
    <meta name="viewport" content="width=device-width,
initial-scale=1.0">
    <title>Internal CSS Example</title>
    <style>
        body {
            font-family: 'Arial', sans-serif;
            line-height: 1.6;
            margin: 0;
            padding: 20px;
            background-color: #f4f4f4;
        }

        .container {
            max-width: 800px;
            margin: 0 auto;
            background-color: white;
            padding: 30px;
```

```
            border-radius: 8px;
            box-shadow: 0 2px 10px rgba(0,0,0,0.1);
        }

        h1 {
            color: #2c3e50;
            text-align: center;
            margin-bottom: 30px;
            border-bottom: 3px solid #3498db;
            padding-bottom: 10px;
        }

        .highlight {
            background-color: #fff3cd;
            padding: 15px;
            border-left: 4px solid #ffc107;
            margin: 20px 0;
        }
    </style>
</head>
<body>
    <div class="container">
        <h1>Internal CSS Demonstration</h1>
        <p>This document uses internal CSS for
styling.</p>
        <div class="highlight">
            This is a highlighted section with custom
styling.
        </div>
    </div>
</body>
```

```
</html>
```

Organizational Benefits

Internal CSS provides superior organization compared to inline styles by centralizing all styling rules in one location within the document. This centralization makes it easier to maintain consistency across elements and allows for the use of CSS selectors, classes, and IDs to target multiple elements efficiently.

The approach enables developers to create reusable style classes that can be applied to multiple elements throughout the document, reducing code duplication and improving maintainability.

#html

```
<style>
    /* Reusable button styles */
    .btn {
        display: inline-block;
        padding: 12px 24px;
        border: none;
        border-radius: 4px;
        text-decoration: none;
        font-weight: bold;
        cursor: pointer;
        transition: background-color 0.3s ease;
    }

    .btn-primary {
        background-color: #007bff;
        color: white;
```

```
    }

    .btn-primary:hover {
        background-color: #0056b3;
    }

    .btn-secondary {
        background-color: #6c757d;
        color: white;
    }

    .btn-secondary:hover {
        background-color: #545b62;
    }

    /* Layout styles */
    .grid {
        display: grid;
        grid-template-columns: repeat(auto-fit,
minmax(250px, 1fr));
        gap: 20px;
        margin: 20px 0;
    }

    .card {
        background-color: white;
        padding: 20px;
        border-radius: 8px;
        box-shadow: 0 2px 4px rgba(0,0,0,0.1);
        border: 1px solid #e9ecef;
    }
```

```
</style>
```

When to Use Internal CSS

Internal CSS works best for single-page websites, landing pages, email templates, and prototypes where all styling needs can be contained within one document. It's particularly useful during the development phase when you're experimenting with styles before moving them to external files.

This approach also proves valuable for page-specific styles that won't be used elsewhere in a larger website, allowing you to keep specialized styling close to the content it affects.

Performance Considerations

Internal CSS offers performance advantages over external stylesheets by eliminating additional HTTP requests, as the styles load with the HTML document. However, this benefit comes at the cost of increased HTML file size and the inability to cache styles separately from content.

For optimal performance with internal CSS, minimize unused styles and consider the trade-offs between reduced HTTP requests and increased document size.

15.4 External CSS

Separate Stylesheet Files

External CSS represents the most professional and scalable approach to styling websites by placing all CSS rules in separate files with the .css extension. These external stylesheets are then linked to HTML documents using the `<link>` element, creating a clean separation between content and presentation.

#html

```
<!DOCTYPE html>
<html lang="en">
<head>
    <meta charset="UTF-8">
    <meta name="viewport" content="width=device-width,
initial-scale=1.0">
    <title>External CSS Example</title>
    <link rel="stylesheet" href="styles.css">
    <link rel="stylesheet" href="responsive.css">
</head>
<body>
    <header class="main-header">
        <nav class="navigation">
            <ul class="nav-list">
                <li class="nav-item"><a href="#"
class="nav-link">Home</a></li>
                <li class="nav-item"><a href="#"
class="nav-link">About</a></li>
                <li class="nav-item"><a href="#"
class="nav-link">Services</a></li>
                <li class="nav-item"><a href="#"
class="nav-link">Contact</a></li>
            </ul>
        </nav>
    </header>

    <main class="main-content">
        <section class="hero-section">
            <h1 class="hero-title">Welcome to Our
Website</h1>
```

```
            <p class="hero-description">Professional
styling with external CSS</p>
            <button class="cta-button">Get
Started</button>
        </section>
    </main>
</body>
</html>
```

The corresponding external CSS file (styles.css) would contain:

#css

```
/* Reset and base styles */
* {
    margin: 0;
    padding: 0;
    box-sizing: border-box;
}

body {
    font-family: 'Segoe UI', Tahoma, Geneva, Verdana,
sans-serif;
    line-height: 1.6;
    color: #333;
    background-color: #ffffff;
}

/* Header styles */
.main-header {
    background-color: #2c3e50;
    padding: 1rem 0;
```

```
    box-shadow: 0 2px 5px rgba(0,0,0,0.1);
}

.navigation {
    max-width: 1200px;
    margin: 0 auto;
    padding: 0 2rem;
}

.nav-list {
    display: flex;
    list-style: none;
    justify-content: center;
    align-items: center;
}

.nav-item {
    margin: 0 1.5rem;
}

.nav-link {
    color: #ecf0f1;
    text-decoration: none;
    font-weight: 500;
    transition: color 0.3s ease;
    padding: 0.5rem 1rem;
    border-radius: 4px;
}

.nav-link:hover {
    color: #3498db;
```

```
    background-color: rgba(52, 152, 219, 0.1);
}

/* Main content styles */
.main-content {
    max-width: 1200px;
    margin: 0 auto;
    padding: 2rem;
}

.hero-section {
    text-align: center;
    padding: 4rem 0;
    background: linear-gradient(135deg, #667eea 0%,
#764ba2 100%);
    border-radius: 12px;
    color: white;
    margin-bottom: 2rem;
}

.hero-title {
    font-size: 3rem;
    margin-bottom: 1rem;
    font-weight: 700;
    text-shadow: 2px 2px 4px rgba(0,0,0,0.3);
}

.hero-description {
    font-size: 1.2rem;
    margin-bottom: 2rem;
    opacity: 0.9;
```

```
}

.cta-button {
    background-color: #e74c3c;
    color: white;
    padding: 1rem 2rem;
    border: none;
    border-radius: 50px;
    font-size: 1.1rem;
    font-weight: 600;
    cursor: pointer;
    transition: all 0.3s ease;
    text-transform: uppercase;
    letter-spacing: 1px;
}

.cta-button:hover {
    background-color: #c0392b;
    transform: translateY(-2px);
    box-shadow: 0 4px 12px rgba(231, 76, 60, 0.4);
}
```

Scalability and Maintainability

External CSS provides unmatched scalability for web projects of any size. By centralizing styles in separate files, development teams can work on styling independently from content creation, enabling parallel development workflows and reducing conflicts.

The modular nature of external CSS allows for organized file structures where styles can be split into logical components: layout.css for structural styles, typography.css for text-related rules, components.css for reusable UI elements, and theme.css for color schemes and branding.

#css

```css
/* typography.css */
@import
url('https://fonts.googleapis.com/css2?family=Inter:wght@300;400;500;600;700&display=swap');

:root {
    --font-primary: 'Inter', -apple-system,
BlinkMacSystemFont, sans-serif;
    --font-size-xs: 0.75rem;
    --font-size-sm: 0.875rem;
    --font-size-base: 1rem;
    --font-size-lg: 1.125rem;
    --font-size-xl: 1.25rem;
    --font-size-2xl: 1.5rem;
    --font-size-3xl: 1.875rem;
    --font-size-4xl: 2.25rem;
    --line-height-tight: 1.25;
    --line-height-normal: 1.5;
    --line-height-loose: 1.75;
}

body {
    font-family: var(--font-primary);
    font-size: var(--font-size-base);
    line-height: var(--line-height-normal);
}
```

```
h1, h2, h3, h4, h5, h6 {
    line-height: var(--line-height-tight);
    font-weight: 600;
    margin-bottom: 0.5em;
}

h1 { font-size: var(--font-size-4xl); }
h2 { font-size: var(--font-size-3xl); }
h3 { font-size: var(--font-size-2xl); }
h4 { font-size: var(--font-size-xl); }
h5 { font-size: var(--font-size-lg); }
h6 { font-size: var(--font-size-base); }
```

Caching and Performance Benefits

External CSS files can be cached by browsers, significantly improving website performance for returning visitors. Once downloaded, the stylesheet remains available locally, eliminating the need to re-download styling information on subsequent page visits.

This caching behavior becomes particularly valuable for websites with multiple pages sharing the same stylesheet, as users only download the CSS once while benefiting from consistent styling across the entire site.

Advanced External CSS Techniques

External CSS enables advanced techniques like CSS preprocessing with tools like Sass or Less, which add programming features to CSS such as variables, nesting, mixins, and functions. These tools compile into standard CSS files that browsers can understand.

#css

```css
/* Advanced CSS using custom properties and modern
features */
:root {
    --primary-color: #3498db;
    --secondary-color: #2ecc71;
    --danger-color: #e74c3c;
    --warning-color: #f39c12;
    --info-color: #17a2b8;

    --spacing-xs: 0.25rem;
    --spacing-sm: 0.5rem;
    --spacing-md: 1rem;
    --spacing-lg: 1.5rem;
    --spacing-xl: 2rem;

    --border-radius-sm: 4px;
    --border-radius-md: 8px;
    --border-radius-lg: 12px;
    --border-radius-full: 9999px;

    --shadow-sm: 0 1px 3px rgba(0,0,0,0.12);
    --shadow-md: 0 4px 6px rgba(0,0,0,0.12);
    --shadow-lg: 0 10px 25px rgba(0,0,0,0.15);
}

/* Utility classes for rapid development */
.container {
    max-width: 1200px;
    margin: 0 auto;
```

```
    padding: 0 var(--spacing-md);
}

.grid {
    display: grid;
    gap: var(--spacing-md);
}

.grid-2 { grid-template-columns: repeat(2, 1fr); }
.grid-3 { grid-template-columns: repeat(3, 1fr); }
.grid-4 { grid-template-columns: repeat(4, 1fr); }

.flex {
    display: flex;
}

.flex-center {
    display: flex;
    justify-content: center;
    align-items: center;
}

.text-center { text-align: center; }
.text-left { text-align: left; }
.text-right { text-align: right; }

.mb-1 { margin-bottom: var(--spacing-xs); }
.mb-2 { margin-bottom: var(--spacing-sm); }
.mb-3 { margin-bottom: var(--spacing-md); }
.mb-4 { margin-bottom: var(--spacing-lg); }
.mb-5 { margin-bottom: var(--spacing-xl); }
```

15.5 The style Attribute

Direct Element Control

The style attribute provides the most direct method for applying CSS properties to individual HTML elements. This attribute accepts CSS property-value pairs separated by semicolons, allowing for precise control over element appearance without creating separate CSS rules.

#html

```
<div style="width: 300px; height: 200px; background-color: #f8f9fa; border: 2px solid #dee2e6; border-radius: 8px; padding: 20px; margin: 10px auto;">
    <h3 style="color: #495057; margin-bottom: 15px; font-family: 'Georgia', serif;">Styled Container</h3>
    <p style="color: #6c757d; line-height: 1.6; font-size: 14px;">
        This container demonstrates multiple CSS properties applied through the style attribute.
    </p>
    <button style="background-color: #007bff; color: white; border: none; padding: 8px 16px; border-radius: 4px; cursor: pointer; font-weight: 500;">
        Click Me
    </button>
</div>
```

Complex Styling Through Attributes

The style attribute can handle complex CSS properties including transforms, animations, and advanced layout properties. This capability makes it suitable for dynamic styling scenarios where JavaScript manipulates element styles based on user interactions or data changes.

#html

```
<div style="
    background: linear-gradient(45deg, #667eea, #764ba2);
    transform: rotate(-2deg) scale(1.05);
    box-shadow: 0 10px 30px rgba(0,0,0,0.2);
    border-radius: 15px;
    padding: 30px;
    margin: 20px;
    transition: all 0.3s cubic-bezier(0.4, 0, 0.2, 1);
    position: relative;
    overflow: hidden;
">
    <div style="
        position: absolute;
        top: -50%;
        right: -50%;
        width: 200%;
        height: 200%;
        background: radial-gradient(circle,
rgba(255,255,255,0.1) 0%, transparent 70%);
        pointer-events: none;
    "></div>

    <h2 style="
        color: white;
        text-shadow: 2px 2px 4px rgba(0,0,0,0.3);
        margin-bottom: 20px;
        font-size: 2em;
```

```
        position: relative;
        z-index: 2;
    ">Advanced Styling</h2>

    <p style="
        color: rgba(255,255,255,0.9);
        font-size: 1.1em;
        line-height: 1.6;
        position: relative;
        z-index: 2;
    ">
        Complex visual effects achieved through the style
attribute.
    </p>
</div>
```

JavaScript Integration

The style attribute integrates seamlessly with JavaScript for dynamic styling, allowing developers to modify element appearance in response to user actions, data changes, or other events. This integration enables interactive features without requiring separate CSS classes.

#html

```
<!DOCTYPE html>
<html lang="en">
<head>
    <meta charset="UTF-8">
    <meta name="viewport" content="width=device-width,
initial-scale=1.0">
    <title>Dynamic Styling Example</title>
```

```
</head>
<body>
    <div id="dynamicBox" style="
        width: 200px;
        height: 200px;
        background-color: #3498db;
        border-radius: 10px;
        margin: 20px auto;
        transition: all 0.3s ease;
        cursor: pointer;
        display: flex;
        align-items: center;
        justify-content: center;
        color: white;
        font-weight: bold;
        user-select: none;
    ">
        Click Me!
    </div>

    <div style="text-align: center; margin-top: 20px;">
        <button onclick="changeColor()" style="
            background-color: #e74c3c;
            color: white;
            border: none;
            padding: 10px 20px;
            border-radius: 5px;
            cursor: pointer;
            margin: 5px;
            font-weight: 500;
        ">Change Color</button>
```

```
        <button onclick="changeSize()" style="
            background-color: #2ecc71;
            color: white;
            border: none;
            padding: 10px 20px;
            border-radius: 5px;
            cursor: pointer;
            margin: 5px;
            font-weight: 500;
        ">Change Size</button>

        <button onclick="resetBox()" style="
            background-color: #95a5a6;
            color: white;
            border: none;
            padding: 10px 20px;
            border-radius: 5px;
            cursor: pointer;
            margin: 5px;
            font-weight: 500;
        ">Reset</button>
    </div>

    <script>
        const box =
document.getElementById('dynamicBox');
        const colors = ['#3498db', '#e74c3c', '#2ecc71',
'#f39c12', '#9b59b6', '#1abc9c'];
        let currentColorIndex = 0;
        let currentSize = 200;
```

```
        function changeColor() {
            currentColorIndex = (currentColorIndex + 1) %
colors.length;
            box.style.backgroundColor =
colors[currentColorIndex];
        }

        function changeSize() {
            currentSize = currentSize === 200 ? 300 :
200;
            box.style.width = currentSize + 'px';
            box.style.height = currentSize + 'px';
        }

        function resetBox() {
            box.style.backgroundColor = '#3498db';
            box.style.width = '200px';
            box.style.height = '200px';
            currentColorIndex = 0;
            currentSize = 200;
        }

        // Add click interaction to the box itself
        box.addEventListener('click', function() {
            this.style.transform = 'scale(0.95)';
            setTimeout(() => {
                this.style.transform = 'scale(1)';
            }, 150);
        });
    </script>
```

```
</body>
</html>
```

Style Attribute Best Practices

When using the style attribute, maintain consistent property ordering and use meaningful values that align with your overall design system. Group related properties together and use shorthand properties where appropriate to reduce attribute length.

Consider the maintainability implications of inline styles, especially in larger projects where changes might need to be made across multiple elements.

#html

```
<!-- Well-organized style attribute -->
<article style="
    /* Layout properties */
    display: block;
    width: 100%;
    max-width: 600px;
    margin: 2rem auto;
    padding: 2rem;

    /* Visual properties */
    background-color: #ffffff;
    border: 1px solid #e9ecef;
    border-radius: 8px;
    box-shadow: 0 2px 4px rgba(0,0,0,0.1);

    /* Typography properties */
```

```
    font-family: 'Arial', sans-serif;
    line-height: 1.6;
    color: #333333;
">
    <h2 style="
        margin: 0 0 1rem 0;
        font-size: 1.5rem;
        font-weight: 600;
        color: #2c3e50;
    ">Article Title</h2>

    <p style="
        margin: 0 0 1rem 0;
        color: #555555;
    ">Article content with proper styling
organization.</p>
</article>
```

Essential Tips

- Keep your CSS organized and maintainable by establishing consistent naming conventions and file structures from the beginning of your project. Use meaningful class names that describe the purpose or content of elements rather than their appearance.
- Always validate your CSS code using online validators or development tools to catch syntax errors and ensure cross-browser compatibility before deploying to production environments.
- Optimize CSS performance by minimizing unused styles, combining similar selectors, and using shorthand properties wherever possible to reduce file size and improve loading times.
- Test your styles across different browsers and devices regularly to ensure consistent appearance and functionality, paying special attention to older browser versions if your audience requires broader compatibility.

- Utilize CSS custom properties (variables) to create flexible, maintainable stylesheets that can be easily modified and themed without extensive code changes throughout your project.

Actionable Strategies

- Start every project with a CSS reset or normalize stylesheet to establish consistent baseline styles across different browsers and eliminate default styling inconsistencies that can cause layout problems.
- Implement a mobile-first responsive design approach by writing CSS for mobile devices first, then adding media queries for larger screens, ensuring optimal performance and user experience across all device types.
- Create a comprehensive style guide or design system that documents your color palette, typography scales, spacing units, and component styles, making it easier for team members to maintain consistency.
- Use CSS preprocessing tools like Sass or Less to add programming features to your stylesheets, enabling variables, nesting, mixins, and functions that make large-scale CSS projects more manageable and efficient.
- Establish a systematic approach to organizing CSS files by separating base styles, layout components, individual modules, and utility classes into distinct files that can be easily maintained and updated.
- Implement CSS linting tools in your development workflow to automatically catch common errors, enforce coding standards, and maintain consistent code quality across your team or project.
- Practice progressive enhancement by starting with functional, accessible HTML and CSS, then adding advanced visual effects and interactions that enhance the user experience without breaking core functionality for users with older browsers or assistive technologies.

List of Recommended Books to Read:

Checkout All My Books

ChatGPT for Authors and Writers Books

ChatGPT Secret Weapon: 5 Steps to Start Writing and Selling Books within 24 Hours

ChatGPT's 2000+ Low-Content Book Ideas: Designing, Marketing Tactics and Proven Strategies to Sell Fast

Unleashing the Power of Amazon Kindle: How to Sell ur First 1000 Copies & Get Reviews Without Breaking a Sweat Earn $1k-$20k/Mon - ChatGPT

AI Video Creators Books

No Camera and Studio? No Problem: Make Money Online with Faceless YouTube Channel, TikTok and Instagram Faceless pages

App Ideas and Development Books

App Ideas for the Future; The Next Big Thing: Ultimate Thousands of App Ideas Handbook

Personal Development, Success and Financial Mindset Books

The 4 Pillars of Wealth Creation

REPEAT AFTER ME; I AM A MILLIONAIRE: THE SECRET OF THE MILLIONAIRES

Time Management Books

Conquering Distraction: Mastering Time Management for Success

From Chaos to Control: Strategic Planner for Busy Professionals/CEO: A Guide for Planning and Productivity

Psychologies Books

The Psychology of Writing: Overcoming Writer's Block and Finding Your Voice

The Psychology of Leadership: Mastering the Art of Influence

The Psychology of Greatness: How to Unlock Your Full Potential

The Psychology of Sales: Mastering the Art of Persuasion

The Power of Positive Thinking: Harnessing the Psychology of Success

The Psychology of Reading: How to Read More and Retain More

www.ingramcontent.com/pod-product-compliance
Lightning Source LLC
LaVergne TN
LVHW071159210926
848482LV00014B/692